# Bicycles, Bangs, and Bloomers

# Bicycles, Bangs, and Bloomers

## The New Woman in the Popular Press

Patricia Marks

THE UNIVERSITY PRESS OF KENTUCKY

Copyright © 1990 by The University Press of Kentucky

Scholarly publisher for the Commonwealth,
serving Bellarmine College, Berea College, Centre
College of Kentucky, Eastern Kentucky University,
The Filson Club, Georgetown College, Kentucky
Historical Society, Kentucky State University,
Morehead State University, Murray State University,
Northern Kentucky University, Transylvania University,
University of Kentucky, University of Louisville,
and Western Kentucky University.

*Editorial and Sales Offices:* Lexington, Kentucky 40506-0336

**Library of Congress Cataloging-in-Publication Data**

Marks, Patricia.
   Bicycles, bangs, and bloomers : the new woman in the popular press
  / Patricia Marks.

    p. cm.
   Includes bibliographical references (p.
   ISBN 0-8131-1704-6
   1. Women in the press—United States—History—19th century.
  2. Women in the press—Great Britain—History—19th century.
  3. Women's rights—United States—History—19th century. 4. Women's
  rights—Great Britain—History—19th century. 5. Feminism—United
  States—History—19th century. 6. Feminism—Great Britain—
  History—19th century. I. Title.
  PN4888.W65M37  1990
  071'.3'082—dc20                      89-25110

To the New Man

# CONTENTS

List of Illustrations ... viii

Preface ... ix

Introduction: Queen Victoria's Granddaughter ... 1

1. Women and Marriage: "Running in Blinkers" ... 24

2. Women's Work: More "Bloomin' Bad Bizness" ... 55

3. Women's Education: "Maddest Folly Going" ... 90

4. Women's Clubs: "Girls Will Be Girls" ... 117

5. Women's Fashions: The Shape of Things to Come ... 147

6. Women's Athletics: A Bicycle Built for One ... 174

Conclusion: The New Woman ... 204

Works Cited ... 210

Index ... 215

# ILLUSTRATIONS

1. "A Sketch from Nature"  25
2. "Cross Purposes"  36
3. "Mr. Punch's Four Prize Middle-Class Wives"  46
4. "Her 'Day of Rest' (The Song of the Shop Girl)"  64
5. "In Days to Come, Churches May Be Fuller"  78
6. "The New Navy, about 1900 A.D."  86
7. "A Study in Natural History"  94
8. "Ladies Not Admitted"  114
9. "In a Twentieth Century Club"  126
10. "Girls Will Be Girls"  126
11. "In the New Age"  162
12. "Our Girls *Have* Altered"  167
13. "The New Women's Men"  172
14. "Hygienic Excess"  180
15. "Fashion à la Shakspeare"  192
16. "Half a Century of Bloomers"  194
17. "The Voice of Modesty"  196
18. Miss Heavytopp's Bicycle Lesson  198

# PREFACE

TO STUDY the late nineteenth-century frame of mind through the satire and caricature that appeared is to put the twentieth century in perspective, particularly in terms of women's expanding sphere. Such matters as education, careers, and sports for women may now seem to be inarguable, but the popular reaction in the 1880s and 1890s that both reflected and shaped contemporary views contributes to the attitudes of the modern generation. What the comic record shows is that despite attacks that ranged from the witty to the vituperative, women nonetheless moved inexorably away from a stereotype that bound them to domestic concerns. A view of late nineteenth-century humor about the "feminization" of the world suggests, as well, the profound influence that Queen Victoria had on the women of her century. The woman who held firmly to the value of hearth and home also ruled the country; in her double role, she prepared the way for her cultural granddaughter, the New Woman, who vigorously campaigned for the opportunity to become engaged in the world.

As a reading of contemporary accounts shows, a variety of social forces propelled the late nineteenth-century woman out of the doll's house created for her protection and delight. The population imbalance that created the "redundant women" changed the marital expectations of the middle class; that so many women tried to enter the labor market produced a scarcity of socially acceptable jobs. The resulting crisis generated pressure on other fields, so that eventually it was not only need but inclination that caused women to enter professions other than teaching or nursing. Again, increased movement outside the home affected dress; tight lacing, high-heeled boots, and long trains or wide hoops gave way to "rational" dress more appropriate for walking or riding in public. The illustrators andsatirists responded to the new look, new ideas, and new manners, many with an apparent delight in the incongruity between the common notion of feminine weakness and submissiveness and the actuality of women's strength of purpose.

Interesting in this regard is the comparison between British and American reactions. On the whole, the Americans, partly because of the genial humor of *Life* and *Chic* and partly because of a pervasive democratic ideal, were more open to change and so depicted the New Woman, as she strode along in bloomers toward college degree and profession, with somewhat less rancor. On the other side of the Atlantic, *Punch*, nostalgic about old-fashioned women, was nonetheless stung to reproach those who took advantage of the shop girl, seamstress, and governess; London *Truth*, which actively reviled the "revolting daughters," feared the disintegration of the social fabric.

The following collection of humorous pieces, placed in the context of selected issues and ideas of the day, was initially gathered during a memorable 1977-78 postdoctoral fellowship at the University of Pennsylvania, sponsored by the National Endowment for the Humanities and directed by David De-Laura, whose erudition and generosity of time and energy I remember with gratefulness and pleasure. There, one of my "fellow fellows"—Jerold Savory, who is now Vice-President for Administration at Columbia College—shared his expertise in nineteenth-century periodicals with me. I am indebted to him not only for his words of wisdom and humor, but for an unwieldy packing box of xeroxes that, passed on to me at a South Atlantic Modern Language Association meeting, contained a treasure trove of British caricatures and parodies.

My research has been assisted as well by grants from the Valdosta State College Faculty Research Fund Advisory Committee, chaired by Willa Valencia, which allowed me to travel to the Library of Congress, to the New York Public Library, and to the Newberry Library. To the helpful librarians there, as well as at the Florida State University Strozier Library, and to the indefatigable reference librarians at Valdosta State College, I owe thanks. I am especially grateful to Thomas E. Dasher, whose unfailing encouragement and very real support for this project in terms of class scheduling and reduced teaching loads furthered its completion.

Finally and always, I am indebted to Dennis, the New Man who shares my life and research.

# Queen Victoria's Granddaughter

It was an awful existence. She had to get up of black winter's mornings to make breakfast for her scowling old father. . . . She remained silent opposite to him, listening to the urn hissing, and sitting in tremor while the parent read his paper and consumed his accustomed portion of muffins and tea. At half-past nine he rose and went to the City, and she was almost free till dinner-time, to make visitations in the kitchen and to scold the servants; to drive abroad and descend upon the tradesmen, who were prodigiously respectful; to leave her cards and her papa's at the great glum respectable houses of their City friends; or to sit alone in the large drawing-room, expecting visitors; and working at a huge piece of worsted by the fire, on the sofa, hard by the great Iphigenia clock, which ticked and tolled with mournful loudness in the dreary room.

—William Makepeace Thackeray

OFTEN COMPARED to a flower, a kitten, or a child, she was modest and pure minded, unselfish and meek. She knew her place well; naturally fitted to the common round of household duties, she could make a home of a hovel by ministering to the needs of her husband, either as uncomplaining drudge or angel on the hearth. Nothing in herself, the littlest and the least of all creation, she achieved greatness not in her own right but in her relatedness as daughter and wife and, if she survived the rigors of childbirth, as mother and grandmother. This Victorian Iphigenia, the "womanly woman," was one of the nineteenth century's most memorable myths, not only because she was fashioned after a Queen who ruled both house *and* country, but because rapid social changes made her existence untenable.

Her less pliant, more outspoken sisters, however, not content with a life so circumscribed by female obligations, drew their skirts in a wider circle. These New Women, who wanted

all the advantages of their brothers, asked for education, suffrage, and careers; they cut their hair, adopted "rational" dress,
and freewheeled along a path that led to the twentieth century.
In the hue and cry that followed the determined figure in
bloomers, the popular press was among the loudest. Indeed,
even when they tried by caricature and satire to tame the ram-
bunctious feminist spirit and return it to its domestic sphere,
humor magazines in Britain and America contributed to pop-
ularizing the goals and manners of the New Woman. She ca-
vorted through the pages of *Life, Puck, Punch,* and *Truth*
perched on bicycles and smoking cigarettes; she looked learned
in judges' wigs and academic gowns and athletic in riding pants
and football helmets. All of her uncomplimentary poses served
to shape a new myth; no longer an Iphigenia, the modern Minerva, a stranger in a strange land, aped the customs of the
"manly" natives in an effort to find herself. To look at the satire,
parody, and caricatures that followed each change in manners,
dress, or behavior between 1880 and 1900 is to glimpse not just
the comic spectrum of public response to the new figure but
the entire panoply of concern about a changing feminine mythology. While such issues as intellectual capacity, physical stamina, gender transference, and domestic sanctity were treated
lightly, they were serious matters for both the women and their
critics; the humorous record is, then, the mirror that allows us
to understand how our predecessors viewed the new phenomenon.

Those who sought to change the parameters of their domestic sphere were no longer thought of as "ladies"; indeed,
they acquired a variety of epithets. "Varmity women," "wild
women," "social insurgents," "manly women": none, perhaps,
was more telling than the last, an oxymoron that lies at the
heart of much of the satire published about the New Woman.
As London *Truth* notes, for example, the new manners expressed a blend of genders: "The charm of a young girl is her
dissimilarity to man, and by conforming to his natural tastes
and pursuits she loses her chief attraction. She becomes a 'pal,'
but she is no longer the idol to be adored and worshipped, the
ideal to be wooed and won" (20 Nov. 1890: 105). Commentators
on both sides of the Atlantic pointed to a reversal of sex roles.

In New York *Truth*, for instance, George B. Luks illustrates a column entitled "The Mannish Girl" with vignettes of "One of New York's Mannish girls out for a morning 'breather' "; she is dressed in tie, vest, jacket, hat, and monocle, and she is smoking. The writer notes that "she begins innocently enough," copying her brother's mannerisms and "cut[ting] off her hair like Maggie Tulliver":

So she falls out of sympathy with her sex. She loses its delicacy; she is reckless of its conventions. That is always the peril of the mannish girl. But the fact that a woman in body, she tries to be a man in mind, exposes her to the animadversions of the ribald.

As she mingles with the world, she feeds a kind of vanity by being mannish. To talk slang, to smoke cigarettes, to ride to hounds, commend her, in a measure, to her male companions. They declare her to be jolly, fetching, stunning. . . . But they rarely marry her.

"That," says the columnist, "is where the maidenly girl has her revenge"; the "mannish girl" is consigned to "eternal spinsterhood or the divorce court" (21 Jan. 1893: 7).

Another fear was directed less toward a reversal of sex roles than toward the advent of a completely new order. As a character in Sydney Grundy's 1894 play, *The New Woman: An Original Comedy, in Four Acts*, says, "A woman, who *is* a woman, doesn't want to be anything else. These people are a sex of their own. . . . They have invented a new gender." Such a completely new order has no place in the most conservative view, well stated by commentator Harry Thurston Peck: "When one comes down to the plain facts of human life on its serious side, it is man who is the finest and noblest and the most godlike figure in the world. . . . He has the physical power to work his will, and this alone is a lasting badge of his superiority; while he has also the moral traits that are fitted to direct and exercise his physical power in the best and most efficient way for the welfare of the world." Peck's "cure" for the new movement appeals to evolution:

The remedy will be applied with swiftness and with certainty. . . . The instinct of self-preservation will compel him to cut short a movement that can only be disastrous to the race. The remedy may be brutal, but it will be effective when it comes, and it will ultimately be put in force with something of the primitive severity of primeval days. In the last resort it is physical strength that rules the world. . . . If [female reformers] should ever bring about a state of things where man collectively begins to be uncomfortable, he will speak the word—a short, sharp word—and that will be the end of it. [161]

By 1899, when Peck proposed his "cure," the movement was well established; the very tone of the excerpt is testimony to the fact that the "short, sharp word" spoken by detractors and satirists alike had failed to return women to the status quo. Indeed, the more serious investigations of gender definition uncover inherent contradictions. One contemporary female writer, examining the permutations of gender language, discovers that a popular dictionary like the *Century* is vague about definitions. While *womanly* is an empty term, defined by a weak synonym—"feminine"—and by its opposition to *manly*, *manly* carries such attributes as "humane, charitable . . . brave, [and] strongminded" (Parrish 775). The conclusion? That if *womanly* is opposite to *manly*, to be feminine is to be neither "humane" nor "charitable"—a resolution that runs counter to the nineteenth century's assumptions about the nurturing role of women. Despite Coventry Patmore's attempt in *The Angel in the House* to define woman through the language of apotheosis (Houghton 377-79), apparently even the womanly woman could not be easily identified; indeed, the openness of definition by negation invites the turn-of-the-century observer to formulate his or her own entry.

In the middle of the century, distinctions were clearer and more generally accepted, especially those between "lady" and "female." As *Punch* comments in response to a *Times* advertisement ("AMATEUR LITERARY LADIES.—Females of good education, are invited to JOIN A COMPOSITION SOCIETY. No remuneration offered, and no expense incurred"):

No well educated lady would accept an invitation to appear in a Society, at the cost upon her entrance of being called a "female." . . . she would know that the word "female" is no synonym for "lady." The term "lady" is applied exclusively to women, and it is not every woman who has properly a claim to it. The word "female" may, however, be applied to other animals; and to call women "females" is to speak of them as part of the inferior brute creation. Fine ladies think it vulgar to be spoken of as "women:" but they had better be called this than bear a synonym with "creatures." [30 July 1859: 51]

Indeed, well into the 1890s, when the terms *New Woman* or *advanced woman* replaced *lady* as a general frame of reference, *Punch* was sensitive to the class connotations of the latter word. In a sketch of a wedding, for example, the humor is about the supersensitivity of the shop-girl bride, who, late of Remnant & Co.'s Ribbon Department, objects to the liturgical question "wilt thou take this Woman" with a furious correction: *"Lady!"* (28 May 1898: 251). Again, other cartoons show that *Punch*'s late-century readership is still amused at the pretensions of the servant class. Phil Mays draws a scene in a pharmacy in which a disheveled woman, her head tied up in a turban, asks for medicine:

Chemist (to battered female, who is covered with scratches): *"The Cat, I suppose!"*
Battered Female. *"No. Another Lydy!"* [21 May 1898: 231]

Similarly, in "Early Morning Marketing," Sarah Jane, complete with shopping basket and armful of packages, addresses a fashionably dressed woman: "I do believe, Mum, as *we*'re the only Lidies in the Plice!" (13 Aug. 1898: 64).

As the century progressed, however, a figure developed who no longer seemed to fit as a "lady." The New Woman—or "Novissima," as *Cornhill* writer E.B. Hall dubs her in 1894— "calls herself a woman. Her mother is content to be called a lady, and is naturally of small account." The "non-lady" Hall describes is dark, uninterested in children, and simply dressed; she is an opinionated name-dropper who tolerates her mother and manages her father by hiding her risqué reading from him. "With mild young men she is apt to be crushing," but in the literary man Calamus, she meets her match:

Calamus happens to be rather a simple-minded young man. He has been everywhere. He has seen most things, and nothing seems to have touched a certain strong purity of thought which he probably acquired in the nursery. . . . She thinks she knows the style of talk that will suit him, and she is apparently wrong. . . . Novissima is intensely earnest, and, in her desire to show him the depth of her knowledge, is not always discreet.

She talks of the future of women, of coming generations and women's influence thereon.

"They had better busy themselves with the beginning of the future generation," says Calamus, in his half-listening way.

"How do you mean?"

"Children," explains Calamus in a single word.

Novissima mentions the name of one or two foreign authors not usually discussed in polite society in their own country, and Calamus frowns. She approaches one or two topics which he refuses to talk about with a simple bluntness.

. . . He is superficially shallow, and refuses to be deep. She is superficially deep, and betrays her shallowness at every turn.

Calamus eventually marries Edith, "with motherly eyes and a clear laugh"; as Hall concludes, Novissima "has tried to prove that woman's mission is something higher than the bearing of children and the bringing them up. But she has failed" (*Cornhill* 70 [1984]: 365-68).

As some tried to show, the New Woman was not necessarily new. *Life* spoofs the idea in "Archeological Studies: The New Woman's Parade," a drawing of an Egyptian frieze in which husbands and crying babies serve as an audience to bloomer girls and smirking sphinxes. More seriously, Edna Seass Stewart writes in the *Arena* of Lady Mary Montague and Abigail Adams, two "Ancient New Women," the first of whom in 1739 "liberated" the House of Lords against an edict barring women from the gallery, the second of whom corresponded astutely with her husband John Adams on political matters and espoused the cause of women's education. These old New Women seem to fulfill the definition that Nat Arling suggests by indirection in the 1898 *Westminster Review*, where he argues that just as "manliness is too often confounded with mere brute strength" and other attributes that show "lack of consideration for the feelings and ways of others," womanliness is falsely equated with timidity and "self-effacement." A real "womanly woman" (as well as a "manly man"), Arling proposes, should have "courage" and "self-respect" as well as "deference to the opinions of those older or wiser," but "modesty" and "independence" in expressing her own (582).

Arling's stance is somewhat atypical; more commonly, women are treated as superior only in their own sphere. Many writers agreed with the popular notion that thought is masculine and sentiment feminine. In Boyd Winchester's view of the New Woman, for example, intellect is ranked last in the list of desirable feminine attributes: "Firstly, in a woman, let us have a pure, earnest, loving heart; then, passing over her mind, let her form and features be as graceful as possible. . . . An intelligent and highly cultured mind . . . is only mentioned as subordinate, just as in a piece of music the feelings and sense are perhaps to be more touched than the faculties pertaining to the understanding or the intellect" (370). Others suggested that since emotion and intellect are present in varying degrees in all humans, proper education does not "unsex" women but rather makes them more "womanly" by developing their natural inclinations. A versifier in *Pick-Me-Up* rejoices in this kind of New Woman as "an angel of delight":

The woman of the future will not trifle with our hearts,
She will find more time to study into sciences and arts;
She will not be too disdainful, irreverent, and proud,
But with all the highest virtues and attainments be endowed.

The woman of the future will be modest in her looks;
She will sing the sweetest ballads and peruse the choicest books;
Her sympathies will widen, and her goodness will extend,
Until the poor shall bless her, and the weak shall call her friend.
[10 Oct. 1891: 27]

Perhaps the most furious controversy over the meaning of the term *womanly* raged among women themselves. Two clusters of arguments—one about the "wild women" and one about the "revolt of the daughters"—emerged in the early 1890s; both are of special interest in shedding light on the manners and attitudes that appealed to the satirists. Mrs. Lynn Linton, essayist and novelist, spearheaded an attack on what she called the "wild women" in a series of *Nineteenth Century* articles in which she develops a definition for the New Woman: "We must acknowledge now as our Lady of Desire the masterful *domina* of real life—that loud and dictatorial person, insurgent and something more, who suffers no one's opinion to influence her mind, no venerable law hallowed by time, nor custom consecrated by experience, to control her actions. Mistress of herself, the Wild Woman as social insurgent preaches the 'lesson of liberty' broadened into lawlessness and license" ("Wild Women as Social Insurgents" 596).

In "The Wild Women as Social Insurgents," Linton modifies the Spencerian argument that increasing differentiation is a mark of culture to suggest that the woman who chooses to blur the "finer distinctions" between the genders is contributing to the downfall of civilization; she attacks smoking, "violent" sports like golf and cricket, and hunting ("an absolutely unwomanly instinct, an absolutely unwomanly indifference to death and suffering"). Above all, she decries the desire of women to work, which, she believes, undertaken for the mischievous desire to shock, causes unemployment among the needy. What she does applaud in "The Partisans of the Wild Women" is the effort of the female entomologist, astronomer, or Grecian scholar, none of whom advertises her accomplishments. The partisans themselves are open to disapproval. Some are "decent"—men who believe that morality is genderless, women who are ignorant and misled—but all are dupes; others, the "mentally unsexed partisans," are emotional and cocksure; still others, with "a strangely suggestive pruriency of imagination," applaud women for being women, not for perfection in their work. On the whole, Linton maintains, "the unsexed woman pleases the unsexed man."

One response that appeared, written in a quiet, reasoned manner, was "A Defence of the So-Called 'Wild Women,'" in which Mona Caird answers Mrs. Linton's arguments point by point. Her basic charge—that Linton not only describes extremes but contradicts herself—is only a small part of the article in which Caird suggests that "the apostles of the new faith" want to replace personal self-sacrifice with work for the common good; overemphasis on motherhood with development of all faculties; and neurasthenia with action. She further suggests that political and social freedom (including limiting family size) is the key not only for women's emancipation, but for the emancipation of all workers.

The logic and tone of Caird's answers are in themselves the antidote to Linton's stridency and are typical of some of the better feminist arguments that appeared. A similar tone is taken by Kathleen Cuffe and Alys Pearsall Smith in their responses to "The Revolt of the Daughters," a two-part article by B.A. Crackanthorpe and M.E. Haweis on what a modern reader would call the generation gap. Linton suggests that mothers are to blame for turning their daughters into "wild women" ("Partisans of Wild Women" 460); Crackanthorpe ventures to suggest that old-fashioned ways of rearing middle- and upper-class daughters do not take the economic situation into account, that such girls must be taught the self-respect that makes independence possible, and that one solution is early marriage on a limited budget (a solution that runs counter to the Victorian custom of late marriage and extensive settlements). Haweis agrees that independence is the answer but takes English education to task as compared to American, which trains women to be self-sufficient; she goes on to propose that the real answer for the daughters' "hostility" to the status quo is work, a "natural duty" prepared for by careful training. The reply of the daughters also calls for independence—from chaperons, for instance, but, more importantly, from a restrictive family life that requires sacrifice of all personal and intellectual goals. The set of papers is, then, indicative of changing mores. Both controversies touch on the same problem: the dissatisfaction of younger women with old social patterns. Both propose similar solutions: independence and work.

Certainly, given the definitions for the New Woman, the phrase "manly woman" becomes the signifier for a variety of mythologies. As Eve or Lilith, or as Mother Nature, woman represents a larger force—of sin or fertility, depending upon the observer's point of view—itself indicative of the nature of the universe; in effect, she is a symbol *of* a symbol, such abstraction perhaps accounting for the *Century* dictionary's unhelpful entry as well as for her own sense of powerlessness.

Given a definition in which strength needed to be concealed by an appearance of "ladylike" weakness, the "womanly woman" subverted the mythology to her own purposes, as Nina Auerbach suggests in *Woman and the Demon*. While her very existence depends on the desire of others to fictionalize her, the nineteenth-century woman invests the myths with both power and life, just as, for example, she transforms the self-effacing "angel in the home" into a ruling spirit, adept at human manipulation. She also, however, plays the mythologizing game; Auerbach's discussion of John Singer Sargent's portrait "Ellen Terry as Lady MacBeth," a depiction of the actress investing herself with Lady MacBeth's crown, illustrates the self-fictionalizing mode that was adopted by many (185-217).

Such a reaction—creating psychological space out of unendurable physical limitations—seems, however, to partake more of the spirit of survival than of redefinition; and certainly, given the medical records of pervasive hysteria (Duffin 26-55), many women, either consciously or unconsciously, wanted to perform the conjuring feat. The overt repudiation of *femina domestica* that cultural history has mythologized as the women's movement can thus be seen as an attempt on the part of women to write their own history, to image themselves forth in their own way, to provide positive content for their definition (if, need be, by adopting the most desirable attributes of "manliness"). Critics like Auerbach are right, of course. Once women begin to create a new self, the self is quickly seen as a new myth. To take one example, the very real, matter-of-fact experiences of women's education and travel recorded by Molly Hughes in *A London Girl of the 1880's*, the third volume of her *Victorian Family*, were translated by the writers of the period into "feminism." The new self that women created was quickly co-opted into a new mythology, that of the "New Woman."

Not until the 1870s in Britain and the 1880s in America did the New Woman appear with any consistency as comic icon in the more popular humor magazines, while the term itself did not gain widespread use until the 1890s. As Ellen Jordan points out, the novelist Sarah Grand first made use of it in the

*North American Review* in March 1894 in "The Bawling Brotherhood," an article that attacks men for perpetuating the "cow-woman" (the household drudge) and the "scum-woman" (the prostitute) for their convenience; Grand observes that "the new woman . . . has been sitting apart in silent contemplation all these years thinking and thinking, until at last she solved the problem and proclaimed for herself what was wrong with Home-is-the-Woman's Sphere, and prescribed the remedy." Ouida (pen name of Marie Louise de la Ramée) picked up the term, capitalized it, and answered Grand's article in May, averring that the "New Woman" is one of "two unmitigated bores," the other being "The Workingman" (Jordan 20-21). In the ensuing controversy, *Punch* published a commentary with the attached verse (19-21): "There is a New Woman, and what do you think? / She lives upon nothing but Foolscap and Ink! / But though Foolscap and Ink are the whole of her diet, / This nagging New Woman can never be quiet!" (26 May 1894: 252).

The term itself, although used in a derogatory way by many feminist detractors, nonetheless carries an interesting connotation. While Jordan notes that the word *new* was much in vogue at the turn of the century when modernism was fashionable (21), "New Woman" also suggests a feminine component to the "New Adam," a component that most detractors—humorists or not—seem to overlook or interpret as London *Truth* does: "By the way, does the advent of the 'New Woman' signify the second Fall? In disobedience to every law of experience has woman been betrayed again into tasting of the tree of knowledge, and is the whole of the painfully established system which we now enjoy to be upset in consequence? The question is worth considering" (4 Oct. 1894: 774). What is perhaps testimony to *fin-de-siècle* distrust of serious social changes and enthusiasm for the superficially new is the insistence that the "Old Woman" (unlike the "Old Adam," who needed regeneration) was unflawed, whereas the "New Woman" (unlike the "New Adam," who carried redemption) was diabolical.

Indeed, some of *Punch*'s reactions to the movement were almost vituperative, as this parody of Shakespeare shows:

"The Seven Ages of Woman"

(*As Sir James Crichton Browne*
*seems prophetically to see them.*)

WOMAN's world's a stage,
And modern women will be ill-cast players;
They'll have new exits and strange entrances,
And one She will play many mannish parts,
And these her Seven Ages. First the infant
"Grinding" and "sapping" in its mother's arms,
And then the pinched High-School girl, with packed satchel,
And worn anaemic face, creeping like cripple
Short-sightedly to school. Then the "free-lover,"
Mouthing out IBSEN, or some cynic ballad
Made against matrimony. Then a spouter,
Full of long words and windy; a wire-puller,
Jealous of office, fond of platform-posing,
Seeking that bubble She-enfranchisement
E'en with abusive mouth. Then County-Councillor,
Her meagre bosom shrunk and harshly lined,
Full of "land-laws" and "unearned increment":
Or playing M.P. part. The sixth age shifts
Into the withered sour She-pantaloon,
With spectacles on nose and "Gamp" at side,
Her azure hose, well-darned, a world too wide
For her shrunk shanks; her once sweet woman's voice,
Verjuiced to Virgin-vinegarishness,
Grates harshly in its sound. Last scene of all,
That ends this strange new-fangled history,
Is sheer unwomanliness, mere sex-negation—
Sans love, sans charm, sans grace, sans everything. [14 May 1892: 230]

The *Punch* verse plays on the common assumption that a
woman's vital energies are sapped by engaging in education
and in politics; that the schoolgirl who overtaxes her intellect
by long hours of study redirects the vital force that prepares
her for motherhood. *Pick-Me-Up* agrees that the New Woman
forfeits everything that is attractive:

Last act of all, a woman *new* but old—
Old in that all the grace of youth has gone,
A thing that wears the outer garb of men,

Yet owneth but man's worsest qualities,
That preaches doctrines, needless and unclean,
The which herself but half doth understand;
She apes all manly sport, disgusting men,
Wears cigarette in mouth, eyeglasses in eye,
Prepares herself a sad unloved old age,
Sans womanhood, sans taste, sans everything. [17 Apr. 1897: 38]

Aside from parody, *Punch* published many valentines, some pining for the woman of old, some suggesting that woman was always a valentine, no matter what. The following two, published four years apart, illustrate that even within that short span of time, the mood has changed: the whimsical acceptance of the new fad has become permeated with a suspicion that gender reversal is a very present danger. In the first example, the versifier offers to allow his Valentine her fancies, if he may have his:

### "To a Girl of To-Day. A Valentine"

My Valentine! say what will take
    Your fancy in these wayward times,
What guerdon I can give will make
    You listen to my modish rhymes?
What fashion of to-day holds fast
    Your heart, that I may give it voice;
Or are the fancies of the past
    The things in which you most rejoice?

Are you "advanced," do you delight
    In politics and wish a vote?
Do you the platform cheers invite,
    I'll cry "Hear, hear!" with eager throat?
I'll vow that you should have a seat,
    And gain the affix of M.P.,
If you will only love me, sweet,
    And by the fireside vote for me.

Are you aesthetic, do you dress
    In terra-cotta or sage green,
Your tender thoughts in verse express,
    And rhymes that very little mean?
I'll yield to all you say and do,

And wear a lily 'mid men's jeers:
If only, Sweetheart, you'll be true,
    As I shall be through all the years.

Be medical, prescribe your pills
    And draughts to cure us when you please,
Your diagnoses of all ills
    Afflicting us must surely please.
'Mid surgeons you may bear your part,
    While LISTER looks on with surprise;
If you'll repair my broken heart,
    With one glance of your healing eyes.

If mathematical, I'll learn
    That awful Algebraic $x$;
With joy to problems I'll return
    That once my schoolboy soul would vex;
If muscular, at tennis strike
    The ball across the net's drawn line—
In short, be anything you like,
    My Pet, if only you'll be mine! [14 Feb. 1885: 77]

The versifier seems to assume that if he humors the new
fashion, old-fashioned virtues—hearth and home, fidelity—are
possible. Four years later his counterpart, who complains of the
shriller tone he finds characteristic of the New Woman, all but
rejects her endeavors:

"A Valentine. To an Advanced Woman"

Lady, in the ancient times,
    I had sung to you of love,
Mingling freely in my rhymes
    Soft allusions to the dove.
Now you'd scorn me if I wrote
    What the old-world poets taught;
For, as your slang goes, your "note"
    Is all philosophic thought.

You are equal now with man,
    Rather better, as it seems;
With amazement do we scan
    All your high ambitious dreams.
You would vote, and then hold sway

In St. Stephens, and methinks
Man must by the cradle stay,
　　While the child has forty winks.

Once we numbered 'mid your charms,
　　Soft low voice and tender yes;
Now you wave a Maenad's arms,
　　On the platform shrieking high.
Where is all the gentle grace,
　　Where the soft seductive glance,
In the bold virago face,
　　Like a *"Pétroleuse"* of France?

You go in for every "fad,"
　　Fancies that fanatics please;
Vaccination's counted bad,
　　Thus you help a dire disease.
Little children, though they learn
　　Ample lessons all the time,
Their poor pittance must not earn,
　　Since it is in Pantomime.

Lady, though you're now enroll'd
　　On committees, talking loud,
Trust me, in the days of old
　　You'd more reason to be proud.
Then no mannish maids we knew,
　　Man for woman's love would pine;
Can a cross between the two
　　Win me for a Valentine? [16 Feb. 1889: 81]

Without *Punch*'s harshness, the *Idler*—a British periodical founded in 1892 by the playwright and novelist Jerome K. Jerome—published an illustrated plea for the "Old Woman" written by F. Mabelle Pearse. The description of the New Woman, clothed in manly style and educated fully, gives way to a Tennysonian plea for woman as the inspiring force:

"To an 'Advanced Woman' "

Divinest Woman, shall I dare in humble rhyme to praise thee,
　　Can words depict thy modern charm of manful coat and hat?
Thy muscle and thy intellect! the ardours that upraise thee!
　　Thy newness day by day! thy mission! but I may not speak of that.

Reformer lion-hearted,
With fashion hast thou parted,
Thy unkempt locks lie limply on thy clear and classic head:
In hygienic clothing,
A waist and heels deep-loathing,
Thy unstayed figure freely flounders, knickerbockered.

With journalistic intellect and mind inquiring, fearless
Of man or devil, heav'n or hell, or even Mrs. Grundy:
To church thou dost but seldom go, nor lov'st the Abbey peerless;
Soul-anchored at the Ethical I see thee oft on Sunday.
Or in occult meditation,
Deep in lore of Eastern nation,
Thou followest the astral track of a Besant or a Stead:
Intellectual gyrations,
Mazes of re-incarnations,
Close wreathe their mystic spells around thy unbewildered head.

In fiction though we seek thee not, full many a time we've found thee,
With chapters of opinions, but a saving love of dress.
Thy heart is all platonic, though thy suitors flock around thee,
And the grave and simple-minded is made graver by thy "Yes."
But—if man finds it well-o
To wed an Aster Yellow,
Or dream Superfluous Woman is to wealth and title blind:
Should he fancy a Marcella,
With her views and lands at Mellor,
I would trust he may be happy—I would pray she may be kind.

O woman of the period, thy accomplishments are legion!
To lecture or to skirt-dance, to frivol or to fight,
To pioneer, to educate, to nurse the leprous region,
—These thy pastimes—but a graver, sweeter task is thy delight:
To proclaim to Man salvation,
Through Woman's mediation:
To show Earth's highest progress through the Woman-soul is found:
Man as intellect material,
Thou as spirit all ethereal,
Ah! 'tis Woman—Woman—Woman—that makes the world go round.
[Sept. 1894: 141]

Like the *Idler* versifier, Mr. Punch also waxed nostalgic for
the woman who eschewed the newer, "mannish" fashions and
who preferred home life to independence:

"A Bachelor's Growl"

Oh, the beautiful women, the women of ancient days,
  The ripe and the red, who are done and dead,
    With never a word of praise;
The rich, round SALLIES and SUSANS, the POLLIES and JOANS and PRUES,
  Who guarded their fame, and saw no shame
    In walking in low-heeled shoes.

They never shrieked on a platform; they never desired a vote;
  They sat in a row and liked things slow,
    While they knitted or patched a coat.
They lived with nothing of Latin, and a jolly sight less of Greek,
  And made up their books, and changed their cooks
    On an average once a week.

They never ventured in hansoms, nor climbed to the topmost 'bus,
  Nor talked with a twang in the latest slang;
    They left these fashions to us.
But, ah, she was sweet and pleasant, though possibly not well-read,
  The excellent wife who cheered your life,
    And vanished at ten to bed.

And it's oh the pity, the pity that time should ever annul
  The wearers of skirts who mended shirts,
    And never thought nurseries dull.
For everything's topsy-turvy now, the men are bedded at ten,
  While the women sit up, and smoke and sup
    In the Club of the Chickless Hen. [18 June 1892: 294]

Such a nostalgic piece for the poorly educated, subservient wife of the old school nonetheless preserves a warm and humorous tone not always characteristic of *Punch*. One contemporary, London *Truth*, consistently attacks the New Woman with considerably more pointedness, looking less to the past than inveighing against modern dress, manners, and attitudes. An excerpt from "Niceness Ad Nauseam!" shows that *Truth*, like Mrs. Lynn Linton, objects to the display occasioned by the new independence of thought and action:

But when "to do good" these "New Women" set out,
They begin with a shrill, introductory shout.
They take, never fear, most inordinate care
*Their* philanthropy's worked in publicity's glare.

The good deed done by stealth's small attraction for them,
Unsensational kindness they sternly contemn.
In their fight against vice they too oft have one plan—
To produce as much hubbub as ever they can.

The womanly instinct which shrinks from display
Has been stifled by them for full many a day;
Their modesty, attribute far above cost,
In their dragon-like virtue is hopelessly lost.
Their charity, if it were ever possess'd,
Has been only too thoroughly curb'd and repress'd;
Whilst their plain common-sense, like a too tender plant,
Has been choked by the growth of unlimited cant.

Still worse, to accomplish their prejudiced end,
To libel and slander they glibly descend.
The women who 'gainst their decrees dare to stand,
With an impudent charge of unchasteness they brand;
All amusement, save such as they sourly permit,
They shrilly denounce as obscene and unfit;
And, slaves to the fads which their follies impel,
Would enslave, if they could, the whole city as well.

And withal they're so dense in their crass self conceit
That they even are able their conscience to cheat.
Thus they little imagine that they, in their way,
Are as weak as the women 'gainst whom they inveigh;
Yet 'tis love of display tempts the daughter of Eve
Too often the path of strict virtue to leave;
And 'tis love of display the "New Woman" incites
To take her misguided empirical flights.

But for women, although in their folly profuse,
We are able to find in their sex some excuse;
They are weak, they have vanity hard to repress,
While of logic 'tis sure they no notion possess;
So some palliation, if but on this ground,
For the newest New Women is possibly found;
But there's not the least need we should bridle our pen
When we come to consider the newest New Men . . .
        [18 Oct. 1894: 878]


Like their British counterparts, American magazines paid
attention to the new phenomenon but were more likely to treat

the new styles and manners as provocative or humorous than as threatening, perhaps because of their democratic bias. Of all of the American magazines surveyed, New York *Truth* was the most conservative; after an abortive run from 1881 to 1884, it was reorganized in 1886 under Davison Dalziel and again in 1891. Through all of its chameleon-like changes, it maintained an interest in fashionable society, acquiring under the editorship of Blakeley Hall in the 1890s a passing reputation as a magazine devoted to the somewhat risqué topics of skirt dancers and bathing beauties (Mott 4: 83-85). Perhaps because it was devoted to a certain kind of female independence, it generally walked the thin edge of disapproval. Sentimental verse is characteristic of *Truth*, although one versifier gives a different perspective, playing on the idea that the New Woman is a Shakespearean shrew who needs taming. The interest of the piece lies in that it was composed by a woman—Ruth Hall—who adopts a male persona:

"The Fin de Siècle Duel"

You fight for a place in business;
    You fight for a chance to speak;
You fight for the right to study
    With men their Latin and Greek.
You fight for a seat in the street car;
    You fight for the Ayes and Noes;
You fight for our reformation;
    You even fight for our clothes.

We laugh at your pert presumption,
    You dear, divine, little shrew!
Yet every man among us
    Would like the taming of you.
We know the one way to conquer,
    Since this dread duel began;
So long as woman is woman,
    So long as man is man;

You may scold, and sneer, and scoff us,
    You may play your Katherine's part;
But Petruchio is victor
    If he but aim at your heart. [23 Mar. 1895: 3]

While even *Puck* (New York, 1877-1918) and *Judge* (New York, 1881-1937) occasionally veered from their primarily political interests to comment on the movement, such a forgiving view was especially characteristic of *Life*, a magazine founded in 1883 by John Ames Mitchell and noted from its inception for its fine graphics and "gentle humor," a humor that, as one historiographer notes, partakes of the "silvery laughter" of George Meredith's Comic Spirit (Mott 4: 556-68). Certainly, however, *Life* bewailed the loss of the old-fashioned, home-making woman, as a typical cover illustrates: a bluestocking wife at a desk surrounded by placards on the walls ("Dare to do right," "Heed they thy hour"), her mascot a lion statuette instead of a domestic dog, asks her husband, "Why do you men like the clubs so well? Is it because they are so homelike?" His reply—"It is because they are not homelike"—suggests the inversion that *Life's* satirists feared. All in all, as the cartoonist E.T. Richards suggests in a double-page spread, "War Would Have Its Compensations," but only "if Life could select the first boat-load to meet the enemy." In the boat, of course, is the New Woman dressed in checkered bloomers and a sailor cap; some of her companions are the actress Lillian Russell and the politician Anthony Comstock who sought to impose "blue laws" in New York.

*Life's* view of the New Woman was ambiguous, however, and many of its attacks, when they came, were whimsical. H.W. Phillips's "Fables for the Times. The Ambitious Hippopotamus" is typical. The illustration by T.S. Sullivant, who draws a splay-footed, winged hippo hovering over a conglomeration of frightened animals, the giraffe hiding his head behind the musk-ox and a small antelope taking refuge under another hippo, tells almost all of the story. The fable recounts the adventures of a hippopotamus who, upon seeing an eagle, "became immediately fired with a desire to fly." Her wish is granted, and "with a pardonable vanity" she flies off to show her friends, but "the effect on the other animals disconcerted the good-natured hippopotamus to such an extent that she lost control of herself and sailed through the forest like an avalanche on a bender. Down went the trees, and crack went the branches, while horror-stricken beasts with bristling hair split the welkin with their shrieks." She swoops home to her favorite mud-bath and splashes down, saying, "Oh, Jupiter! take 'em off! . . . I now see that the hippopotamus was not intended to fly." The "Immoral" attached to the fable gives the antifeminist bias: "It takes more than bloomers to make a man" (14 May 1896: 389).

Like *Life*, the short-lived, sophisticated *Chic* (New York, 1880-81) devoted a number of lighthearted columns and verses to the new phenomenon. The humorist John Kendrick Bangs, who founded *Chic*, also wrote for *Life* with the same whimsical topicality that the following shows:

"The New Profession"

I have learned the fastest dances,
    And I've caught the baby stare,
And I throw about my glances
    With the very newest air;
I've been taught the Langtry giggle,
    Which gives so much "chic" to talk,
And the Sarah Bernhardt wriggle,
    And the Lady Lonsdale walk.

Yes, I used to have a passion
    For old China and high art,
But they're going out of fashion,
    So I've had to change my part;
For I think it is the duty
    Of a girl to keep ahead
Of the style, and be a beauty
    Where the English once have led.

. . . I [now] go in for plain speaking,
    With a spicy touch of slang;
It's the style—there's no more sneaking,
    I just sing out with a bang.
For it's every girl's true duty,
    And quite in the English way,
To profess to be a beauty—
    Not to mind what people say.

I have learned the art of chaffing,
    All the men think it's so "cute,"

And a way of loudly laughing
     That is just the thing to suit,
With a jaunty air of pertness,
     Like a soubrette's on the stage—
In London their alertness
     Makes our Yankee girls the rage. [22 Sept. 1880]


Some early New Woman verses describe what the eighteenth century might have called a "scribbling woman," a bluestocking who, discontented with her lot, devoted her days to writing querulous articles. And while certainly many took to their pens to air their grievances, others took to the streets to pursue their individual talents, making a public statement by their dress and manners and by their increasing education, changing marriages, and agitation for suffrage. The chapters that follow give an overview of the New Woman as the comic press in Britain and in America saw her. The record shows that while the liberated sisterhood on both sides of the Atlantic is portrayed with the caricaturist's universal delight in the unexpected and *outré*, the Americans treat their own more sympathetically, especially in the case of bloomers and bicycles. Indeed, in many cases, the American press seems more to be laughing *with* the New Woman than *at* her, an attitude that demonstrates a degree of acceptance, at least of the myth, if not of the New Woman's substance.

At the turn of the century, then, women were newly fictionalized in a way that superficially touched upon some of the more serious problems engendered by the old myth. The neurasthenia that plagued the intelligent and frustrated woman, Alice James and Virginia Woolf only two well-known examples; the lack of adequate employment that contributed to, for example, rising rates of prostitution as well as to doomed utopian schemes of emigration and communal settlements (Sigsworth and Wyke 77-99; Hammerton 52-71; Dare 195-99): these darker pictures underlie both George Du Maurier's statuesque, complacent modern woman in the pages of *Punch* and Francis Attwood's charming bicycle girl in *Life*. What the caricaturists seized upon were the changes in marriage and careers, clubs and sports, and clothing and manners that signaled changes in perception. And who is to say whether the fashion-conscious Old Woman, adopting a modified version of waist-coat and bloomers, did not find herself walking more freely— and thus thinking more freely?

# ONE

# Women and Marriage
## *"Running in Blinkers"*

"Is Marriage a failure?" old mivvies are asking. Of course, that de-
pends;
But a dashing young feller like me, with good looks, and good 'ealth,
and good friends,
Knows a trick that's worth two on it, CHARLIE. While life goes on
nutty and nice,
And the ochre slings in pooty slick, it is blooming bad bizness to splice.
—*Punch* 29 Sept. 1888: 156

SO OPEN a declaration against the Victorian ideal of domestic
bliss by 'Arry, *Punch*'s cockney maven, is more than just a class
phenomenon; other "dashing young fellers" in all walks found
the expense of setting up an establishment a strong deterrent
to marriage. In the 1880s, when the women's movement began
to receive almost constant notice in the press, 'Arry's lighthearted profession of bachelorhood represented a serious threat
to the growing number of superfluous women. *Punch*'s "Sketch
from Nature" of a neatly dressed, middle-class girl standing
wistfully in front of a sign that reads "No Reasonable Offer
Refused" (Fig. 1) is indicative of the situation at the end of the
century, when an increasing number of women failed to fulfill traditional expectations to marry and to rear children.
Such women were frequently called *redundant* in discussions
of the time, a term that suggests not only their status of
personal alienation but the prevailing attitude toward their
employment in the public sector. Many became governesses or
nurses, two socially acceptable, if relatively unremunerative,
careers that masked economic necessity with acceptable
nurturing roles; perhaps many more, both unnamed and unnum-
bered, became dependents—poor cousins or sisters or aunts—

Fig. 1. "A Sketch from Nature." *Punch*, 12 July 1884: 22.

in extended families. At the lower end of the social scale, women worked side by side with men in the factories and in the mines or eked out their existence as seamstresses. The harsh economic reality was that, for many, prostitution was the only way to provide daily bread.

The plight of such redundant women was treated in Parliament and pulpit, but the combination of factors that caused a dramatic increase in the number of young women for whom marriage was not an option was too complex for immediate solution. On the one hand, better health and nutritional practices increased the life span and fertility of women; on the other, British foreign wars decimated the young male population (Peterson 6). The disease rates shifted as well. Before 1880, for instance, tuberculosis had accounted for a 50 percent death rate for females between the ages of fifteen and thirty-five; later, the disease began to strike more men than women. The changing statistics seemed to justify neo-Spencerian medical opinion that British women, as the flowers of civilization, received more careful medical supervision than men (Johansson 169-70). It is interesting to speculate, however, whether the increase in feminist activity had an effect not only on these but on all mortality rates, either by freeing women from the virtual paralysis of body and will called neurasthenia or by causing them so actively to reaffirm their status as "womanly" women that they received the medical attention they were supposedly entitled to. Whatever the combination of forces, as the number of unmarriageable women increased, so did the number of women in the work force, many "emancipated" not from desire but from need.

The situation in the United States was similar, as the pamphlet *Too Many Women* suggests. This commentary on a report that appeared in the *New York Herald* on 16 November 1886 gives 125,000 women in the city as self-supporting, with one-third unemployed, another one-third destitute, and 20,000— almost the same number as those legitimately working—engaged in prostitution. The author of the pamphlet, who blames modern novelists for impeding evolution by fictionalizing the fragile, sickly beauty as ideal woman, calls for a form of eugenics: "In the great redundance of women there is fortunately one beneficial feature. It affords an opportunity of selection of those best fitted to become wives. If once a process of selection of the fittest was general, more attention would be given to the proper training of young girls" (53).

Eugenics was clearly in the air, whether discussed seriously in a pamphlet such as this or provocatively under the banner of social Darwinism that George Bernard Shaw so flamboyantly waves seven years later in *Man and Superman*: "If a woman can, by careful selection of a father, and nourishment of herself, produce a citizen with efficient senses, sound organs and a good digestion, she should clearly be secured a sufficient reward for that natural service. . . . Even a joint stock human stud farm (piously disguised as a reformed Foundling Hospital or something of that sort) might well, under proper inspection and regulation, produce better results than our present reliance on promiscuous marriage" (725-26). Clearly, Jack Tanner's eugenic diatribe was not an immediate answer; the Roebuck Ramsdens who tossed Tanner's *Revolutionist's Handbook* in the trash can in Britain would have been just as likely to do so in New York. A similar idea appears in the British *Pick-Me-Up*, where one writer decides that what is needed to solve the problem of redundant women is "The Science of Marriage." Since opening the professions to women reduces the number of men who can make an adequate income to support a wife, the writer makes the Shavian suggestion that a state-funded Bureau of Heredity be established: "When science had sufficiently attended to the matter it would only be necessary to keep a few armies of matrimonial gardeners, who should select the leading types, and bring about skilfully corresponding matrimonial unions. . . . Then the Bureau would be able to grow statesmen, poets, and philosophers as easily as we can now grow cucumbers" (1 Nov. 1890: 68-69). What is interesting about the proposals, whether made seriously or tongue in cheek, is their lack of class bias; writers are talking less about rearing a stronger, more efficient working class than they are about strengthening the human race. Such proposals reflect a generalized scientific cast of mind that showed itself in a variety of ways—in the call for "hygienic" marriages, for instance, and for women's athletics and dress reform. Perhaps one of the most important factors in the women's movement was just this increasingly modern idea about fitness for marriage and propagation, because it helped to reinterpret the Victorian conception of female beauty in a more realistic light.

While such talk of eugenics was a way of dealing with an overwhelming social problem futuristically, some reformers had more practical proposals. Emigration, an immediate, although partial solution to women's unemployment, was one of these. Fostered by the feminist *English Woman's Journal*, proponents sought to send well-trained women to the colonies, not only to ameliorate the immediate social crisis but to provide long-term personal benefits, such as education, experience, and an improved standard of living. Aside from those eager to attempt any kind of subsistence work, a number of populations were affected: the genteel but unemployable gentlewoman, whose old standby—running a dame school—became impracticable as teacher preparation schools opened; the educated teacher; and the trainable or the skilled at handiwork or domestic service. One contemporary commentator claimed that, all in all, 405,000 women were redundant and available for emigration in 1862 (Hammerton 53-54, 58).

Even though most adherents of the movement discouraged the idea that they were fostering a lonely hearts club in disguise, the notion persisted. Public opinion accused even the feminist editors of the *English Woman's Journal*, Bessie Parkes and Barbara Bodichon, of running a marriage bureau (Hammerton 59), and certainly the satirists treated the connection as self-evident. After Lord Lorne's speech on female emigration to Canada, for instance, *Punch* published a sketch of a becurled and homely belle reading from a newspaper and saying enthusiastically to her Gorgon of a mother, " 'The further West the Young Woman went, the more offers she got!' Oh, Mamma, let us go to Canada, as far West as possible!" (31 Dec. 1881: 301).

The idea of emigration, however, was intended to help those who were truly in need. Despite *Punch*'s many jokes at the expense of the lower classes and of women who forsook the home to be independent, its reformist streak proved in this instance to be even stronger than its attitude of *noblesse oblige*. One example is its mid-century response to the issue of starving needlewomen; it not only proposed and supported practical

ideas at home but also furthered the idea of emigration. Its
stance is well defined by an 1850 commentary, "Our Female
Supernumeraries. In a Series of Views" (1). From the "commercial" man's point of view, the "muslin home-market
is . . . in depression"; the cynic complains that women have
always caused mischief, while the "alarmist" fulminates
against a "petticoat government"; the scholar worries about
the feminization of England; and the naturalist believes that
"redundant females [need to] take wing, like the hen chaff-
finch." *Punch's* "Own View," which ends the article, is different: "It is lamentable that thousands of poor girls should starve
here upon slops, working for slopsellers, and not only dying
old maids because dying young, when stalwart mates and solid
meals might be found for all in Australia. . . . It remains with
the Government and the country to find them wings."

One kind of "wing" was suggested by a letter in the London
*Times* on 1 March 1850 (6c), in which the writer recommends
establishing a registry of reliable workers to counter the crisis
in unemployment blamed, in part, on the efforts of the charity
schools to supply sewing services. In the same year *Punch* supports the idea in "The Hidden Needlewomen," suggesting a
registry in every post office so that the "suffering creatures"
could alleviate "the dietary of thrice-drawn tea-leaves and but-
terless bread" (117). A more radical solution was effected in
June, when sixty-one needlewomen sponsored by Sir Sidney
Herbert's Needlewoman Emigration Society embarked for Australia. The "words of affection, exhortation and farewell" and
encouragement of "order, cheerfulness, command of temper,
and general amiability of demeanor" (*Times* 28 June 1850: 7c)
with which they were sent off reflect a typical mid-Victorian
attitude that personal rectitude will be rewarded, an attitude
later codified by Samuel Smiles, whose books on "Self-Help,"
"Character," "Thrift," and "Duty" became middle-class by-
words.

*Punch* took up the idea with a mixture of seriousness and
quixotism, speaking movingly for those who otherwise had little voice. In its remarks and illustrations, *Punch* fostered the
view that emigration would help to solve problems of vice,
unemployment, and redundancy at home, yet it did so by pro-

viding an idealized picture of life in the colonies, a picture
colored by middle-class values about marriage and possessions.
In 1850, for instance, it depicted "The Needlewoman at Home
and Abroad," a double-panel illustration in which a ragged
woman "at home" in England is accosted by a well-dressed
man outside a gin shop, while abroad she happily bounces a
baby on her knee in a comfortable room, as her farmer husband
and young son look on (15). Accompanying the illustration is
"The Needlewoman's Farewell" (14), a poem about the Aus-
tralian emigration. It is written from the viewpoint of the
woman, who accuses "Hard step-mother, O England, and nig-
gard of thy care" of confining its workers to hovels until they
died or resorted to prostitution:

> . . . And so we strove with straining eyes, in squalid rooms, and chill;
>   The needle plied until we died—or worse—oh, Heaven, have
>     pity!—
> Thou knowest how 'twas oftener for want we sinned, than will—
>   Oh, nights of pain and shameful gain, about the darkling city!
>
> Body and soul we gave for food, nor yet could we be fed;
>   Blear-eyed or blind, we pored and pined, and battled like our neigh-
>     bours;
> And the city roared about us, and over each weak head
>   Washed the wild waves, till in our graves we rested from our la-
>     bours.

The real hope that spurs emigration is revealed in one of the
later stanzas:

> Now speed thee, good ship, over sea, and bear us far away,
>   Where food to eat, and friends to greet, and work to do await us—
> Where against hunger's tempting we shall not need to pray—
>   Where in wedlock's tie, not harlotry, we shall find men to mate
>     us. [1850: 15]

Despite the optimism with which the bevies of "redundant"
women were sent to the colonies, the Victorians considered
emigration—like work—to be a poor alternative to marriage.
One writer, in a spirit of triumphant compromise, predicts that

controlled emigration will lead to more marriages. Since lowered job competition will raise the market value of "redundant" women left behind, he suggests, more women will find respectable jobs and not be forced into prostitution; thus, men will be less likely to obtain female companionship on "illicit" terms. "As soon as their sole choice lies between marriage and a life of real and not nominal celibacy," writes W.R. Greg, "the apparent redundancy of women . . . will vanish as by magic" (quoted in Helsinger, Sheets, and Veeder 2: 136). Another anodyne, which skirted the ideas of eugenics and emigration altogether, was proposed by Walter Besant. Writing about the dire effects of an influx of gentlewomen on the labor market, he poses a mercantile twist to the French practice of providing daughters with a *dot*. British parents, he says, should purchase deferred annuities for their daughters, making them more attractive to prospective suitors and saving them from genteel poverty (and the labor market from them) should they remain unmarried. *Punch* responds whimsically to the idea:

"Husbands and Husbandry"

In England Trade is dull and slow
And girls are portionless, and so
Unto the altar men won't go
    Of Hymen, burning uselessly.

But BESANT sees a novel way
Of making marriage brisk and gay,
Commanding British sires to slay
    The Demon of Celibacy.

In that good time, as Walter B.
Explains, all maids shall wedded be,
And hardened bachelors with glee
    Shall join in amorous rivalry.

He tells us of the plight we're in
When girls who wish to, *cannot* spin,
And hundreds madly strive to win
    Each post of well-paid drudgery.

And fiercer still that fight shall glow,
While youths hold back, and "have no go,"

Because the maidens have no *dot*,—
    So much for modern chivalry!

And more and more will suitors bold
The offer of their hands withhold,
Until their sweethearts they behold
    Endowed with a sufficiency.

The dulness deepens. On, ye Sires,—
Whoe'er to sons-in-law aspires—
And save your girls from fruitless fires
    By saving half your salary! [7 Apr. 1888: 158]

The wide range of proposed solutions, from the serious to
the silly, suggests how near to the public's consciousness the
problem lay. For almost all women, marriage was worth pursuing in economic and social terms; it promised not only social
standing but also some degree of financial protection. The difficulty was in finding a husband or, as *Punch* would have it,
in slaying the "Demon of Celibacy." Hand in hand with the
population inequity, the dearth of opportunity to meet prospective suitors and the cost of a wedding itself worked against
women of marriageable age. The situation was especially difficult for "respectable" girls in domestic service who were usually barred from entertaining male guests in their employers'
houses. *Punch* treats the problem lightly in "A Sunday Story,"
in which a mistress takes her maid to task:

> *Mistress (severely).* "I understand, Mary, that, instead of going to
> Church this Morning, you were seen in Hyde Park!"
> *Mary.* "Oh, please, 'M, I went to the Service in the Open Air!"
> [26 Mar. 1887: 154]

As the illustrator shows, however, the "pew" for "the Service
in the Open Air" is a park bench, and the "congregation" a
young man in livery. A year later in "London Idyls," the caption
to a nicely realized sketch of a courting couple guarded by
Bobbies seems to make amends for the earlier joke. The caption
comes from a serious letter published in the London *Times* ten
days earlier: "It is no use shutting our eyes to the fact that the
Parks take the place of drawing-rooms for a large part of the

community. . . . Until Masters and Mistresses are willing to
provide a reception-room for the 'young men' of their five or
six maid-servants, the Parks must be their trysting-ground, and
therefore ought to be kept free of rowdyism. Respectable young
people of the class to which I allude deserve as much protection
from 'gangs of men and women' as do the residents of our city"
(16 June 1888: 282).

The difficulty of courtship was matched by the expense of
marriage; it often took years for a young man to afford even a
modest establishment. Molly Hughes, whose autobiographical
trilogy *A Victorian Family* recounts growing up and marrying
in the final decades of the century, writes matter-of-factly that
she waited ten years for her fiancé to finish his law training
and go into practice. Hughes was fortunate, however; she pursued a full-time teaching career while she waited for her Arthur.
Her situation was perhaps more representative than not, although *Punch* generally sees middle-class pretension and female rapacity as the culprits, as one cartoon of a wooing couple
shows in "Safe Bind, Safe Find!":

> *Young Spoonbill.* "Ah, my dearest Miss Shillinworth, if I may—I
> have long wished for this sweet opportunity, but I hardly dare trust
> myself now to speak the Deep Emotion—But, 'n short, I Love you!—
> and—your—your Smile—would shed—would shed—would—"
> *Miss S.* "Oh, never mind the wood-shed! How's your Aunt's Money
> invested? and where are the Securities deposited?!!"
> [17 Nov. 1883: 230]

More sentimentally, the magazine deplores the false financial expectations that stand in the way of true affection. In so
doing, *Punch* was actually contributing to the realignment of
the class structure that it seemed otherwise to support. In "Love
à La Mode," for instance, the woman is clearly wealthier than
her suitor:

He

The moonlight's on the sea, and on her hair;
She is a real beauty! How they'd stare,
The boys, if I brought home a wife—but there,
  What bosh it is to think of love and marriage;

She'd want a house, we'll say in Grosvenor Place,
Ascot and Goodwood, one must go the pace,
And such a fashionable lady's face
    Must smile upon the world from out a carriage. . . .

        She

The moonlight's on the sea. What idle tales
The poets tell of moonlight. What avails
My love and his?—for love in these days fails,
Though girls would risk it to gain love's one guerdon.
He thinks that I want diamonds; and I,
Who for his sake and love's would gladly die,
Know that between us must for ever lie
    His coward fear lest life should prove a burden.
    [14 Sept. 1889: 121]

Finally, and certainly more typical of the magazine's attack
on snobbery, *Punch's* caption for a sketch of a butcher chatting
with his customer suggests how completely middle-class ma-
terialism has influenced all classes. When the customer congratulates Mr. Ribbes on his upcoming marriage, the butcher
replies: "Much obliged, but I dunno so much about Congratu-
lations. It's corstin' me a pretty Penny, I tell yer. Mrs. Ribbes
as is to be, she wants 'er *Trousseau*, yer know; an' then there's
the Furnishin', an' the Licence, an' the Parson's Fees; an' then
I 'ave to give 'er an' 'er sister a bit o' Jool'ry a-piece; an' wot
with one thing an' another—sh's a 'eavy Woman, yer know,
Thirteen Stun odd—well, I reckon she'll a corst me pretty near
*Two-an'-Eleven a Pound* afore I git 'er 'Ome!" (25 Mar. 1893:
133).

The butcher's woes are comical, but they represent a very
real problem. Whether trivial or profound, the proposed solutions failed to resolve 'Arry's complaint, that "it is blooming
bad bizness to splice." Despite the expense of marriage, however, the impetus to marry increased as the opportunities for
women to meet male counterparts on a more informal basis
grew rapidly. The middle-class woman could look to more than
church and family as sources of introductions; increased education and travel, career options, and, ultimately, a general public recognition of her growing independence broadened the

scope of her personal relationships. If she did marry, she underwent a rite of initiation into sexuality that brought with it a host of responsibilities: nursing the sick, rearing children, running a household, and arbitrating moral behavior. If she remained single, she joined a growing company of women who had to forge a new female identity unless they wished to remain a perpetual and eventually superannuated "young person" within the normal framework of the Victorian family. The very presence of a group that either could not or would not comfortably fit the norm arbitrated by Mrs. Grundy, the popular British embodiment of nineteenth-century mores, eventually changed the sense of what a woman might expect in courtship and marriage. The more conventional attitude persisted, of course, but discussions about the scope of marriage and the roles of the partners, legal rights, medical practices, and lifestyle had their parallels in the comic press. There were, as the caption to one *Punch* cartoon suggests, new ground rules to marriage:

"Two Sides to a Question"

"Oh, Flora, let us be man and wife. You at least understand me—the only woman who ever did!"
"Oh yes; I understand *you* well enough, Sir Algernon. But how about your ever being able to understand *me?*" [26 Sept. 1896: 147]

Some *Punch* satirists took refuge in the idea that the New Woman had changed in outer garb only; true love, they were convinced, would restore the natural order. This point of view is illustrated in "The Old, Old Story," in which two onlookers spy a perfect match:

*The Colonel.* "Yes; *He* was Senior Wrangler of his Year, and *She* took a Mathematical Scholarship at Girton; and now they're Engaged!"
*Mrs. Jones.* "Dear me, how interesting! and oh, how different their Conversation must be from the insipid twaddle of Ordinary Lovers!"

THEIR CONVERSATION.

*He.* "And what would *Dovey* do, if Lovey were to *die?*"
*She.* "Oh, Dovey would die too!" [20 Dec. 1884: 294]

Fig. 2. "Cross Purposes." *Punch*, 2 December 1882, 258.

In "Cross Purposes," another cartoon based on a similar idea, a bespectacled bluestocking flirts with a Savoy Row gentleman complete with monocle and cane (Fig. 2): "He had gone in for Fashion, She for Mind and Culture. They met. He listened and loved. She saw and was conquered. They both secretly resolved to make themselves worthy of each other in every respect." "Their Next Meeting," as the illustrator shows, finds her in high-heeled boots and a bustle and him with a book tucked under his arm, in the slouch hat and shabby overcoat of the scholar (2 Dec. 1882: 258).

The question of courting the New Woman was not so easily resolved, and the spate of cartoons and satires suggests a popular confusion about the nature of the new phenomenon. An extended discussion appeared in the 1894 *Idler*, where the article entitled "How to Court the 'Advanced Woman'" bears an Aubrey Beardsley illustration, the choice of artist rather than the drawing itself a hint, perhaps, that the editor found the New Woman sexually ambiguous. Angus Evan Abbott gives a whimsical narrative about courtship, moving from the "cavewoman through her more mercantile aspects—woman as Chattel," as "Souvenir," and as "Pound of Tea" or dowry—to the present-day "Man-Woman," "for whom Man will not risk his life, whom Man will not buy, whom Man will not take as a gift, nor can Man be bribed to receive" (Sept. 1894: 193-94).

Notably absent among the female writers assembled to respond to the question of how to court the New Woman is the feminist apologist Eliza Lynn Linton; on the other hand, Sarah Grand, emancipated novelist and mayoress of Bath, promotes a conservative view when she proposes that "respect" will win the day. The relationship between the sexes should be one of mutual toleration, she decrees; every woman should "render, by a thousand little feminine ways, a life more comfortable, which is generally spent in shielding her from discomfort." Grand, then, defines the "Advanced Woman" in a maternal way—"one who says little, and is constantly, yet unobtrusively, ameliorating the condition of her fellow mortals, be they men or women" (Sept. 1894: 204)—that would not be uncomfortable to old-fashioned readers. Mary Chevalita Dunn, writing under the pen name of George Egerton, temporizes less; while

she believes that man's superiority has been "purely
... economic" and that woman is "always his Superior" because of her physiological control over the very existence of
the human race, she sees rapprochement in shared differences.
Intelligent women, she suggests, enjoy old-fashioned wooing
and find that in this "world of compensations," a man's "restful
companionship" may pair happily with a woman's intellectual
life (Sept. 1894: 195-96).

This relatively mild-mannered and sometimes droll article
only touches on what seems to be the real issue about modern
courtships, the fear that were women to take the initiative,
gender roles would become confused. Such concern, that men
will be emasculated by feminine aggressiveness, is the theme
of *Life*'s "A Woman of the Future." In this satire, W.J. Lampton
writes in the persona of Miss Eliza Linger (a name that evokes
Eliza Lynn Linton), who, on a moonlit June night, woos her
desired husband. Herbert has "the coy grace of an old fashioned
girl": he blushes, he speaks shyly, he "laugh[s] with a cute
chirp, as of a bird." For Eliza, he is her "more than wise charmer
of womankind," without whom she would "wander away and
be lost to the career which is so grandly opening before [her]."
Her avowal is patterned on a nineteenth-century romantic hero's speech: "As for myself, there are no heights to which I may
attain that with me Herbert shall not go as a husband whose
great love makes him the equal of his wife in all the honors
the world may confer upon her. 'A perfect husband, nobly
planned, / To love, to comfort and command' " (16 May 1895:
326-27).

The ending couplet is borrowed from Wordsworth's "She
Was a Phantom of Delight," a poem that in itself might be used
as a commentary on the nineteenth century's changing understanding of women. The progress of the original, which records
the poet's increasing understanding of the woman he writes
about, coincidentally parallels the progress of the popular response to the feminist movement. The object of the poem, first
"A lovely Apparition, sent / To be a moment's ornament" (ll.
3-4), is then seen as a "Spirit," "A Creature not too bright or
good / For human nature's daily food" (ll. 17-18); in these
guises, she seems initially the innocent, graceful maiden of

Victorian idealization and then the domestic goddess. Finally, given intellect and self-discipline, she comes into her human estate:

And now I see with eye serene
The very pulse of the machine;
A Being breathing thoughtful breath,
A Traveller between life and death;
The reason firm, the temperate will,
Endurance, foresight, strength, and skill;
A perfect Woman, nobly planned,
To warn, to comfort, and command;
And yet a Spirit still, and bright
With something of angelic light. [ll. 21-30]

British satirists, unlike their American counterparts, whose humor was both broader and more whimsical, were perhaps even more concerned about gender transference. *Pick-Me-Up*, for example, predicts that the New Man will reject the new morality:

We've talked about the Woman who Did—

What quite a lot of women do;
And then of One who was Forbid
    Because she said she Wanted To.
Enough, and more, we have debated
    Their cause, even if 'tis worth a penny,
While no one yet has celebrated
    The Man who Isn't Having Any.

Then come, my muse, and let us sing
    The praises of this tempted hero,
For man is now the bashful thing,
    And woman the gay cavaliero.
She does the wooing, frames the plan,
    Assures him there is none to stop her.
All's frank and free—but then the man
    Objects that it would be improper!

School-girls with satchels of wild oats
    Have come to make mankind their prey;
And some have dofft their petticoats
    As being rather in the way.
To prove that they are frank and free,

Lord knows what else they would not doff;
But *voila!* When they turn to see—
The Newest Man is making off! . . . [11 Jan. 1896: 236]

These somewhat generalized complaints are paralleled by more focused ones that women have become so legalistic that they have destroyed romance. Jay Hambridge's cartoon of an "Up to Date" courting couple, published in New York *Truth*, represents the fear iconographically. In the left frame, he is about to declare his love; in the right frame, she presses two electric buttons in her belt and says, "Now you may propose, if you wish," the buttons causing a camera and microphone to pop up on her sleeves (17 Aug. 1895: 89). The concern over the female assertiveness and journalistic scrutiny pictured here is a mask for the fear that woman's nature has changed radically. In one satire *Punch* blames the change on modern education that has so warped women's emotional responses that they must rely on legal means to acquire husbands. Differing considerably in tone from *Life*'s "gentle satire," then, the prophetic "Love-Making in 1891. (When Women shall have obtained their Rights)" shows the New Woman, educated in all matters except those of the heart, interrupting her suitor's romantic flights with learned commentary. The word *dearest* evokes a lecture on the law of real and personal property; *moonlight*, on modern astronomy; and *nightingale*, on natural history.

*Edwin.* Believe me, dearest—
*Angelina.* Pardon me, Edwin, but is that the best adjective you can use? The word "dearest" implies that I have cost you a great deal—have been very expensive. Now when I prepared our settlements with my Solicitor I—[*Explains the Law of Real and Personal Property.*]
*Edwin.* Thanks, darling, your lecture has been delightful. But see, the moonlight tinges the trees without—
*Angelina.* Moonlight? I am glad you have mentioned the moon. Do you know that our planetary system is—[*Exhaustively canvasses the whole system of modern astronomy.*]
*Edwin.* Wonderful! But the nightingale has begun her sweet singing—
*Angelina.* Really! That reminds me, you told me the other day that you knew little or nothing of Natural History. I have an excellent

memory, and will recite a few chapters of White's *Selborne* to you. [*Does so.*]

Edwin, who dozes through much of the conversation, finally extricates himself:

> *Edwin (tearing himself away)*. Farewell, dearest—I should say my own one, or rather *femme sole*. Good-bye until I see thee again. [*Exit to attempt to escape to America, to avoid damages for a Breach of Promise of Marriage.*]
> *Angelina*. Fortunately I have taken my Medical Degree, and can read his mind like an open book! [*Exit to her Solicitor to restrain him!*]
> [10 Dec. 1881: 273]

Despite the changing courtship patterns of the New Woman, the more conventional preconceptions about marriage persist until the end of the century, the difference being, perhaps, that conservative essays in the 1890s tried to defend maintaining the marital status quo by proving "scientifically" that a woman's primary function was maternal and that her own vitality and that of succeeding generations would be sapped if she directed her interests elsewhere. In this regard similar preconceptions underlie two very different works, "Hints to Make Home Happy," published in mid-century *Punch*, and *Domestic Duels: Evening Talks on the Woman Question*, published in 1898. Both assume that the home is woman's domain and that her husband and family are her vocation; neither takes account of the status of the redundant woman.

In keeping with *Punch*'s satirical tone, the 1844 "Hints" essay recommends to the average husband that he "take frequent opportunities of praising features and personal peculiarities which are as different as possible from [his] wife's," use the fireplace fender as a footstool, be careless about when he appears for dinner (and about whom he brings with him), complain about his wife's pastry, and generally stay out late with his cronies. "In short," the essay concludes, "on all occasions consult studiously your own inclinations, and indulge, without the least restriction, your every whim and caprice; but never regard your wife's feelings at all; still less make the slightest allowance for any weakness or peculiarity of her character; and your home will assuredly be as happy as you deserve that it should be" (186).

To the wife, the essayist recommends a policy of appeasement before marriage and carelessness about personal appearance afterward. A reliance on curlpapers and flannel dressing gowns at home and extravagant clothing outside; a nervous disposition; a neglect of politeness; and either negligence or overfastidiousness in housekeeping: all combine to keep a husband in line. The conclusion is paired to that of "Hints" to husbands: " . . . bear these grand principles in mind—that men must be crossed and thwarted continually, or they are sure to be tyrants; that a woman, to have her rights, must stand up for them; and that the behaviour which won a man's affections, is by no means necessary to preserve them" (208). The reverse of these recommendations is the writer's recipe for a loving relationship based on the ageless ingredient of mutual respect; but even in 1844, the phrase "women's rights" seems to premise marital discord.

Fifty-four years later, in 1898, one finds the conventional view more pointedly framed in *Domestic Duels*, in which the persona "Mr. Notion" undertakes to reeducate his wife. Mrs. Notion argues for equality, questions why the wife should be a "domestic drudge," and complains that men "love to patronize and protect us; but we are tired of being protected and coddled into weakness, inferiority, and nothingness." Mr. Notion answers these feminist complaints by citing women's "own peculiar and appropriate sphere, where God has placed them" and by arguing the sacred inviolability of the home. "In her care and keeping are immortal spirits, and their precious physical casements," he exclaims: "Here all the sciences converge. Biology, psychology, physiology, hygiene, logic, rhetoric, theology, ethics, chemistry, physics, architecture, zoology, botany, mathematics, philology, astronomy, history—here all have a practical application" (Girvin 12). The home, in short, becomes a microcosm of the sciences—presided over by one who has only informal training. Mrs. Notion laughs at the idea of domestic science, but she is eventually convinced by her husband's logic.

One of Mr. Notion's main points, that physiology predetermines women to marriage and motherhood, was a popular assumption and one that threatened the self-identity of the redundant woman. The physiology argument was double-edged; it painted a flattering picture of woman's sensitivity while denying her intellectual capabilities. The conclusion that "woman is less reflective . . . than man" is based, then, on her constitution: "Woman's nervous system is more highly organized, closely connected in all its parts, and intimately related to the reproductive region than that of man. With her, sensation is much more potent than with him, and all her parts are more sympathetic. Her skin possesses the quality of reproducing at every part that which is felt at a single point. She attains puberty sooner than man, and the substance of her brain is less dense and consistent" (58-59).

A similar argument about woman's responsiveness and talent for practical matters rather than for theoretical study was pursued to a different conclusion by some feminists, who, like Mona Caird, looked to woman's nature and asked why, if her primary function was motherhood, she was endowed so bountifully with other attributes and abilities. Caird suggests that the development of extramaternal interests is more natural than an exclusive focus upon motherhood and urges that a fairer balance among interests would make better mothers of those suffering from nervous strain (817-20, 825). In all of these comments, one can see the beginnings of a new life-style that includes personal time not just as a necessity but as a right. One of the most practical approaches was proposed by Honnor Morten, who recommends a utilitarian life-style that sounds remarkably modern. Rather than pretending that the "domestic drudge" is "a happy, beauteous queen," Morten suggests that women create personal time and streamline domestic chores by adopting French ways—preparing continental breakfasts instead of English breakfasts, serving cold cuts for lunch, and ordering main meals from restaurants. Morten calls, moreover, for the elimination of extra pots and pans and such kitchen gewgaws as fluted molds enjoyed for aesthetic rather than for practical reasons (73-76). Similarly, the author of "Are Women Companionable to Men?" suggests that women's confining sphere is what makes them limited. They are unprepared for real companionship because they "are thrown upon themselves and one another, confined to their narrow round, shut out from the larger life their husbands lead" (Browne 454). Those who are companionable, however, are unconventional, "usually of superior rank and distinct individuality. The men are finer, more illuminated; the women [are] stronger, larger than average, and they must not be shackled by conventionality or dread of echoes" (452). The writer connects physiology with behavior and, by tone, at least, seems to hold society culpable for stifling women's individuality.

Such serious—and, to modern eyes, reasonable—arguments and suggestions were tentatively reflected in the press by quips that recognized that types of women and men other than the ideal did exist. This "advanced" view, a kind of substratum to the status quo, appears in *Punch*, which gives its readers a more modern Mrs. Notion:

"Difference of Opinion"

*Jones (reading aloud).* " 'A true, good, noble Woman is ever ready to make herself a Door-mat for the Man she loves!' . . . Ah, Dolly, *those* are the Women who make the best Wives!"

*Mrs. J. (who is not of this type).* "Yes, dear—and the *worst Husbands!*" [29 Aug. 1891: 102]

Again, *Punch* deals with the question of wifely submission—or lack of it—in a humorous inversion of Henrik Ibsen's Nora, who decided that being a doll-wife was unsatisfying. The *Punch* cartoonist E. Hopkins transposes this idea to a different setting in "Ibsen in Brixton," a lower-class suburb of London, where a sour-faced matron says to her astonished spouse, "Yes, William, I've thought a deal about it, and I find I'm nothing but your Doll and Dickey-Bird, and so I'm going!" (2 May 1891: 215).

On the whole, *Punch* shows a development in attitude about the woman question, a development perhaps partly due to the nature of the sophisticated humorist who is quick to see the shortcomings in both sides of a question. In fact, *Punch*'s view of the American wife, that she is liberated for the sake of her offspring, is perhaps closer to the truth than the conventional picture that the American *Puck* presents. For *Puck*, the pretty, old-fashioned girls marry; the unattractive ones campaign to change the terms of marriage. In "The Athletic Girl and the Millionaire—A Tale of Too Much Up-To-Dateness," a pictorial essay, the captions tell the tale: "She did her best to jump into his affections with her diving accomplishments ... And she thought she had touched his heart with her fine fencing ... But she saw him landed at last by a quiet girl, who did nothing athletic at all" (4 Sept. 1895: 48). What may happen after such a marriage is "Overdoing Things—The Tendency of the Day," an illustration of unattractive and unkempt housewives bearing placards reading "Essay on the great superiority of the female mind" and "Our great mission must not be hindered by household drudgery." As *Puck* comments, "Lots of our married women-folks are overdoing the 'Elevation and Advancement idea" (15 Jan. 1896: 376-77). Why the pretty, home-loving, "quiet" girls should become vociferous ten-stone feminists was never directly answered by *Puck*. Well before these complaints occur, however, *Punch* gives a contrasting picture of the American woman. In "Four Prize Middle-Class Wives" illustrated in the *Almanack for 1890* (Fig. 3), the American wife is playing lawn tennis, "that the little ones might be sound in Wind and Limb"; the French wife is thriftily keeping the books for her husband's business; the German wife is cooking a hearty dinner; and the English wife, Mrs. van Trump, is "reading Browning and Herbert Spencer—to be an Intellectual Companion for George P. van Trump, and his English Friends" (5 Dec. 1889). As stereotypical figures, these are a blend of the conventional and the liberated, and the humor is more accepting of athletics, work, and intellectual pursuits than it was two decades earlier.

Even the more biting attacks on certain aspects of the modern marriage were elaborate and persistent enough to show that new modes could not simply be dismissed. One common attitude seemed to hint that what was needed was an anthropological study of the new, barbaric customs. Rising concern

Mr. Punch left Mrs. Jones playing Lawn-Tennis with Mr. Jones—that the little Jones might be sound in Wind and Limb.

He found Madame Dubois keeping Monsieur Dubois' Books—in order that he may prosper and grow rich, and spare an extra Clerk.

He found Frau Müller cooking Sauerkraut and Sausages—that Herr Müller should eat of the best and cheapest and most digestible.

He found Mrs. van Trump reading Browning and Herbert Spencer—to be an Intellectual Companion for George P. van Trump, and his English Friends.

Fig. 3. "Mr. Punch's Four Prize Middle-Class Wives." *Punch's Almanack for 1890.* Courtesy of the General Research Division, New York Public Library, Astor, Lenox, and Tilden foundations.

about divorce rates, for instance, seems to have prompted one
matron to suggest wedding rings applied as tattoos. *Punch*
quotes from her letter in the 23 May 1894 issue of the *Pall
Mall Gazette*: "The operation of tattooing could, with all rev-
erence, be performed by an expert in the vestry after the Church
service. . . . This custom will help to insure peace, respect, and
happiness to many homes and hearts." The suggestion spurs a
*Punch* versifier to envision a modern service presided over by
members of the medical profession:

> . . . Nor think, if I don't have the ring
>    That our marriage a failure will verge on!
> No, sweetest, instead I shall bring,
>    As "best man," a young friend who's a surgeon.
>
> While he marks us with circlet of blue,
>    If you like, he'll no doubt chloroform us—
> We're the first wedded pair to tattoo,
>    And we'll make a sensation enormous!
>
> In the vestry, perhaps, 'twere as well
>    To go through this manicure-ordeal;
> Besides ('tis a secret I tell),
>    We can there take, if nervous, a cordial!
>
> Thus with fingers that tingle, and smart
>    Our mutual wedlock we'll make fast;
> And *won't* it be nice when we start
>    Shaking everyone's hands at the breakfast!
>
> Thence we'll go to the dentist, my pet,
>    Then on to be well vaccinated—
> Altogether we'll never forget
>    The day when, tattooed, we were mated! [2 June 1894: 264]

The same hygienic theme is pursued seven years later as
*Punch* responds to a report in the *British Medical Journal* that
the Wisconsin legislature was considering a bill to require couples to demonstrate freedom from disease:

> "Preliminaries"
>
> Tell me, MARY, ere I woo thee,
>    Ere to ask your hand I kneel,

What ancestral faults pursue thee—
  Every hidden taint reveal.

In their old traditions ferret
  For the crimes to which they're prone,
Lest their ills which you inherit
  In their turn your children own.

Does your doctor's diagnosis
  Show of lunacy a trace?
Or has dread tuberculosis
  Been inherent in your race?

Might their bygone misbehavings
  Make you less from vice to shrink?
Did your forefathers have cravings
  After opium or drink?

But if you your stock can warrant
  As from immemorial time,
Not inclined to vice abhorrent,
  Free from tendency to crime;

Yes, when to your lover wary
  All this you can guarantee,
'Twill be time enough, sweet MARY,
  Then to think of wooing thee. [13 Feb. 1901: 131]

Such modern ideas of testing were satirized at the turn of the century, partly because they interfered with the popular, romantic notion of love that had gained strength over the previous decades; perhaps testing seemed a variation on an older understanding of marriage as a matter of "progeny and property," as one writer, James Bell, puts it (quoted in "Live Questions" 196). The versifiers seem to be reacting to an expansion of the relationship's civil ramifications to include the medical, many of which were relatively novel to the readers.

As with medical questions, the satirists seemed to treat the 1882 Married Woman's Property Act as another step in the desentimentalizing of marriage. The major objection was a persistence of the idea that women, because of their physiology, were too irrational to handle their own financial affairs properly and would surely misuse their legal powers. The *Times*, how-

ever, calls the abrogation of legal rights for married women a
"primitive doctrine" only made up for by equity lawyers who
devised a system of conveyances and settlements such that
"common law . . . [was] virtually suspended" for all but the
lower classes. The new Act was an expansion of the 1870 version, which freed a husband from his wife's premarital debts
(and in 1874 made him partly liable) and which allowed a wife
to keep her own earnings; this last stipulation was one that
Caroline Sheridan Norton had fought for earlier in the century
when her divorced husband, the Honorable George Norton,
sued to gain possession of her literary proceeds. After 1882,
however, a married woman was legally entitled both to hold
and to dispose of property, to make contracts, and to seek civil
remedies (including suing her own husband). Although the
*Times* believed that "affection and custom" would cause portions of the law to be ignored, it, like *Punch*, warned that trust-
ing, gullible women would be vulnerable to the "snares
of . . . schemers" (1 Jan. 1883: 7).

Typical of the satirical attacks on women's ignorance of
legal matters, "Ladies' Law" in *Punch* presents the "feminine"
viewpoint: "A mortgage," for example, "is a sort of thing that
causes a house to become the possession of a dishonest Agent,
who is usually a Solicitor," and "a nice Solicitor never contradicts a Lady, and therefore knows the law infinitely better than
the disagreeable fogies, who are so obstinate. And, lastly, the
best way to learn the real provisions of the law, is to study a
modern novel by a lady Authoress" (13 Aug. 1887: 65).

Indeed, *Punch* believes, most women are too ignorant to
recognize even a beneficial settlement:

"So Selfish"

*Husband (with pride).* "My Love, I've been effecting—I've insured
my Life today for Ten Thousand Pou—"

*Young Wife.* "Just like the Men! Always looking out for themselves! I think—you might have insured Mine while you were about
it!" [4 Sept. 1886: 118]

As the magazine implies, there are two interpretations for the
law, neither palatable. In two scenarios, *Punch* explains "How

It Is Expected to Work"—Angelina threatening criminal proceedings against her Edwin, who has paid his tailor with her
funds—and "How It Is Sure to Work"—Angelina foolishly giving her inheritance to her husband, who squanders it on doubtful stock (13 Jan. 1883: 21). Altogether, *Punch* adopts an attitude
that seems an uncomfortable compromise between the paternalism that would protect the weak and the satire that would
defend against the empowerment of women.

The question of the emancipation of women from the stereotype of Victorian fragility proves to be, then, a pervasive
one, especially where marriage is concerned. In itself, the relationship presented a paradoxical mixture, well illustrated by
a *Punch* cartoon that carries an ambiguous title:

"A Warning"

*Archie (to his Sister, who has been reading him Fairy Tales).*
"Won't there be a lot of *Us*, if none of us go and get Married? Worse
than *Hop o' my Thumb!*"
*Sister.* "Yes; but you know *I* mean to be Married!"
*Archie.* "Do you mean to say you'd go and live alone with a Man
after reading *Bluebeard!*" [9 Apr. 1892: 174]

The ceremony that married a woman both freed and entrapped
her. Married, she experienced some loosening of censorship, as
a new bride shows in this *Punch* quip: "Oh, Edwin dear! Here's
*Tom Jones*. Papa told me I wasn't to read it till I was Married.
The Day has come . . . at last! Buy it for me, Edwin dear" (5
Dec. 1891: 270).

On the other side of the picture, like Ibsen's Nora, she might
not be gaining freedom but rather surrendering, not just a dubious opportunity to enter the workplace, but her very identity.
Despite the comfortable assumption that the Edwins would
acquiesce in their wives' heartfelt wishes, the very existence
of—or necessity for—the Married Woman's Property Act suggested that "affection and custom" might entail not protection
but rather abuse. Indeed, an indication that the times were
truly changing is the discussion that raged in a number of 1888
periodicals over the question "Is Marriage a Failure?" Responses ranged from the serious to the satirical, from readers'

polls to considered statements from pundits of the day. In the United States, *Cosmopolitan* published a series of responses, and the *New York Times* reported that the *Daily Telegraph* had received over 27,000 letters about the subject in a space of seven weeks. In Britain, *Pick-Me-Up* polled its readers, who won prizes for the best answers (and who mentioned petty misunderstandings about finances and in-laws as the primary sources of marital problems); *Punch* invoked 'Arry, whose summation of the discussion reveals not only popular prejudices but perceived problems.

In "Live Questions: Is Marriage a Failure?" *Cosmopolitan* took its own poll on the question, publishing a series of letters from, for instance, an unmarried woman, a happy wife, a Chinese man, a bachelor, a poet, and a jurist. In one letter, James Bell contends that marriage is purely a "business affair," which, while on the whole is successful, may be a failure for the individual. The jurist Belva Lockwood calls for "absolute equality of the woman in the marriage relation," while the poet Edna Wheeler Wilcox defends Mona Caird's view that "women must be educated to become more liberal-minded; men must be compelled by public censure to lead purer lives" (196-200).

Because the *Telegraph* article is based on such a wide pool of letters, it may be more representative of the average reader than the considered replies in *Cosmopolitan*. Most of the newspaper's respondents believed that early marriage—under twenty-one for men and under nineteen for women—should be discouraged, especially among the working classes; that divorce should be made easier for "desertion, lunacy, confirmed inebriety, conviction for disgraceful crimes, . . . [and] established incompatibility of temperament"; and that the marriage service should be reformed to change passages that "shock young minds and disconcert older ones" (*New York Times* 30 Sept. 1888: 1). What emerges is a pastiche of old and new beliefs. To discourage early marriages was an attempt, on the one hand, to encourage middle- and upper-class couples to wait for a proper establishment but, on the other, to discourage lower-class couples from having large families. Again, to make divorce easier for the causes listed suggests the wide range of mistreatment that the unhappily married spouse had to endure;

to change the passages in the marriage service devoted to procreation suggests the persistence of prudery. As far as the *Times*
writer is concerned, however, the *Telegraph* poll left out mention of two serious deterrents to marriage: a "devastating flood
of children" and the population inequity—800,000 more
women than men.

*Punch* involved itself in the argument both directly and
indirectly. In "Marriage Evidently Not a Failure," a country
wife ties the shoes of her husband, who is too stout to bend
over comfortably (15 Sept. 1888: 130). More obliquely, *Punch*
affirms the same idea by means of one of E.J. Milliken's poems,
in which 'Arry, in high dudgeon, writes to his friend Charlie
about marriage. To be sure, the humor of the 'Arry poems resides partly in the dialect and partly in the upper-class point
of view aped by a cockney. 'Arry, however, provides something
more—a "hate figure" extracted, as Milliken notes, from
"street boys, costers, cheap clerks, counter-jumpers, excur-
sionists, music hall performers and audiences, and mechanics."
Indeed, as Milliken himself realized, " 'Arryism" became a by-
word for " 'the *spirit of Caddishness* rampant in our days in
many grades of life, coarse, corruption, revolting in all' "
(quoted in Prager 152). 'Arry's comments on marriage as a failure, then, incorporate the worst aspects of the *Telegraph* discussion—too many children, too little work, divorce leading
to promiscuity—yet, because he is an antihero, they also affirm
*Punch*'s unstated assumption that despite the "woman problem," marriage is, after all, a success:

" 'Arry on Marriage"

Run in blinkers at my time of life? Try the tandem with *me* in the
shafts?
Not likely! I likes a short run with the trimmest of tight little crafts;
But one consort over the course like, is not 'Arry's form by a lump;
'Ow could you imagine, dear boy, as yours truly 'ad gone off his
chump? . . .

"Is Marriage a failure?" old mivvies are asking. Of course, that depends;
But a dashing young feller like me, with good looks, and good 'ealth,
and good friends,

Knows a trick that's worth two on it, CHARLIE. While life goes on
    nutty and nice,
And the ochre slings in pooty slick, it is blooming bad bizness to splice.

Look at swells! *They* ain't in no dashed 'urry to church themselves
    out of good fun;
And wy? Clear as mud, my dear feller! The cash keeps 'em fair on the
    run.
When they do get stone-broke prematoor like, as 'appen it may to the
    best,
Then they looks for a Missus with money, and rucks in along o' the
    rest.

'Arry taunts an old friend of his, who had "a *hapron*
on . . . and kicksies as must ha' been cut by his wife." Clearly
domesticated, Bob is also penniless and cuts a poor figure next
to the irresponsible, dashing bachelor.

"Wot, *is* Marriage a failure?" I chuckles. "Oh, cheese it, old feller!"
    sez Bob,
And—he swore 'twas a cold in the 'ead, but I'm blowed if it wasn't a
    sob.
"Seven mouths, and six weeks out of work, mate! In Queer Street,
    and cleared of the quids!
I should just make a 'ole in the water, if 'twon't for the wife and the
    kids." . . .

"The kids is the *crux* of the question," says Mrs. LYNN LINTON. In
    course!
BOBBIE BINKS could ha' told her that, CHARLIE, and put it with dollops
    more.
She's a-teaching 'er grandmother, she is although she's a littery swell,
And as to "the State" steppin' in, yah! the State knows its book fur
    too well.

If the country took care of the kids, and diworce was made easy all
    round,
Wy, *I'd* marry, mate, early and often, and so would lots more, I'll be
    bound.
But, oh my, wot a mix, my dear CHARLIE! Free Love and Free Contract?
    Oh, yus!
The Guvment as Grandmother's dear, mate, but wot would it cost as
    a Nuss? . . .

No, CHARLIE, the dowdy-domestic, pap-bowls, p'ramberlators, and
    that
Is not *my* idea of the rosy, so Meg don't 'ook *me* for a flat.
If it ever *should* run to a Wife, and—well, trimmings, perhaps I may
    marry,
But till I can splice *ah la* Toff, CHARLIE no double-'arness for
    'ARRY.     [29 Sept. 1888: 156]

'Arry was not alone in worrying about the economic con-
sequences of marriage; hidden under the cockney slang and
posturing are some of the very real concerns that contributed
to the women's redundancy problem. The expectation of marrying *"ah la* Toff"—with a society wedding and well-furnished
establishment; the availability of "short runs" with Megs and
Molls; the inevitability of a large family and the cost of food,
clothing, and shelter: all of these added to the "superfluity" of
women to force a new conception, not just of marriage but of
women's nondomestic role. Many middle-class women, then,
had to face the probability that despite their upbringing, despite
their belief in physiological destiny, they would *not* marry;
unprepared and unwilling, they would have to be factored into
the economic system.

TWO

# Women's Work

*More "Bloomin' Bad Bizness"*

Man for the field and woman for the hearth;
Man for the sword, and for the needle she;
Man with the head, and woman with the heart;
Man to command, and woman to obey;
All else confusion.
   —Tennyson, *The Princess*

THE POPULATION inequity, coupled with the disinclination
of the 'Arrys and Edwins to marry, caused many women to
move from what they themselves considered their proper
sphere—the home—into the workplace. Received opinion gave
this sphere mythical proportions: both derided and glorified, it
was exacting in obligation and liberal in wealth of influence,
narrow in intellectual rigor and broad in emotional demands.
Exactly those qualities that were said to make women excel at
domestic obligations were also said to limit them in the workplace: their emotional, intuitive responses, their innocence, and
their lack of education were inappropriate for a hard-bitten
business world in which money, rather than personal relationship, was the goal. During the last twenty years of the century,
it was not so much that woman's nature had changed but that
the public perception of her strengths had become redefined.
Improvement in education paved the way for a general reassessment of women's status; indeed, in the hands of the reformers, women were better prepared both for independence
and for the old-fashioned sphere.

Education in a finishing school was small preparation for
undertaking a career or for managing a household; rather, it
validated an entire set of societal attitudes, not only about what
women were capable of, but about what they ought to be like.

In fact, the distance between two ideals—that of the virginal schoolgirl garnering accomplishments to delight her future spouse and that of the responsible matron serving as lifeline to a household bustling with husband, children, relatives, and servants—must have been the measure of disillusionment for many a young, marriageable girl. The hapless Doras whose undisciplined households made life miserable for their David Copperfields, the Rosamunds whose embroidered trousseaux, keepsake albums, and elegant flaxen braids were unable to keep their Lydgates from bankruptcy: these were the women who, as Charles Dickens and George Eliot portrayed them, failed to bridge the gap. Indeed, George Bernard Shaw, in making the case for the instinctive vitalism of Creative Evolution, counterpoises in *Man and Superman* the uselessness of finishing school education with a woman's true vocation. As Jack Tanner, responding joyously to Violet Robinson's supposedly illegitimate pregnancy, says: "Here is a woman we all supposed to be making bad water color sketches, practicing Grieg and Brahms, gadding about to concerts and parties, wasting her life and her money. We suddenly learn that she has turned from these sillinesses to the fulfillment of her highest purpose and greatest function—to increase, multiply, and replenish the earth" (3: 540). Shaw, of course, sanctifies woman's sphere in his own way, seeing in the work of procreation the key to human survival and progress. "Is there anything meaner than to throw necessary work on other people and then disparage it as unworthy and indelicate," he asks in the "Epistle Dedicatory" (3: 497); the nineteenth-century feminist might answer, however, that even ennobling the work still meant "throwing it" upon one person, and an unprepared one at that.

The distance between the accomplishments of the ideal girl and the tasks of the real housewife or redundant woman contributed not only to the revamping of women's education, then, but also to a pervasive change in attitude about women's self-sufficiency. This change was furthered by the founder of the North London Collegiate School for Girls, Frances Mary Buss, who tried to prepare her students for the growing problem of women reared for marriage and then left without resources in an inhospitable marketplace. Her curriculum was shaped by a twofold goal: not only preventing "the misery of women brought up 'to be married and taken care of,' and left alone in the world destitute," but also achieving a balance between domestic proficiency and the skills for an independent livelihood (Gorham 143).

Buss's own early years were typical. She was educated at home while her brothers were sent away to school, and she began work as a teacher at the age of fourteen. What sets her apart, however, is that she stubbornly pursued her own education, becoming one of the early pioneers whose life speaks to both conservative and liberal beliefs about women's work: on the one hand, that any career entailing service and ministration is a "natural" outlet for women and, on the other hand, that pursuing a career, no matter what, is a right. Buss's background makes her insistence that a female student accepted at the North London Collegiate School for Girls demonstrate not only academic aptitude but needlework skills not surprising. This requirement for plain work, which Buss demanded as the middle ground between art and necessity, surprised such well-prepared students as Molly Hughes, who was mortified to find that she had failed the buttonhole test although she could explain the tides and fill in a blank map of Africa (Hughes 3: 10). The endless worsted that the enervated Lady Crawley knits out of boredom in *Vanity Fair*, the needlework with which Jane Osborne passes "an awful existence" as she sits under the Iphigenia clock, the samplers and the lacework produced at finishing schools: this was the kind of useless labor that failed to prepare a woman for independence. For Buss, plain sewing was a fact of life.

Such a need for practical accomplishment matched the need for self-sufficiency on the part of the middle-class woman, whom the specter of penniless dependence on a relative's charity oftentimes drove into the workplace. With few skills and many frustrated expectations, she might become a governess, a combination of baby-sitter, nurse, seamstress, and instructor, with little pay and long hours. An excerpt from a letter from Charlotte Brontë to her sister Emily illustrates a typical situation: "The children are constantly with me," she writes, and adds that she is so overwhelmed by "oceans of needlework . . . I never in my whole life had my time so fully taken up" (quoted in Helsinger, Sheets, and Veeder 2: 188-89). The position of the seamstress, factory worker, or shop girl was worse; indeed, as the market was flooded with cheap, unskilled labor, the tenor of the satirical commentary changed. Once women were clearly in the workplace for good, writers became concerned not just with the loss of the old-fashioned girl but also with the exploitation of the modern woman. As early as 1843, *Punch* began its course of chivalric (albeit sometimes grudging) humanitarian protection with the publication of Thomas Hood's "Song of the Shirt." Rejected by other periodicals, the poem seemed to jar with the jolly mood expected of the Christmas issue, yet was immensely popular (Prager, 50-51). Its appeal is evident in a single stanza:

O! Men, with sisters dear!
    O! Men! with Mothers and Wives!
It is not linen you're wearing out,
    But human creatures' lives!
        Stitch—stitch—stitch,
    In poverty, hunger, and dirt,
Sewing at once, with a double thread,
    A Shroud as well as a Shirt. [1843: 260]

The measure of the distance that women had come almost fifty years later might be taken by London *Truth*'s indignation over a more sophisticated kind of abuse—the salary inequity, not between men and women, but between skilled and unskilled women. After a *Chronicle* report that female typists at the War Office were hired for fourteen shillings a week for a seven-hour day, while charwomen received twelve shillings for a five-hour day, *Truth* published the following:

"Woman's Latest Triumph"
Here is encouragement for those
    Who, though the weaker vessels,
Still boldly try a part to play,
And hold their own and make their way,
    Where man contends and wrestles.

Here is encouragement, I say,
    To women to be clever—
Listen! and I will tell them what
    They'll gain by their endeavour!

Let them essay to raise themselves
    By dint of education;
Let them toil on, by night and day,
Till they have learned type-writing, say;
    Then, what's the consummation?
Why, then, employed by Government,
    And men-clerks' duties sharing,
They'll find that they're paid less per hour
    Than those who do the charing! [5 Mar. 1891: 476]

Whether the root problem was lack of men or lack of employment, interest in the latter explanation gained momentum as the century passed. Buss, Parkes, Bodichon, and a host of others demonstrated that women could be self-motivated and socially productive, but these early reformers also displayed a conservative bias: the belief that preferred careers for women were those that involved ministering to men. Such a bias is reminiscent of the extreme view espoused by W.R. Greg, who writes in the *National Review* that "female servants . . . fulfill both essentials of woman's being; they are supported by, and they minister to, men" (quoted in Helsinger, Sheets, and Veeder 2: 138). Bessie Parkes's 1859 letter to the *Times* about a job registry for middle-class women bears traces of this attitude; it is, as well, interesting for its tone of exclusivity (Parkes suggests charging a small fee) and social responsibility. The registry is proposed for "ladies" who want "remunerative employment in charitable institutions, as nurses in hospitals, matrons in workhouses, teachers or superintendents in industrial schools; likewise for those who desire to obtain situations as secretaries, clerks, or bookkeepers. Other kinds of employment will in all probability gradually suggest themselves in accordance with the needs of society" (12 Nov. 1859: 7f).

The suggestion to encourage women to apply for even these poorly paid positions did not, however, meet with popular approbation. *Punch* published a spoof letter in reply to Parkes in which "Fanny Hooker" complains that dressing, shopping, dancing, needlework, and music are occupation enough: "so long as girls have *husbands* to get they want no *other field* of employment" (3 Dec. 1859: 226). Again, *Punch*'s later report on "Work for Woman," ostensibly a summary of a meeting of the Society for the Employment of Women chaired by the Earl of Shaftsbury, is really an excuse for a series of pointed comments about women's frivolous habits. Women need employment because their "taste for a profusion of finery" coupled with high taxes makes them too dear for husbands to support; their propensity for writing long letters qualifies them for legal copying, if they can control their tendency to underline words for emphasis; and (in a typical pun) their millinery experience trains them to set caps at printing, as well as to become printers' angels, instead of printers' devils (14 July 1860: 20).

These early retorts seem, when set against the very real problems redundant women faced, socially irresponsible; yet, as the years passed and the abuses became increasingly evident, *Punch* seems more deliberately to assume the mantle of protector. During that time protests against factory conditions were heard not only in Britain but in America, where the problem grew incrementally worse as the century progressed. In the 1820s women were ignoring teaching positions for clean, attractive, well-paying factory jobs (the factories in Lowell, Massachusetts, serving as the paradigm); by the 1850s the same factories were plagued by the British problems of long hours, unhealthy conditions, and below-subsistence pay (Helsinger, Sheets, and Veeder 2: 120). More seriously, even well-intentioned reforms sometimes backfired. A primitive kind of maternity leave that barred nursing mothers from their jobs to prevent neglect of the newborn caused a sharp increase in the number of abortions (Helsinger, Sheets, and Veeder 2: 133).

These and other problems were seen by *Punch* in the 1890s as symptomatic of deeper social evils. A number of versified commentaries appeared; one of the most comprehensive was "A Dream of Unfairly-Treated Women (A Long Way After the Laureate)," a parody of Tennyson's *Dream of Fair Women* (2 Aug. 1890: 20). Harry Furniss's accompanying banner, reminiscent of the Cruikshank covers for Dickens's novels, shows a variety of ogres, like Bumbledom (from Mr. Bumble, the corrupt parish beadle in *Oliver Twist*), Profit, the Sweater, the government, and the police force, imposing restraints and duties on weeping, weary nurses, seamstresses, and shop girls. These poorly paid members of "slaveydom," the cartoon suggests, remain respectable at the price of hunger and disease; it is the Gaiety girl, curling her devil's tail toward the word *freedom*, who, smiling and well fed, flaunts a bag of gold.

The poem, which draws a dreary picture of women's employment at the end of the century, supports striking "for good cause":

Turning I saw, ranging a flowery pile,
  One sitting in an entry dark and cold;
A girl with hectic cheeks, and hollow smile;
  Wired roses there she sold . . .

Again I saw a wan domestic drudge
  Scuttering across a smug suburban lawn;
Tired with the nightly watch, the morning trudge,
  The toil at early dawn.

And then a frail and thin-clad governess,
  Hurrying to daily misery through the rain.
Toiling, with scanty food, and scanty dress,
  Long hours for little gain.

Anon a spectral shop-girl creeping back
  To her dull garret-home through the chill night,
Bowed, heart-sick, spirit-crushed, poor ill-paid hack
  Of harsh commercial might!

The poem seeks to move the reader through description rather than polemic; indeed, the illustrations give a more explicit social indictment than the poem, which presents an unsolvable problem in archaic, discordant language. "Dislodg[ed] from her throne love's household pet" becomes one of the "Work-ridden vassals of [the world's] Mammon-god," her temptation the "Maenad-masked betrayer, base, impure" of prostitution:

It smiled, it beckoned—whither? To the abyss!
  But of that throng how many may be

By the gay glamour and the siren kiss
  To where sin's soul-gulfs yawn?

How many? No response my vision gave.
  Make answer, if ye may, ye lords of gain!
Make answer, if ye know, ye chiders grave
  Of late revolt, and vain!

Dream of *Fair* Women? Nay, for work and want
  Mar maiden comeliness and matron grace.
Let sober judgment, clear of gush and cant,
  The bitter problem face! [2 Aug. 1890: 50]

The "bitter problem" that the poem recognizes is, in part, what Henry Mayhew discovered in 1849 in his street interviews (Helsinger, Sheets, and Veeder 2: 152-53); prostitution not only paid better than factory labor, but it was frequently a path to respectability and marriage. In contrast, the idea that a sister of the streets cannot retrace her steps (a pervasive theme in literature and art) is a pretense firmly held by the middle class as well as by religious groups, such as the Anglican sisterhoods that recommended isolation and contemplation as reform measures (Vicinus, *Independent Women* 74-84). It is Auerbach who points out that both the spinster and the prostitute are related; both are outcasts, but by that fact both are to some degree freed from conventional behavior. For the Victorians, she argues, the prostitute goes one step further, opening the way to transfiguration on the part of those who deal with her (150-84). Certainly, the prostitute, who was thought "redundant" in many senses of the word, inspired a variety of passionate responses.

One such response was occasioned by the Contagious Diseases Acts (1864 in Britain; 1867 in America). Unlike the religious sisterhoods, proponents and opponents of the Acts alike focused on protecting the prostitute's rights. On the one hand, conservative supporters argued the possible "redemption" of the prostitute as one rationale for mandating examination for venereal diseases; as they contended, former prostitutes, as the new middle class, regularly produced *legitimate* children whose health it was in the interest of the state to protect. On the other hand, reformers such as Caroline Dall and Susan B.

Anthony, proponents of the "new Abolitionism," complained that the Acts demeaned all women; not only did they recognize prostitution as an "industry" (thereby lowering the wage scale in "respectable" trades), but also they abrogated women's civil rights, for any woman walking alone was legally open to the charge of prostitution, and all were supposed infectious until proved otherwise (Helsinger, Sheets, and Veeder 2: 156-64).

*Punch* supported the idea that social conditions, rather than inborn traits, were responsible for creating prostitution; not-so-veiled references to financial rewards and the life-style of the Gaiety girl appear in many poems calculated to shake the socially complacent reader into altering conditions in the workplace so that a woman could choose respectability without starvation. Social change thus became a moral imperative. The magazine's condemnation of those who depended upon the working classes to keep the country's economic wheels spinning surfaces in its championing of the shop girl, the figure whom O. Henry did much to sentimentalize in America. In 1893 the magazine published "Her 'Day of Rest' " (Fig. 4), an updated "Song of the Shirt" in response to a quotation from the Debate on Early Closing for Shops: "As one poor shop-girl said:—'After the fatigue and worry of the week, I am so thoroughly worn out, that my only thought is to rest on a Sunday; but it goes too quickly, and the other days drag on so slowly!' " The verse mimics a feverish and rambling meditation brought about by overwork:

    "Her 'Day of Rest' "

    (The Song of the Shop-Girl)

    Eight o'clock strikes!
    The short day's sped,—
My Day of Rest! That beating in my head
Hammers on still, like coffin-taps. He likes,
Our lynx-eyed chief, to see us brisk and trim
On Monday mornings; and though brains may swim,
And breasts sink sickeningly with nameless pain,
*He* cannot feel the faintness and the strain,
    And what are they to him?

Fig. 4. "Her 'Day of Rest' (The Song of the Shop Girl)." *Punch*,
8 April 1893: 158.

The shop girl, who should, by reason of gender, be protected, is rather treated like a beast of burden, the versifier points out; she is like a vestal virgin, arrayed for the sacrifice, and her only resource is prostitution:

> Only the Comus wand
> Of an unhallowed pleasure offers such
> Freedom, and with it pollution in its touch. . . .

> Oh that long standing—standing—standing yet!
> With the flesh sick, the inmost soul a-fret,
>     Pale, pulseless patiences, our very sex,
> That should be protection, one more load
>     To take, and chafe, and vex.
> No tired ox urged to tramping by the goad
>     Feels a more mutely—maddening weariness
> Than we white, black-garbed spectral girls who stand
> Stonily smiling on while ladies grand,
>     Easily seated, idly turn and toss
>     The samples; and our watcher, 'neath the gloss
> Of courtly smugness jarring menace, stalks
> About us, creaking cruelty as he walks.

> Stand! Stand! Still stand!
> Clenched teeth and clutching hand,
> Swift blanching cheek, and twitching muscle tell
> To those who know, what we know all too well,
>     Ignored by Fashion, coldly mocked by Trade.
>     Are we not for sacrifice arrayed
> In dainty vesture? Pretty too, they say
> Male Gabblers, whom our sufferings and poor pay
>     Might shock, could they but guess
>     Trim figures and smart dress
> Cover and hide, from all but doctor-ken,
> Disease and threatening death! Oh! men, men, men!

For the shop girl, then, all that is possible, says the versifier, is to continue until the end:

> *Stand*—till hysteria lays its hideous clutch

> On our girl-hearts, or epilepsy's touch
>     Thrills through tired nerves and palsied brain.

Again—again—again!
*How long?* Till Death, upon its kindly quest,
    Gives a true Day of Rest! [8 Apr. 1893: 158-59]

For *Punch*, death—that Victorian refuge from despair and shame—was not always the conclusion in poems like these; as in the earlier "A Dream of Unfairly-Treated Women," the "siren kiss" of prostitution was often invoked as an unsentimental but realistic alternative. In "Only a Shop-Girl," for instance, a versifier traces the career of a country girl "married by law" in London, who is deserted by her handsome husband once her long hours as a store clerk diminish her attractiveness. Fired from her job because she lacks both spirit and appropriate clothing, she sacrifices her reputation by going on stage:

What a sermon is here! Is Morality dumb? Or why doesn't Virtue
    whine and preach
At a woman who's driven from shop to the stage, and discovers that
    honesty's out of her reach!
She thinks once more of the days at home! as down on her pillow she
    sinks her head;
She sees her sisters jauntily fine, and hears her little one cry for bread!
And then comes love—not the old, old love, as she felt it once in the
    country lanes—
But a passionate fever of gilded youth,—who reckons the cost, and
    who counts the gains?
Still, a dinner or so in a time of need! and a soft new dress for a lovely
    form,
Are things that most women are grateful for,—they are sails of life
    that weather the storm.
Only a Shop-Girl fallen away!—by the road of life! Samaritan, stop!
Only a Shop-Girl! Waiting the end! Only a Girl of the Shop!
    [18 Nov. 1882: 239]

*Punch*'s call for a Good Samaritan was typical of the Victorian belief that charity would solve a variety of social problems ranging from hunger to vice. On the one hand, giving both money and goods seemed to stave off the very real threat of revolution caused by a disparity between the haves and the have-nots. On the other hand, it demonstrated the possession of a good heart, for sentimentality, as Fred Kaplan points out in *Sacred Tears*, was taken to be the expression of a moral nature. While charity was indeed practiced on behalf of starving needlewomen and reformed prostitutes, workers in factories and shops were considered to be less needy. Unionization and government-sponsored reform had a long and troubled history, however, as Lee Holcombe's *Victorian Ladies at Work* shows. The first effective union to include women was the National Union of Shop Assistants, formed in 1891. In a series of inadequate Parliamentary bills, the first such union failed in 1873 partly because shop work, the investigating commission argued, was hardly as "fatiguing" or as "unwholesome" as factory work (117-32).

Other kinds of work were seen to be even less deserving of either charity or regulation primarily because they were service areas, by definition natural outlets for womanliness. Little aid was available for governesses, for instance, many of whom came from families that, in less than "reduced" circumstances, would themselves have undertaken ordinary charitable efforts. Indeed, such women were caught in a psychological trap: to be paid for a "feminine" service like teaching or nursing frustrated their own and others' expectations of womanly behavior while guaranteeing an independence that they would perhaps have preferred to avoid. *Punch* became one of the Good Samaritans of the press, speaking out for those who labored at so high a human cost. As the magazine comments, the Olympian labors called for by the prospective employers require mythical strength: "There are two employments, the one reserved for masculine, the other kept exclusively for feminine aspirants, in which were a Briareus [the giant who helped Zeus overthrow the Titans] one of the employed, he would soon find his hundred hands full of the duties that devolved on them. Not only are the persons filling these positions required to devote their brains and bodies to the service, but they find they have to be, as far as humanly is possible, ubiquity personified and coupled with omniscience." The first "Briarian" employment is engaged in by newspaper special correspondents; the second, by governesses (29 Oct. 1859: 176). The journalist had, at least, some measure of personal independence, while the governess endured a position that was grueling and ultimately unrewarding. As the records of the Governesses' Benevolent Association show, over half of the applicants for a £20 annuity faced retirement in their fifties without any income (Vicinus, *Independent Women* 23). Working, for these women, provided daily room and board but little else.

Five years after the Governesses' Benevolent Association was founded, *Punch* proposed a "Governesses' Benevolent Institution" for training the female Briareuses to cope with the idiosyncrasies of their situation. Again, as in the case of *Punch*'s defense of the shop girl, the middle and upper classes are taken to task for their inhumane demands. In its satire, *Punch* notes that the Institution should contain a number of training rooms in which the governesses will be both reviled by servants and tested by "refractory children . . . selected from the most purse-proud families, and their mammas will drop in every now and then, daily, and reprimand and find fault capriciously and unjustly with their preceptress, so as to inure her to such treatment." At evening parties the trainees, allotted £20 a year to dress, are to be snubbed for their shabby appearance (1846: 216). Indeed, any reader acquainted with Ruth Pinch in Dickens's *Martin Chuzzlewit* will recognize the indignities suffered by the governess without "the slightest innate power of commanding respect" from children taught by their parents to degrade their teacher. Reports from the beginning of the century show that the situation had not improved; a journal entry from Nellie Weeton, who began teaching at the age of twelve, records a poignant and not exaggerated complaint: "O Brother! sometime thou wilt know perhaps the deprivations I have undergone for thy sake, and that thy attentions have not been such as to compensate them. For thy sake I have wanted food and fire, and have gone about in rags; have spent the flower of my youth in obscurity, deserted, and neglected" (quoted in Hellerstein, Hume, and Offen 343).

The abuse that such women were subject to because of the demands of the marketplace was publicized in the 1840s and 1850s when *Punch*'s editors published and responded satirically to a series of actual advertisements for governesses. Perhaps to readers of the day, *Punch*'s comments were particularly telling because the "young women of good families" to whom the advertisements were addressed were popularly considered to be a protected, special group. The consistency of the work and salary descriptions, as well as the tone of paternalism, suggests a generally accepted standard. Such "sisters of misery," then, might expect the following in 1848: "WANTED, in a *Gentleman's* family, a *Lady*, who can be well recommended as NURSERY GOVERNESS. She must be fond of children, clever with her needle, active, intelligent, and good-tempered in the discharge of her duties. *No salary will be given.* Travelling expenses and washing paid, with every domestic comfort. Address, stating age, to R.L., Mr.—, Dundee" (78). Or, in 1851, "A Young Lady is wanted to assist in the care and education of three little girls, between the ages of four and seven. Accomplishments are not required; but she must write a good hand, and work well at the needle. As opportunity would be afforded for improvement, it is thought that board and washing, with £5 pocket-money, would be a fair remuneration for the first year" (52).

By 1890, the idea that a governess exchanged her time and talents for a home-away-from-home and that she had found a safe haven that paid mostly in "improvement" or in protection from the vicissitudes of public labor had changed radically. In that year a governess whose duties had been unfairly increased not only sued her employers but won the case. As a *Daily News* article of 12 June 1890 reports, a day governess was fired after she requested a holiday; she received twenty-five shillings a month plus board to teach grammar and music to three children and to take care of several infants and was asked, with no salary increase, to do the work of the cook and the scullery maid, who had given notice. When she sued successfully for a month's wages, *Punch* celebrated on her behalf in "A White Slave":

. . . So all day long with urchins three Miss HARKER toiled in chains,
And she poured the oil of learning well upon their rusty brains,
And she practised them in music, and she polished up their sense
With the adverbs and the adjectives, and verbs in mood and tense.

And they said, "She's doing nicely, we will give her something more
(Not of money, but of labour) ere we show her to the door,

Why, we've got two baby children, it is really only fair
That Miss HARKER should look after them, and wash and dress the
      pair.

"And, Miss HARKER, it will save us such a lot of trouble too,
If, when our servants leave us, they can leave their work to you
So you'll please to cook our dinner, let your motto be *Ich Dien*,
(No, no, you needn't thank us) and you'll keep our dishes clean.

"And, of course, you'll do it daily—what was that you dared to say?
You would like to rest a week or so, and want a holiday?
Who ever heard such nonsense? Well, there's one thing we can show,
Not politeness, but the door to you—Miss H. you'd better go."

So she went, but brought her action, and I'm thankful to relate
That when the case was argued she hadn't long to wait.
"Costs and judgment for the plaintiff, the defendants' case is fudge,
Pay her monthly wage, she's earned it and deserves it," said the Judge.

There be Englishmen in England, sleek men, and women too,
Who tie their purse-strings tighter than tradition's grasping Jew.
What care they for fellow-feeling, who for profit try to lure
Fellow creatures to their grindstone for the faces of the poor?

And they set some wretched slave to work her fingers to the bone,
Then sullenly deny her bread, or give at best a stone;
And after she has grubbed and scrubbed, they insolently sneer
At one who dares to ask for rest on £15 a-year. [21 June 1890: 289]

Although such satire did attack obvious abuses, the real
answer to the problem—a change in the perception that careers
were more than avocations or substitutes for marriage—was
slow in coming. Perhaps those activities that seemed to be the
outgrowths of domestic functions were the most difficult to
professionalize. Women who wished to become physicians, for
instance, were significantly hindered by the view that nursing
was a more appropriate choice because it was an extension of
a womanly desire to minister to the sick and the helpless.
Those who saw nursing as a lifelong vocation faced obstacles
other than low pay, not the least of which was overcoming the
stereotype of the lower-class nurse fixed in the public imagination by Dickens's snuff-taking, gin-swigging Sairey Gamp
and her refrain—"leave the bottle on the chimley-piece, and
let me put my lips to it when I am so dispoged."

Even the healing passion that drove Florence Nightingale to the Crimean War and then to a late career in public health (Gorham 127-29) came under fire from the satirists who suggested that nursing was a mask for selfishness and husband hunting. "Charity That Beginneth Not Where It Should," as one *Punch* cartoonist suggests as late as 1889, should begin at home, in taking care of parents rather than in becoming a hospital nurse. A young, well-dressed woman explains to a Dutch-uncle figure why she wants to find an occupation: "Well, you see, it's so dull at home, Uncle. I've no Brothers or Sisters—and Papa's paralysed—and Mama's going blind—so I want to be a Hospital Nurse" (7 Dec. 1889: 267). Again, as two young women in fashionable walking costumes pass a group of top-hatted young men, they converse:

"Happy Thought. A Vocation!"

*Eva.* "I suppose those extremely nice-looking Young Men are the Students, or House-Surgeons, or something?"
*Maud.* "No doubt. Do you know, Eva, I feel I should very much like to be a Hospital-Nurse!"
*Eva.* "How strange! Why the very same Idea has just occurred to Me!" [21 May 1887: 246]

The struggle to change popular preconceptions took place from the 1850s to 1880s, when Florence Nightingale and her followers attempted to reform the large, influential hospitals. During this "pioneer period" when training programs were instituted and medical reforms were multiplying, it became clear that if women were to succeed they would need to accept the given hierarchy, working under male doctors or under strong matrons. Nightingale's initial dream of nurses working alongside of doctors was frustrated by power politics. As Martha Vicinus points out in *Independent Women*, the turn-of-the-century shift from martial metaphors to maternal metaphors in the reform literature indicates a development in ideology that is only superficially regressive; as the decades passed, women moved from waging a front-line battle against the status quo to a deeper professionalism that called them to care for their patients regardless of the political message (88).

While female nurses were always in some sense considered indispensable, the woman who wanted to achieve independent status as a medical doctor faced both discrimination and patronizing humor. In America, women were not allowed to attend anatomical classes, and, when such classes were opened selectively in Britain in the 1870s, female students were greeted with riots and personal vituperation, as contemporary accounts report (Hollis 102-3). Perhaps because such women were less obviously in need of protection than, for example, seamstresses or shop girls and perhaps because, given their obvious dedication and years of schooling, they presented a serious threat to male professionals, even *Punch* failed to respond helpfully. When, for example, in 1848 *Punch* congratulated the first female medical student in America, Elizabeth Blackwell, who was granted not a degree but the title of "Domina" by New York's General Medical College, the magazine suggested that her studies were "qualifying [her] for that very important duty of a good wife—tending a husband in sickness" (117). Such women had little need of their own professional identity, many agreed, because they would be ministering to their own families. That sentiment appears in "An M.D. in a Gown":

... Young ladies all, of every clime,
    Especially of Britain,
Who wholly occupy your time
    In novels or in knitting,
Whose highest skill is but to play,
    Sing, dance, or French to clack well
Reflect on the example, pray,
    Of excellent MISS BLACKWELL.

Think, if you had a brother ill,
    A husband, or a lover,
And could prescribe the draught or pill
    Whereby he might recover;
How much more useful this would be,
    Oh, sister, wife, or daughter!
Than merely handing him beef-tea,
    Gruel, or toast-and-water.

Ye bachelors about to wed
   In youth's unthinking hey-day,
Who look upon a furnish'd head
   As horrid for a lady,
Who'd call a female doctor "blue;"
   You'd spare your sneers, I rather
Think, my young fellows, if you knew
   What physic costs a father!

How much more blest were married life
   To men of small condition,
If every one could have his wife
   For family physician;
His nursery kept from ailments free,
   By proper regulation,
And for advice his only fee,
   A thankful salutation. [1849: 226]

*Punch* similarly congratulates the first woman whc completed a medical degree in Paris, an option pursued by Emily Blackwell; as the author of "Physicians in Muslin" points out, Dr. Emily's surname "is immaterial," since it will one day be changed by marriage, when, combining the compassionate attitude of the nurse with the knowledge of the doctor, she will be "a treasure indeed" (5 Apr. 1856: 133). The same theme is invoked in a cartoon entitled "Lady-Physicians" that compares the medical profession to a marital hunting ground, especially for the handsome patient: "Who is this Interesting Invalid? It is young Reginald de Braces, who has succeeded in Catching a Bad Cold, in order that he might Send for that rising Practitioner, Dr. Arabella Bolus!" (23 Dec. 1865: 248).

    That the fair physicians may not, however, prove so attractive is at the heart of another satirical commentary, in which support is given to the hopeful female doctor, but only tongue in cheek. In "A Foul Word for the Fair Sex," *Punch* reprints a statement, reportedly from a *Scotsman* article arguing against female physicians: "Man is made for work; his is the strong arm to expel poverty, to bring comfort to the door. Woman is made, in common with bitter beer and tobacco, to urge him on to exertion, to soothe him in defeat." The dandified "Albany

Fitz-Brummell" takes umbrage on behalf of "Lovely Woman," but goes on: "How could one whisper a soft nothing to an ear that had been hardened by the chaff of medical students and the language of the schools: or how could one press tenderly the fingers which had just been spreading a big blister, or dispensing a black dose?" (14 Nov. 1863: 203).

Five years later one of the few supporters for "Physicians of the Fair Sex" appears, perhaps partly in reaction to the efforts of Sophia Jex Blake, who campaigned in Edinburgh for an entrée into the profession. In response to Elizabeth Garrett, featured in the *Lady's Own Paper*, "Chip" invokes the reverse of the matrimonial arguments against women's careers. Some women object to "matrimonial servitude," he says; their plainer sisters suffer from the unwillingness of men "so dull as not to see that a plain face will never spoil." Most women lack nerve, not intelligence. The crux of the matter, he argues, is that "the medical corporations . . . are afraid of female competition. . . . they are no better than Trades' Unions" (22 Feb. 1868: 81). The same argument is used in Honnor Morten's study of "Woman's Invasion of Men's Occupations," in which she charges that women were barred from medicine but not from nursing because "men did not want women to secure the higher position and the higher fees" (44).

Like the medical profession, the legal profession attracted women of unusual determination who not only threatened the careers but challenged the self-esteem of their male counterparts. Along with members of the nursing profession, female lawyers fought an unflattering stereotype fostered by the existence of a leisured female class whose prurient interest in the courts made a legitimate interest suspect. *Punch* makes fun of these onlookers in the courts, comparing them to Madame DeFarge knitting the names of the guillotine victims under the scaffold in Dickens's *A Tale of Two Cities* (31 Aug. 1889: 106) and lampooning them in verses like "A (Law) Court Lady":

I like to listen to—well all that sort
Of thing one wouldn't hear except in Court.
I'm of the class that's "privileged." The Judge
Can't turn me out of Court, so I don't budge,

But sit to hear wigg'd barristers with three tails
Describe what journals call "Disgusting details,"
At which, next day, they scarcely dare to hint.
So, being deprived of reading it in print,
I go to Court to hear what I can't read,
And I enjoy it very much indeed. [23 Nov. 1889: 252]

Another way that popular sentiment spoke against the entrée of women into law was the familiar cavil that the field
entailed argumentation rather than ministration, the operation
of the head rather than the heart. In 1854, for example, one
waggish "Old Bachelor" in *Punch* suggests that the most lu-
crative and beneficial connection between women and the law
is in helping legal students in "trying emergencies": "If a number of women were to go through the Inns of Court every morning with the charitable object of sewing, stitching, and mending
all imperfect garments, they would realize a very large income"
(149). As late as 1893, another versifier, in responding to the
Report of the Lady Commissioners on Women's Labour, ele-
vates the shop girl by using a law motif in "To Hebe," a wait-
ress:

Be it counter, be it bar,
You can "dress" it—you're its star,
Bright, and *most* particular! . . .

Hours are long, and meal-time short,
Mashing bores, who think it "sport,"
Say the things they didn't ought!

Gather, then, the tips that fall;
Don't let vulgar chaff appal;
To the Bar you've had your "call"! [18 Nov. 1893: 229]

The general attitude toward female adjudicators was, then,
either flippant or conventional, although from time to time the
periodicals print an uncharacteristic remark about the need for
women barristers. *Punch*'s own early reaction is mixed. In 1855
it attacks the decision of the American Emma R. Coe to study
law by publishing a series of shibboleths: women cannot keep
secrets, will not patronize sister barristers, will balk at wearing

periwigs. In the same year, however, it published a diatribe against wife beaters that includes a mention of female lawgivers: "All brutes guilty of beating their wives, should be committed by Lady Magistrates, tried before a Lady Chief-Justice, convicted by Gentlewomen of the Jury; and when sentenced, to be given into the custody of strong-minded women. Punishment upon marital brutes will never be duly carried out, unless by functionaries chosen from the sex so tryingly outraged. To the hands of the avenging Beauties would we render up all the offending Beasts" (29 Sept. 1855: 131). The argument that women may open the legal system to female victims is posed more seriously by the *Buffalo Democracy*: "There are many delicate circumstances which woman can only confide to her own sex, and besides, the presence of ladies may civilise the bar, and lead lawyers to deal tenderly with witnesses on cross examination" (24 Feb. 1855: 74).

The point of view published in the American paper was liberal; ordinarily, the special capacity that woman had to engage in human relations was seen as a detriment when it was translated into social action and professional involvement. This attitude was evident in the case of the female theologian; just as the female physician pushed the notion of the ministering angel to unacceptable lengths, so the female minister, although following an apparently natural career marked by purity and inspiration, seemed to subvert her "natural," more subordinate role.

One solution was ministering within a community of women. In Britain, where the evangelicals and nonconformists flourished, so did woman's ministry, as it did in America (Helsinger, Sheets, and Veeder 2: 175-76). Anglicans, however, favored a less public role; indeed, the differences between the types of communities set up to succor the poor and fallen illustrate the century's double focus. Low-church communities housed "deaconesses" who emphasized home visitation; high-church communities offered meditation and seclusion as the antidote to street habits (Vicinus, *Independent Women* 46-47). Activity of a more formal nature, such as ordaining female ministers and priests, was frowned upon on both sides of the Atlantic, however. As early as 1837 a pastoral letter—"The

General Association of Massachusetts (Orthodox) to the
Churches Under Their Care"—suggests that women go against
nature in usurping male religious roles. The responses, John
Greenleaf Whittier's tirade among them, include "The Times
That Try Men's Souls." This excerpt, beginning with an allu-
sion to Alexander Pope's *Essay on Man*, implies that once
women step out of their place on the Great Chain of Being, the
entire social order is at risk:

Confusion has seized us, and all things go wrong,
 The women have leaped from "their spheres,"
And, instead of fixed stars, shoot as comets along,
 And are setting the world by the ears!
In courses erratic they're wheeling through space,
In brainless confusion and meaningless chase.

. . . They insist on their right to petition and pray,
 That St. Paul, in Corinthians, has given them rules
For appearing in public, despite what those say
 Whom we've trained to instruct them in schools;
But vain such instructions, if women may scan
And quote texts of Scripture to favor their plan.

Our grandmothers' learning consisted of yore
 In spreading their generous boards;
In twisting the distaff, or mopping the floor,
 And *obeying the will of their lords*.
Now, misses may reason, and think, and debate,
Till unquestioned submission is quite out of date.

. . . Oh! shade of the prophet Mahomet, arise!
 Place woman again in "her sphere,"
And teach that her soul was not born for the skies,
 But to flutter a brief moment here.
This doctrine of Jesus, as preached up by Paul,
If embraced in its spirit, will ruin us all.
 [quoted in Helsinger, Sheets, and Veeder 2: 178]

Fourteen years after the pastoral letter, the first American
female theologian, Antoinette Brown (ordained in 1853), was
graduated from Oberlin, but the question was far from settled.
Most who felt called to the ministry redirected their talents by
joining church groups or by writing hymns or novels. Reactions

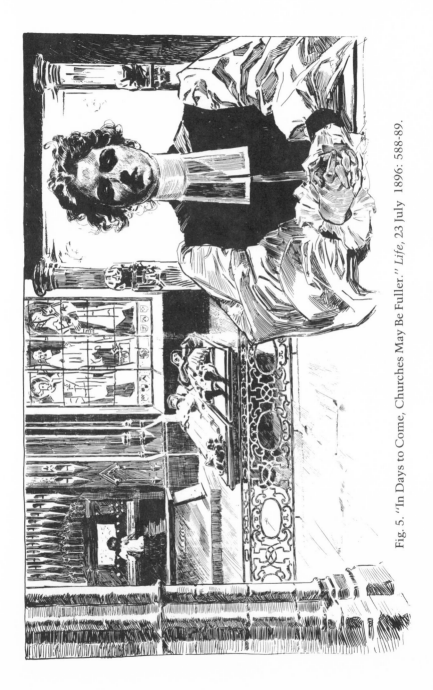

Fig. 5. "In Days to Come, Churches May Be Fuller." *Life*, 23 July 1896: 588-89.

in the American press were twofold by the turn of the century. *Chic*, for instance, perhaps deliberately focuses on the connection between the feminist issues of prostitution and theology. On the cover of the 22 February 1881 issue, "The Next Move" features a priest in red-striped stockings hearing confessions. Far from being feminist, of course, the cover implies that a woman prostitutes herself by aspiring to the pulpit; the drawing also seems to suggest that to encourage female religious leadership is tantamount to throwing young men to the Scarlet Woman of Rome—the Catholic Church.

On the other hand, although no less unwilling to ignore the theological arguments that even today bar many women from the pulpit, *Life* looks at the other side of the question, as its reputation as a "gentle satirist" might imply. Charles Dana Gibson turns his hand from the *embonpoint* and panache of the "Gibson Girl" to vestments, producing a church interior with stained glass and effigies, but putting Cupid to work at the organ (Fig. 5). The caption—"In Days to Come, Churches May Be Fuller"—implies part of *Punch*'s pervading theme, not so much that a woman's career is a stepping-stone to marriage, but that her auditors and viewers perceive it as such.

*Punch*, however, more adept at religious politics, early takes the opportunity to poke fun at both bishops and bluestockings when it reports that the Scotch Episcopal Synod adjourned rather than carry on business in front of ladies who were present and refused to leave. The sword is double edged. On the one hand, Mr. Punch suspects that the synod "is of the nature of a free-and-easy, at which the Bishop presides in an arm-chair over a bowl of whisky-toddy, and calls on the constituents to sing songs, which are not exactly anthems"; on the other hand, Mr. Punch wonders, "Why should the Bishop have deprived [the women] of any gratification they might have experienced in listening to what they could not have understood, if anybody else could have understood it" (21 Aug. 1858: 75). A more characteristic reaction, however, appears in a cartoon entitled "The Church Congress," a gathering of attentive young ladies, one of whom says, with an eye to matrimonial possibilities, "More curates are what we want" (2 Dec. 1865: 255). On the whole, then, the periodicals did not take women's interest in religion as a serious career option. Rather, because women were supposed to be "pure," they were shown to be religious (rather than theological); and because their purpose was marriage and procreation, they were presumed to be interested in the clergy—as husbands.

As the record shows, women who endeavored to enter the professions fared poorly in terms of satirical attacks, the single step taken away from the hearth becoming a giant's step into public scrutiny. Female lawyers, physicians, and theologians, however, faced considerably less mention than would-be female authors. Here the satirists were on firm ground, wielding the pen against those who wished to wield a pen. Perhaps because writing seemed an easy way for many women to undertake a career without leaving the home, it augured ill for the sanctity of the domestic sphere, supposedly safe from the taint of business. Writers as disparate as William Schwenck Gilbert and Nathaniel Hawthorne commented disparagingly on female scribblers, the bluestockings of their set, from "that singular anomaly, the lady novelist" on Ko-Ko's "little list of society offenders" in *The Mikado*, to Hawthorne's praise for Hilda, heroine of *The Marble Faun*, who gives up trying to produce original art, "pretty fancies of snow and moonlight; the counterpart in picture of so many feminine achievements in literature!" (chap. 6). Such "feminine achievements" (which a dispassionate glance shows to include the works of Hawthorne's contemporary George Eliot, for example) were characterized by the satirists as inflated romantic verbosities with little plot and less significance.

The authors of such works were frequently depicted as uncommonly plain old maids with a taste for gossip; where the face was good-looking, the brain was lacking. The clubman contributed to this persistent view, as *Punch* shows in the cartoon entitled "Love's Labour Lost; or, Laying it on too Thick!" in which "The Colonel" decides that the "very passionate love-story" which he is reading was written by a woman—"a doosid ugly one to the bargain!" because it is not only "improper" but "so full of abject and grovelling worship of the male sex. . . . No good-looking woman ever thinks about us like that!" (21 Apr. 1894: 186). The idea that the act of writing causes an authoress to forfeit her feminine purity surfaces regularly. Bernard Partridge's *Punch* sketch of the fashionable married couple makes this point well:

> *He.* "I see your friend, Mrs. Overton, has written a Society Novel."
> *She.* "Oh dear!—and I always thought she was such a *nice*-minded Woman!" [8 Feb. 1896: 69]

The female author is seen, then, either as a love-hungry spinster, living her life vicariously through her works, or as an innocent young lady, writing about matters she knows nothing about and making herself unattractive in the bargain. *Punch*'s "Passionate Female Literary Types" illustrates the first kind:

> *Miss Waly (Author of "Boots and Spurs and a Baritone Voice!")* "Honestly, Lucilla, have you ever met the Man you couldn't love?"
> *Miss Thrump (who wrote "Oh, the Meeting of the Lips!")* "No, Clarissa! Have you?"
> *Miss Waly.* "Oh, never, *never!* And I earnestly trust *I never shall!*"
> [12 May 1894: 225]

Unlike such practiced hands, a somewhat different stereotype grew up about the youthful bluestocking. *Punch*'s Evard Hopkins depicts a fashionable woman visiting her writer friend, who wears a frumpish dress and spectacles:

> "Fiction—Present Style"
>
> *Gertrude.* "You never do anything now, Margaret, but go to all sorts of Churches, and read those old Books of Theology. You never used to be like that."
> *Margaret.* "How can I help it, Gerty?—I'm writing a Popular Novel!" [13 Feb. 1892: 83]

Other writers seem to suggest that youthful authoresses might better attend to their fashions and feminine wiles than to their foolscap. Appearing in Chicago *Figaro*, Clara Hemingway's skit "A Business Arrangement" features an editor who rewrites an inferior piece of writing for the sake of the author's beautiful eyes (11 May 1893: 194-95). Likewise, *Punch*'s Tony Wilkinson creates a kindly publisher, if only for the sake of the joke. His sketch depicts a Gibson-like figure dressed in the height of fashion:

> *Pompous Publisher (to aspiring novice in literature).* "I have been reading your manuscript, my dear lady, and there is much in it I think—ahem!—very good. But there are parts somewhat vague. Now you should *always* write so that the *most ignorant can understand.*"
>
> *Youthful Authoress (wishing to show herself most ready to accept advice).* "Oh, yes, I'm sure. But, tell me, which are the parts that have given you trouble?" [13 Mar. 1901: 201]

To judge from the satirists, then, female writers were either too knowing or too innocent, too masculine or too feminine. As serious novelists, they were often taken to task for their overly gloomy view of human nature, a view attributed by the satirists to a false realism that makes up in luridness what it lacks in knowledge. *Punch*, for example, quotes a comment made by David Christie Murray at the Article Club: "The present pessimistic and hopeless kind of fiction, written by a lot of schoolgirls, who did not know what life was, was not going to last." The problem seems to be a combination of youth and inexperience, as well as an ignorance of aesthetics and the English language. *Punch* refers the modern writer to the classical proportions practiced by the French painter David as well as to the standard works of the grammarian Lindley Murray:

"To a Novelist of the Modern School"

Fair novelist, whose youthful pen,
    Steeped in the dismal style prevailing,
To unsophisticated men
    Life's dubious mysteries unveiling,
With fervid fancy's seared and scarred,
    A-throb with pessimistic hurry,
The laws alike you disregard
    Of DAVID and of LINDLEY MURRAY.

For us, who in the world have spent
    Some scores of winters—often wasted—
While, on life's pathway as we went,
    Its pleasant fruits we oft have tasted,
You, preternaturally wise,

In saddest, gloomiest effusions,
Strip off existence's disguise—
　　For you at least have no illusions.

Yet at the worst we fain would hope—
　　Though, judging thus the world unkindly,
You drag us with you as you grope
　　Amid its mazes madly, blindly,
And teach us everywhere to see
　　Horrors and miseries in plenty—
That, gentle maiden, you may be
　　Wiser perhaps when you are twenty. [18 Jan. 1899: 34]

In a longer poem, *Punch* reacts to the *Westminster Gazette*'s news of a private Russian library of 18,000 volumes written only by women, suggesting that this "pure and chaste" collection sets up a new pantheon that brings neither a blush to the cheek nor an idea to the mind. In place of Dickens and Thackeray, for instance, and in place of "Q" (Douglas Jerrold, *Punch*'s liberal satirist), Anthony Hope, and Rudyard Kipling, the library contains works by Mary Elizabeth Braddon (perhaps her most popular, *Lady Audley's Secret*), herself a *Punch* contributor; the poetess Felicia Hemans; Marie Corelli (among her works *The Sorrows of Satan* and *The Master Christian*); and Ouida, the pseudonym of Marie Louise de la Ramée, who published over three dozen novels).

### "Authoresses"

No SHAKESPEARE here hath quibbled
　　In jests best left unsaid;
No CONGREVE waxes ribald
　　In plays that can't be read;
But here the heart may gladden
The hours that such would sadden
With ANNIE SWAN, Miss BRADDON
　　And Mrs. WARD instead.

No wild Byronic passion
　　In this chaste study rings;
No KEATS in dubious fashion
　　Proclaimeth dubious things;
Yet need we not man's pity,

For hark, how sweetly pretty
The pure and pious ditty
  That holy HEMANS sings!

With firmness all unyielding
Far from our shelves we spurn
The wicked works of FIELDING,
  SWIFT, RICHARDSON and STERNE.
No gorged digestion sickens
On THACKERAY or DICKENS;
To Mother CAREY's chickens
  For lighter food we turn.

Consistent still we banish
  Man-writers of to-day;
Q., HOPE and KIPLING vanish
  Far from our shelves away;
For wherefore should we need a
PETT-RIDGE while we can read a
CORELLI, GRAND, or OUIDA,
  A GYP or MAXWELL GRAY?

Here in this haunt of virtue,
  Here in this Vestal shrine,
No work of man shall hurt you
  With humour masculine:
This pure and chaste collection
Owes all its sweet perfection
And virtuous complexion
  To fingers feminine. [27 Nov. 1901: 384]

   This feminine—rather than feminist—library might be appropriate for the dame school that Gilbert and Sullivan's Princess Ida sets up; by 1901 *Punch*, however, objects to the library's
narrowness and implies, at least, that both "Byronic passion"
and "humour masculine" provide an important edge to reading
enjoyment. A similar complaint, that female writing lacks
gusto and depth, was common in the case of the female journalist, who was, however, generally seen to pose a more formidable challenge. Indeed, the imputations of the *Punch* versifier pale considerably next to the condemnation of the
American Jessie M. Wood, who wrote for *Life* in the 1890s. The
"Newspaper Woman," "whom for polite reasons . . . we should

prefer not to call an adventuress," is, as he claims, given to alliterative pseudonyms, like "Jennie Jot-it-down" or "Rita Rite-it-up" as she gleefully reports her "eccentric" exploits: "In narrating her follies, a complete absence of such adult literary ingredients as grammar, style and common sense, united to a certain naive but flamboyant egotism, convinces the reader that she is an irresponsible little kitten who doesn't know any better." Wanting exploits, she writes fashion articles: "A strong outburst of morality will be sandwiched in between a description of a collarette and that of a flannelette combing jacket. . . . This shows the depth of the female literary mind." Finally, to supplement lack of news, she makes up anecdotes: "As interviewer the newspaper woman shows how splendidly she has developed that quality which first led our mother Eve to interrogate the serpent. In this branch of the profession she displays great mind-reading powers, and in publishing the interview she translates the laconic reticence of the interviewed lion into several columns of what she knew he wanted to say and somehow didn't. . . . If she doesn't put what you have said to her into one of her articles, you may be very sure that it was only because it was too stupid to print" (7 May 1896: 372).

Many of the ephemeral publications that appeared at the end of the century suggest that Wood's column has some measure of truth. His remarks, however, are confined to the shallowness of the female journalist's mind, a shallowness that proper education might have repaired; for other satirists, her main threat is that she blurs gender lines. In undertaking a male endeavor, she adopts male habits, engaging in a kind of "dress-for-success" code. She is depicted as intelligent and unsentimental; she smokes, swears, and prefers common sense to flowery compliments. She has, in short, as *Punch*'s lovelorn newspaperman discovers, given up the recognizable trappings of the "lady":

"To a Lady-Journalist"

Then ladies of the Press bar compliments
(At least *I* seldom find they will permit any!)
    So I'm impelled to write plain common sense,

Fig. 6. "The New Navy, about 1900 A.D." *Life*, 16 April 1896: 310-11.

As near as may be, and on no pretence
Aspire to high-flown ode or "lover's litany"!

But still you've *asked* me, and I'd much regret
Not to oblige you promptly, if I know a way;
  The more so, as you've just dropped in to get
  A cup of tea and smoke a c-g-r-tte.
(By Jove, I hope I haven't giv'n the show away!)

Well, I've not *said* much, but I've thought the more:
If I were fulsome in your praise, why, "Drat it!" you'd
  Most probably remark, or "What a bore!"
  So, therefore, please between the lines explore—
Twas *you* who bade me thus descend to platitude!
  [15 June 1895: 281]

Aside from the caricatures and satires that cluster around certain professions, many scattered responses to the idea of women in the marketplace were published. Doctor, lawyer, Indian chief: perhaps the last was the only vocation not touched on. Although even a reformer like Nat Arling, who supported opening all professions, balked at the idea of women's engaging in manual labor or entering the military (583), the cartoonists especially seemed to draw fun from shocking their more conventional audience. Women were thus depicted in professions in a way that today seems almost prophetic. In 1890 Lady "Barberesses" were shown shaving and trimming hair and beards in *Punch* (19 Apr. 1890: 186), while a female armed forces was suggested in 1896 by *Life*'s illustrators, Charles Dana Gibson and William Walker, who envisioned women revolutionizing the military in squadrons of their own. In one drawing, "A Council of War in the Days to Come," Gibson girls dressed in boots, kilts, and marching hats gather for a conference; surrounded by swords and medals and other paraphernalia of war, they primp in front of a mirror, sing and play the piano, drink coffee, and feed a small kitten, using a war map to catch the spilled milk (6 Aug. 1896: 100-101). Likewise, Walker's "The New Navy, About 1900 A.D." is presided over by a stout and invincible-looking captain; officers and crew on the gunboat are attired in a variety of bloomer outfits to designate rank (Fig. 6). In both, the satire is gentle, touching lightly on the readers' preconceptions and fears, but certainly more humorously than bitterly. The feminization of the armed forces seems less an issue than the novelty of the costumes.

Anchored firmly in their readers' preconceptions, then, popular periodicals nonetheless furthered the late-century revolution by publicizing the occupations they satirized and caricatured. Periodicals like *Punch* and *Life* with the power to sway public opinion generally avoided supporting the crusade for vocations, entering generally when humanitarian issues were involved, as, for example, in the case of wages for seamstresses and governesses. Some ground was gained, of course, as inhumane factory conditions were shown to be the norm, not the exception; yet the argument about equal pay is still present today. Indeed, it might be argued that the shop girl, forced into the marketplace against her will and thrust into public view because of her substandard working conditions, did as much as the pioneering suffragettes to broaden woman's sphere of influence.

To be sure, the helpfulness of the satire directed toward women's issues either in opening the professions or in effecting social reform varied enormously and depended, in part, on the attitude of the satirist. The series that appeared in *Pick-Me-Up* in 1889, for instance, gives "Visions of the Future" in which women were lady barristers, cabwomen, guides, boxers, policewomen, barbers, and the like; yet these "glimpses" are scarcely feminist in any sense, the drawings by Raven Hill featuring glimpses of stocking and coy poses that suggest provocation rather than professionalism. The costumes, moreover, are almost always recognizable uniforms feminized with skirts rather than with bloomers. Even the female band members, boxers, and clowns wear tutus; the lady dragoons seem to be wearing tights and miniskirts. More serious are the "Social Idylls" sketches by C. Smitham-Jones that appeared sporadically, a lady curate on 22 December 1888 and a bewigged Queen's Counsel on 3 May 1890; while these show handsome, intense women who are somewhat older and very much in command, Raven Hill's frivolous approach is more common.

Generally speaking, then, women who chose to widen their sphere through a career or who were forced into employment

because they were "redundant" were often depicted as improper, incapable, or unfeminine, especially if they were members of the middle class. Those who argued seriously against
women in the marketplace sometimes assumed that they were
dealing with a passing phenomenon, a fad engendered by a new
myth, that being a "bachelor girl" and living a Bohemian life
were preferable to the ordinary course of marriage and family.
Winifred Sothern argues, in fact, that the price paid for work
and freedom is high, that "false glamour" misleads unprepared
women into the city to earn what is barely a living wage (282-
83). To be sure, some serious writers encouraged women to
work for a variety of reasons: such activity cured adolescent
restlessness (Haweis 434); taught women appropriate self-value
(Crackanthorpe 425); returned them to their "natural" sphere,
idleness being a product of the industrial revolution (Arling
584); and guaranteed respect, since social status is a function
of financial status (Caird 814). On the whole, though, the question of women's work was closely linked to the question of
marriage and education. While the woman who could not marry
often needed to work to support herself, the professions were
closed to those without training. And as long as the argument
over the proper use of women's talents persisted, acquiring an
education required not only intelligence but courage to face all
shades of social and family disapproval.

# THREE

# Women's Education

## *"Maddest Folly Going"*

They intend to send a wire
    To the moon—to the moon;
And they'll set the Thames on fire
    Very soon—very soon;
Then they learn to make silk purses
    With their rigs—with their rigs,
From the ears of Lady Circe's
    Piggy-wigs—piggy-wigs. . . .
    These are the phenomena
    That every pretty domina
    Is hoping we shall see
    At her Universitee!
    —W.S. Gilbert, *Princess Ida*

FROM THE cockney 'Arry to Gilbert and Sullivan, women's education might well have seemed the "maddest folly going." Indeed, in an age in which sons had tutors or were sent away to school and daughters had governesses, when finishing schools provided the most surface of polishes, women's education had small value, although it was, in monetary terms, extremely expensive. The idea, moreover, of women establishing more than a dame school to teach young children seemed unreasonable; not only did they themselves lack the advantages of male training, but their prospective students were expected eventually to marry. Received wisdom suggested that serious studying sapped a woman's reproductive strength, thus impairing her very raison d'être; doctors argued over the "nature" of women, some declaring that since a woman's cranial capacity was smaller than a man's, intellectual endeavors were not only unwise but unnatural.

    Against these and other arguments and preconceptions the

"pretty domina" had to contend. Not the least of her problems was the sense that she was not just wresting a commodity—education—away from her brothers but also attempting to become, so to speak, the author of her own story. In so doing, she was literally planning for the contingency of not marrying, a state that no young lady might admit to pursuing but one that every young lady expected. She was, in fact, entertaining the notion of an independent life, one in which she might earn her own sustenance by using her head as well as her heart.

Education, then, provided the safety net between marriage and work, but adequate education was slow to develop. The new frontier—America—initially offered more to its sons than to its daughters. Early education might be summed up by saying that boys were taught to read and write, girls to read and sew; generally speaking, in New England towns the teachers were available to girls only after their brothers had been taught, and on the plantations, where central schooling was not feasible, southern women were educated with their brothers only at the pleasure of their fathers. After the Revolution the wealthy educated their daughters in finishing schools on the English plan (Douglas 85-87). Once such institutions as Mt. Holyoke, Oberlin, and Wesleyan were established, women had real academic alternatives. Although attacked for their high-schoolish curricula by the educator Catherine Beecher, they paved the way for "Vassar's folly," Antioch, and Wellesley, schools that emulated Harvard's standards. By the end of the century, the argument had shifted more to whether women should be allowed to practice the professions after acquiring law, theology, and medical degrees than to whether they should be educated at all. In fact, in 1908 M. Carey Thomas—the president of Bryn Mawr (1894-1922)—was able to make the following triumphant—if quixotic—pronouncement: "In the twenty-five years covered by the work of the Association of Collegiate Alumnae the battle for the higher education of women has been gloriously, and forever, won" (Kraditor 90-94).

In England the battle was long fought as well. While middle- and upper-class boys received some instruction in the classics at boarding or day schools, their sisters were cared for by the selfsame governesses whose low pay, indifferent backgrounds, and heavy work load had made them *causes célèbres* in *Punch*. While young men were distinguishing themselves by earning prestigious degrees, their female counterparts were sent out among the Miss Pinkertons of the finishing schools; not until 1920 at Oxford and 1948 at Cambridge were women allowed to take degrees or achieve full university membership (McWilliams-Tullberg 120). And while married men were in the full flush of their careers, wives were supervising governesses and sending daughters to finishing schools—thus beginning the cycle anew.

At the heart of the battle waged against the self-perpetuating system was the question of gender identification, both in the distinction between what was considered "womanly" and "manly" and in the social stratification indicated by the terms "ladylike" and "female." As the century progressed, the tendency was to insist upon the difference between "female" and "lady," the latter usually suggesting a class identification. Generally speaking, the "womanly woman" centered her affections in the home and was both the guiding spirit and the submissive wife; if she was "ladylike," she conducted herself modestly and properly, with regard for the feelings of others. That "dame" schools were especially sensitive to the nuances of terminology is made clear by *Punch*; in a small cartoon of a "Lady Visitor" to a school, the quip is based on the Victorian superdelicacy that put paper frills and skirts around furniture legs, that transformed "legs" into "limbs," and that made "unmentionables" out of underwear.

"Quite Correct"

*Lady Visitor (looking out on playground).* "Ah, there are all the girls, and my little girl among them! What are they doing?"
*Schoolmistress.* "They're making a snow-woman."
*Lady Visitor.* "A Snow what!"
*Schoolmistress.* "*My* young ladies are not allowed to make a snow-man!" [9 Mar. 1895: 120]

One illustration of the semantic arguments that occurred was published by London *Truth* as a response to a news item in the *Westminster Gazette*. According to the report, a disturbance was occasioned by a Wandsworth prison board member who persisted in calling "female Guardians" "women" rather than "ladies." The versifier gibes equally at the "lady" and the women's rights advocate, at the end maintaining his preference for "good old English women":

"A Word for 'Woman' "

What do our sisters say to this?
   Are they such matters prim in?
And do they mean to urge the plea
That "women" cannot "ladies" be,
   That "ladies" can't be "women"?

We fancied it was *"Women's* Rights"
   That they put forth their might for;
But must we from to-day conclude,
After this Wandsworth interlude—
   'Tis *"Ladies'* Rights" they fight for?

Do they despise the good old name,
   And think its meaning "shady"?
And hold that, when this world began,
Though Adam was the first made "man,"
   Eve was the first-made "lady"?

And these "New Women," of whose fads
   We get such long recital—
Do *they* intend a change to make,
And for all time to come to take
   "New *Ladies*" as their title?

By all means let them, if they choose,
   This new demand be grim in:
Let the "New *Ladies*" have their will
If only they will leave us still
   Our good old English women! [10 Jan. 1895: 71]

While the satirists had fun with the intricacies of language, many "good old English women," unmarried and without hope of inheritance, faced a crisis of expectation that their education was inadequate to provide for. The periodicals, however, quick to attack both the social pretensions of the "lady" and the aspirations of the feminist, did service to the latter by lam-

Fig. 7. "A Study in Natural History." *Punch*, 23 July 1898: 34.

pooning the inadequacies of the finishing school, which seemed devoted to providing its students with a smattering of skills that might be useful in snaring a husband. In *Punch* Reginald Cleaves illustrates not only the prevailing attitude about education and marriage but also the conflict between the New Woman's attire and the old mythology. His girl of the period, dressed nattily in fedora, tie, and walking suit, nonetheless asks to be allowed to "go abroad to finish." Her mother, veiled and bedecked in an older fashion, answers, " 'No. It's time you were married; and men don't care how ill-educated a woman is.' " Ripostes the daughter: " 'You shouldn't judge everybody by Pa, Ma!' " (19 May 1894: 231). Again, "A Study in Natural History"—A.S. Boyd's cartoon in *Punch*—suggests the real reason for the finishing schools: young Leonidas, eyed by a "boarding-school 'crocodile' "—a "formidable" group of fashionably dressed maidens out for a stroll—suddenly perceives himself to be the intended victim (Fig. 7). The same sort of attitude prevailed across the Atlantic, even at the turn of the century. In *Life*, a well-dressed young lady confronts her mother about her education:

> *Daughter (home from a seminary):* "We no sooner learn a little about one subject, Mamma, than we stop and turn to another."
> *[Mother.]* "You must remember, dear, that I am fitting you to enter society." [26 Oct. 1899: 323]

Even such shallow training aroused the fears of the old guard, who remembered their younger days with nostalgia. However outmoded in the 1890s, even a finishing school education would have seemed advanced in, for instance, the 1840s. One measure of the distance women's education had come may be seen in an 1842 *Punch* valentine to an "Accomplished Young Lady." In this verse the writer expresses a popular belief that even excellence in music, embroidery, and "ladylike" verse would develop the intellect to the detriment of feeling:

You sing with a thrilling expression,
 That makes all your auditors tremble,
And warble out "Del cor tradisti,"
 Like Grisi or Adelaide Kemble.

Tis divine—though some ill-natured folks,
    Full of envy, snarl out in their rage,
" 'Tis a pity this clever young lady
    Wasn't brought up at once for the stage."

You embroider such exquisite patterns
    For ottomans, sofas, and chairs;
And I hear you have finish'd a carpet
    That stretches up two pair of stairs:
Though the same set of commonplace people
    Opine 'twould be better by far,
If these wool-working clever young ladies
    Took stalls at the Lowther Bazaar.

You write the most ladylike poems;
    And I hear that (*incog.*), now and then,
The *Assemblée's* elaborate columns
    Are graced by the fruits of your pen.
They are brilliantly soft, I allow;
    But with all the respect for a blue,
The world thinks 'tis sometimes a pity
    You find nothing better to do.

There are many opposed to such measures,
    Who hint from the right you depart,
In cramming the *head* with such treasures
    And wholly forgetting the *heart*:
But hearts have long ceased to exist,
    So I deem your affections are free,
And the chance is not one to be miss'd,
    Then, fair one, my VALENTINE be. [69]

    In the 1840s education of the "head" seemed to mean proficiency at embroidery, tapestry, singing, and versifying, all subjects still taught at the end of the century in fashionable schools. In the middle of the 1890s' educational reform movement, however, the situation was reversed, with one writer complaining that modern education ignored such domestic niceties as fine sewing, housework, and cooking, all of which might solve the servant problem and provide "free" clothing for the family (Unite 854-55). Indeed, as *Punch* suggests, the problem was in part created by irrelevant schooling that made all women unfit for their positions; educated middle-class women became dissatisfied with the domestic sphere, and the servant class put on airs. *Punch's* humorist in the *Almanack for 1881* provides a glimpse of the problem in an interview between the mistress of the house and a fashionably dressed serving girl:

"Culture 1881"

*Mistress.* "As you've never been in Service, I'm afraid I can't engage you without a 'character.' "
*Young Person.* "I have three School-Board Certificates, Ma'am—"
*Mistress.* "Oh, well—I suppose for Honesty, Cleanliness—"
*Young Person.* "No, Ma'am—for 'Literatoor, Joggr'phy, an' Free 'And Drawrin'!"

Not only have the lessons not succeeded in changing the status of the servant, the cartoonist seems to say, but what she has learned is of no help in earning a livelihood.

To marry and to enter society: neither of these presupposed the need for intellectual development for the middle-class woman, an irony that the satirists exploited. Many products of finishing schools recognized the irony as well. The suffragist Frances Power Cobb, whose later social work and reform writing, including *Darwinism in Morals* and *The Duties of Women*, belie her early training, writes of her Brighton boarding school:

. . . a better system than theirs [the Misses Runciman and Roberts] could scarcely have been devised had it been designed to attain the maximum of cost and labour and the minimum of solid results. It was the typical Higher Education of the period, carried out to the extreme of expenditure and high pressure. . . . But all this fine human material was deplorably wasted. Nobody dreamed that any one of us could in later life be more or less than an "Ornament of Society." That a pupil in that school should ever become an artist, or authoress, would have been looked upon by both Miss Runciman and Miss Roberts as a deplorable dereliction. Not that which was good in itself or useful to the community, or even that which would be delightful to ourselves, but that which would make us admired in society was the *raison d'être* of each acquirement. Everything was taught us in the inverse ratio of its true importance. At the bottom of the scale were Morals and Religion, and at the top were Music and Dancing. . . .
[quoted in Hellerstein, Hume, and Offen 73-74]

Given the poverty of instruction for women in the classics and in the hard sciences, however, *Punch* was similarly skeptical on other grounds of the lasting effect of "finishing" education. On 14 March 1885, for example, George Du Maurier published a cartoon captioned "The Higher Education of Women" that depicts two women and their escort in a theater box. One, looking at her playbill, exclaims, "Only fancy! *As You Like It* is by Shakespeare!" (126). Eleven years later on 18 January 1896, a female astronomer informs an astonished acquaintance that Jupiter, the evening star, is "exactly two yards and a half to the right of the Great Bear." She knows that the distance is correct because, as she exclaims, "I've measured it carefully with my umbrella!" (34).

Such complaints about the inadequacy and frivolity of women's education were commonly framed by the satirists, yet women like Frances Power Cobb, who had succeeded in educating herself, were also likely to be attacked for their success. *Life* warns that rather than simply appearing foolish, the bluestocking who parades her knowledge may find herself ostracized, not so much because her knowledge is envied, but because she has lost attractive womanly qualities. This danger is illustrated by one cartoonist, who draws a spinsterish figure with the profile of the pulpit orator Henry Ward Beecher:

"I resemble the late Mister Beecher,"
Said this wonderful masculine creecher.
   She then started classes
   To lift up the masses
At which vacant chairs were a feecher. [7 Apr. 1900: 288]

For most commentators, this kind of gender transference means that the lessons of the heart are forgotten in favor of the lessons of the head; sentiment and warmth give way to rationality and practicality. In *Life*'s "Cinderella Up to Date," for instance, three sisters discuss a wedding. "Yes," says one, "we, who have been through a private seminary and a college, have been taught to observe, and it is natural that, between us, nothing should escape our observation." In the course of discussion, two of the sisters evaluate the "styles" of the relatives and estimate their probable worth; they discuss the bride's dress at length. Finally, Cinderella speaks up:

> "I saw all you saw, and more," she said.
> The sisters gazed at her superciliously.
> "Indeed!" they chorused. "What did you see that we didn't see?"
> "I noticed the groom," said Cinderella. [20 July 1899: 45]

The question of the relationship between education and marriage was a recurrent one. Even toward the end of the century, many sympathizers with the educational reform movement emphasized woman's special mission. Chicago *Figaro* reprinted a plea by Mrs. Van Rensselaer for a broad education, rather than a specialized one, to prepare a woman to be "a companion for intelligent men and a help to those who are not" and to prepare her to participate in her grown children's lives (13 Aug. 1892: 428). In the same periodical, even Harriet C. Brainard's more liberal stance that women no longer need defend their right to higher education is moderated by the idea that "nothing [is] withdrawn from the sacred conception of the home and the womanly presence there" (16 Apr. 1892: 116). In England, too, the earlier Victorian idea that women should not pursue knowledge for its own sake broadened toward the end of the century into the belief that "the hand that rocked the cradle" should belong to one who was well educated enough to raise future leaders. M. Carey Thomas makes this apologia as late as 1908: "If 50 per cent. of college women are to marry, and nearly 40 per cent. are to bear and rear children, such women cannot conceivably be given an education too broad, too high, too deep, to fit them to become the educated mothers of the future race of men and women to be born of educated parents. Somehow or other such mothers must be made familiar with the great mass of inherited knowledge which is handed on down from generation to generation of civilized educated men" (quoted in Kraditor 95).

As proponents of this compromise position, many educators threaded the generally accepted behavioral norm for women through their reforms, thereby making them more acceptable.

Such well-known figures as Frances M. Buss, headmistress of North London Collegiate School, and Constance Maynard, of Westfield College, insisted on the importance of femininity (Gorham 107), which, in part, meant nurturing a homelike atmosphere through filial duty, attention to moral values, and cultivation of the emotions. Molly Hughes, one of Miss Buss's most promising students, ceased to teach once she married and records in *A London Home of the 1890's* the pride with which she settled into her domestic duties.

Even such concessions to prevailing attitudes as those made by the reformers were not enough to still the critics' fear that women's special nature would be ruined by too much education. One satirist in *Pick-Me-Up*, noting the superhuman combination of domestic and intellectual attributes expected of the "modern" woman, concludes that she is an Admirable Crichton. On the one hand, she knows Latin and Greek and is conversant with the philosophers: "She has read her Herbert Spencer, / Her Kant, and Schopenhauer; / And in logic she's a fencer / Of unquestionable power." On the other hand, she is a domestic goddess:

She instructs the untrained servant
　　To perform his task with ease;
And, if called on, will wax fervent
　　Over infantile disease.

She can cook and wash and mangle
　　(Tho', perhaps, she'[d] rather not),
Play lawn-tennis, ride, and angle,
　　And is quite a champion shot. . . .  [14 June 1890: 172]

Not everyone made the synthesis between education and woman's mission, however; the more vociferous complained that domestic concerns would become easily obscured by intellectual pursuits, especially when those pursuits had a scandalous edge. Both Zola and Ibsen appear as bellwethers of corrupting modern influence, as in *Pick-Me-Up*'s sketch of a bluestocking leaning against a copy of Zola's *Nana* with her feet propped on a Bible (29 Apr. 1893: 73). Likewise, *Punch* sums up such fears in a verse illustrated by a thumbnail sketch showing a female scholar contemplating a play by Ibsen, while scattered around her lie notes and books, among them Zola's naturalistic novel *Thérèse Raquin*:

"A Fair Philosopher"

Ah! Chloris! be as simple still
    As in the dear old days;
Don't prate of Matter and Free Will,
    And IBSEN's nasty plays.
A girl should ne'er, it seems to me,
    Have notions so pedantic;
'Twere better far once more to be
    Impulsive and romantic.

There was a time when idle tales
    Could set your heart aflame;
But now the novel nought avails,
    Philosophy's your game.
You talk of SCHOPENHAUER with zest,
    And pessimistic teaching;
Believe me that I loved you best
    Before you took to preaching.

There's still some loveliness in life,
    Despite what cynics say;
It is not all ignoble strife,
    That greets us on our way.
Then prithee smooth that pretty brow,
    So exquisitely knitted;
Mankind in general, I trow,
    Can do without being pitied.

We'll linger over fans and frills,
    Discuss dress bit by bit,
As in days when the worst of ills
    Were frocks that would not fit.
'Twas frivolous, but I'm content
    To hear you talk at random;
For life is not all argument,
    And *"Quod est demonstrandum."* [23 Jan. 1892: 41]

Two years later, a stronger, less nostalgic complaint focuses on the progressive woman, who, the versifier contends, copies the follies of man; she seeks college degrees that make her a "feminine Baboo of Arts" and that are, in the long run, irrelevant to her womanly nature and position, as these excerpts from "Words to the Wise Women" show:

Learn all you wish to learn, exult in learning,
For Hymen's torch keep midnight oil a-burning,
Bulge your fair foreheads with those threatening bumps,
Ungraceful as an intellectual mumps,
Be blatant, rude, self-conscious as you can,
Be all you feign—and imitate—in Man.
Spurn all the fine traditions of the past,
Be New or nothing—what's the gain at last?
You know as much, with hard-eyed, harsh-voiced joy,
As the shock-headed, shambling fifth-form boy;
Adding, what his sound mind would never please,
An Asiatic hunger for degrees.
True learning's that alone whereon are based
Clear insight, reason, sympathy, and taste.
Not relic-worshipping of bones long dry,
Not giving puppet-life to $x$ and $y$,
And walking haughtily a fair world through
Because some girls can't do the sums you do. . . .
    Meanwhile our faith looks on, devoid of fear,
Facing the hatchet of the Pioneer.
Still will the storm, in Nature's potent plan,
Be temper'd to the shorn, or bearded man.
Your sex will still be perfect in its place,
With voice of melody and soul of grace.
Pose, lecture, worry, copy as you will,
Man will be man, and woman woman still! [8 Dec. 1894: 275]

The nostalgic yearning for the old-fashioned frivolous and ornamental female was coupled with the use of "fact"—some of it documentable—to support the mythology. Using statistics about brain weight and anatomical structure, critics of the New Woman demonstrated that women lacked intellectual capacity and receptivity to education. Other writers, obviously concerned about the adverse effects of intellectual endeavor on female fertility, concluded that women's education should be different—less intensive and less lengthy—than men's. One example of a closely reasoned argument appears in *Popular Science Monthly*, where George J. Romanes uses a Darwinian analysis to support his argument for separate and different education for women: "Seeing that the average brain-weight of women is about five ounces less than that of men," he notes, "on merely anatomical grounds we should be prepared to expect a marked inferiority of intellectual power in the former. Moreover, as the general physique of women is less robust than that of men—and therefore less able to sustain the fatigue of serious or prolonged brain action—we should also, on physiological grounds, be prepared to entertain a similar anticipation." Romanes comments "that the inferiority displays itself most conspicuously in a comparative absence of originality" and "that a woman's information is less wide, and deep, and thorough, than that of a man" (384). He concludes not that women need more education to enhance their powers but that they are incapable of pursuing anything but superficial study.

One facetious answer to the kind of argument framed by Romanes appears in *Judy*, where a versifier, inverting the usual argument, suggests that philosophers are needlessly perplexed by the differences between men and women:

Indeed, the argument's so brief
    'Tis past ere well begun;
It is that woman *has* a mind,
    And man, alas! has none.

Dear woman changes oft her mind—
    She's neither wrong nor strange;
But man is constant still, because
    He has no mind to change. . . . [6 Apr. 1887: 164]

More serious answers came from the "ornaments of society" themselves, who, realizing that body weight and brain weight are proportional and that superficiality of information is the fault of poor schooling, not genetics, found a number of ways to protest against the stereotype. One line of reasoning sought to prove that the intellectual capacities of men and women differ because of social expectation; even less intelligent men have a better opportunity to develop than exceptional women, not only because of the intellectual activities open to them, but because they are expected to excel. The argument continued that brilliant men are just as liable to lapse into contented ordinariness as their feminine counterparts and that since even men can be "good," virtue is not necessarily sex linked (Simcox 391, 398-400).

With the popularization of Mendel's law, however, the argument shifted from brain size to brain composition, from quantity to quality; if a child inherited equally from mother and father, then even female offspring would be likely to possess some "superior" male genes. This "proof" of women's capability did not answer all objections to education. Among the many factors that mitigated against the new intellectualism was the fear that unprotected girls, uprooted from their homes, would be unable to deal with the dangers of independence at college. One writer lays the blame on the upbringing of young girls and compares British education unfavorably with that offered in America: "An English girl travelling without her mother or old friend . . . is looked at a little askance by well-bred people . . . because it is assumed that, having the usual English education, she is either not fit to take entire charge of herself or—it is too late to matter." On the other hand, in America "there are physiological classes held for the wise and decent instruction of the girls in the main responsibilities pertaining to physical life" (Haweis 435).

Again, in England the concern that with general education women of different classes would not only be treated equally but would form "unsuitable" friendships was very real; such indiscriminate mixing threatened the very class system itself, to say nothing of the meaning of the word *ladylike*. A further stumbling block to admitting women to degrees at Oxford and Cambridge was the attendant social and administrative privileges. University membership granted the right to be considered for university positions and full voting rights on university matters (McWilliams-Tullberg 120), and male members were loathe to share the power. Clearly, a woman who chose to acquire a university education challenged the physiological, psychological, social, and political status quo. As women's colleges like Girton and Newnham, Vassar and Wellesley grew in

influence and as the arguments over separate but equal education, examinations, degrees, and housing became more rau-
cous, the press reacted in kind, for the most part conservatively.
*Life*, both concerned about and charmed with the notion of "girl
graduates" invading men's professions, published a series of
drawings of attractive female ministers and lawyers, yet it held
firmly to the belief that a woman's mission was husband and
home. "Some Timely Words" is typical; male graduates are
reminded that through the "hard work ahead" they should "be
temperate, be upright, be diligent." Women, however, are addressed quite differently: "And you, dear girls! If a qualified
man offers, please marry him. That is the best service you can
render the world. Meanwhile, look around and see what there
is to be done, and try to do your share of it. There's plenty to
do, and if it puzzles you how to get at it, console yourself with
the knowledge that the problem what to do with a college-bred
woman between the time she leaves college and her wedding
day is mighty complex, and stumps the doctors and puts the
most sagacious parents to their trumps" (24 June 1897: 534-
35).

In the same season, however, *Life* also published a commentary by Harriet Caryl Cox suggesting that women are their
own worst enemies in the tug-of-war between education and
marriage, intellect and love. It stands as one of *Life*'s few en-
couragements to women to persist in their academic endeavors,
although Charles Dana Gibson did join the argument in pro-
posing "A 'Word to the Wise' " to a statuesque woman seated
at dinner between two insipid beaux: "Have a Book in Case
you are Bored," he advises (29 Mar. 1900: 250-51). Cox's vignette, a discussion between a pretty, sociable girl and her Intellect, is more to the point, however. The speaker says that
she "hates" her Intellect, which warns her whenever she is
nicely "enjoying" herself: "You make me 'unusual,' 'remarkable,' 'brilliant,' " she says, "and I hate it. . . . I don't want to
be a person with Intellect. I'd rather be just silly, and commonplace, and look pretty, and be like other girls." She is
"bored" with being liked for her mind: " 'But I am you,' retorted
the Intellect, stirred at last. 'We are inseparable. I am what
makes you and the people who admire me are admiring you. I

*am* you, and you can't get away from it.' " The girl believes
that by falling in love, she will eradicate her Intellect and enter
a "world of dearest delight." But the Intellect warns that love
changes one's perspective for the worse: "That which is not
will seem to be, and that which seems substance will be but
shadow. There will be no cruel awakening when the falling
petals reveal the worm-eaten rose, for without me the awakening cannot come." The Intellect's final warning that true delight cannot exist without consciousness convinces the girl,
and she and her Intellect "are at peace once more" (15 Apr.
1897: 308-9).

In contrast to this gently feminist warning, *Life* more char-
acteristically suggests as late as 1900 that love is inevitable and
supreme and that no matter how rigorous the education, Cupid
conquers. Montrose J. Moses takes this stance in a mock speech
by Love itself:

"Love's Address"
(Before Any College, Male or Female)
Ladies and Gentlemen:
I have not been allowed to enter
    This learned centre
Knowingly, because I am not the kind of knowledge
    They spread at College;
Unfathomed, but felt, I need no dissertations
    On my frequent visitations,
For beneath the cap and gown of learning,
    I come, analysis spurning,
        And appeal to the heart—
        That vital part
    Which Professors cannot reach
        To teach.

I invade the laboratory, where grim vessels
    And grinning mortars and pestles,
Stand in harmony with the student's face;
    I enter and take my place
Beside him at the laboratory table,
    And give him a touch of Mabel,
        Or any other maiden;

And his hands, vessel-laden,
Are my slaves, self-poised, while he,
   Ruled by me,
   Gazing into infinite space
    With a softer face,
   Forgetful of his chemical test;
   Forgetful of the fluid and the rest:
Feels his heart begin to beat the faster
   And knows I am the master!

I go where a maid is bending,
   In unending
Study of a flower under the microscope,
   In the hope
   Of making a rose more a rose
    Through what she knows.
   I know a rosebud in her hair
Would be a thousand times more fair;
   I send the color to her face,
    With subtle grace;
And she—ah, well—I creep into her heart,
   And make her start,
And read into the rose, a world the microscope
   Would have no hope
    Of analyzing
    Or devising.

There are those who can fathom anything, and see
   Everything but me;
There are those who, pondering over ponderous lore
   Would fain explore
   My realm; still, I need no teaching—
   I am far-reaching.
   Unseen, I come and enter
   This learned centre,
And do my will as best I can,
   With maid and man;
   And so
   They know
Without study, as much of Love, as they
   do of knowledge
    Gained at College. [24 May 1900: 441]

Unlike many of its other counterparts, *Life* more gracefully accepted the assimilation of women into the public sphere by temporizing, implicitly sanctioning women's education by creating a new mythology about the college girl while insisting on the primacy of love and marriage. One reason may be related to its undisguised patriotism and its belief that American women, fostered by the atmosphere of liberty and progress in their native land, were capable of doing anything. *Punch*, on the other hand, was more uncomfortable in finding a place for the "girl graduate"; its writers devoted more of their time to wonderment at the phenomenon than to praise for her achievements. When London University allowed the first female graduates to march in the academic procession, for instance, *Punch* recorded the event with mild amazement, suggestively stereotyping them as Aspasia, the Greek courtesan who was famous for her literary salons:

"Girl Graduates"

Girl Graduates! They realise
   Our Tennyson's old fancies,
And winning Academic prize,
   They scorn seductive dances.
Here come the feminine M.D.s,
   Of physic fair concocters,
Who write prescriptions with such ease,
   The "violet-hooded Doctors."

And here are those who won success
   In fields supremely classic,
Who read of NEOBULE's dress,
   Of Horace and his Massic.
Here female rhetoricians tell
   How useful many a trope is;
And men will learn, perchance too well,
   If girls are all βοῶπις.

How strange to some folks it must seem,
   This modern Convocation;
ASPASIA rules the Academe,
   Once man's exclusive station;
And those who bow beneath her yoke,

The strongest men and sternest,
May try to think that she's in joke,
And find her quite in earnest! [3 June 1882: 257]


By 1883, when *Punch* began to notice Aspasia with due
regularity, some of its pictorial commentary became more biting. The magazine moved away from the philosophy of Charles
Keene, an early artist who refused to show women in uncomplimentary poses because, as he said, " 'he could not be hard
on the sex' " (Spielmann 141), to more direct attacks. Unlike
*Life*'s satire, which never questioned the rectitude of its college
women, many of *Punch*'s innuendos impugn the intellectual
woman. Linley Sambourne's sketch for the *Almanack for 1883*
shows *Punch*'s editorial preference for the old-fashioned girl.
The device for the caption "Long Vacation ends. Mistress of
Arts" is a bespectacled female graduate accoutered in cap and
gown; carefully holding up her skirts to display (probably blue)
stockings, she proudly flourishes a scorpion's stinger. In the
background a cherubic Mr. Punch parades with a modestly attired lady of the period.

Just three years later "Professor Punch" (à la Harry Furniss)
hints that young women resident at Cambridge might find other
occupation than reading for degrees. Like many of *Punch*'s cartoons, this one is based on a newsworthy controversy: a letter
to the London *Times* by the founder of Girton College, Emily
Davies, who deals with some of the objections to granting women
degrees. That the Tripos examinations may not be the "ideal
course of higher education for women" was easily answered;
out of 160 students at Girton and Newnham, twenty-five (between 1880 and 1887) would have qualified for first-class honors, despite their initial lack of preparation for university
studies. Again, in exchange for degrees, Davies says, women
were willing to accept restrictions that barred them from sitting on university policy-making bodies. The more problematic
objections were based on veiled fears of sexual misconduct.
"Having a considerable number of young women resident in
Cambridge with no other occupation than reading for an ordinary degree might be very serious," one critic contended;
similarly, for men and women "to mix without special restric-

tions would evidently be unwise. . . . at best, the maintenance of discipline would be rendered more difficult." Davies's answer was simple: while women were "guests" of the university, "the Senate could at any time apply a remedy if the occasion arose" (25 Jan. 1888: 7f).

The suspicion that the female scholar's primary occupation is husband hunting is illustrated by *Punch* in a series of cameos surrounding a black-robed don preventing a curvaceous, fashionably dressed woman from receiving her degree. In the sketches a lecture is an excuse for canoodling; serenades disturb the Quadrangle at night; College Hall dinner is tête-à-tête; romantic plays predominate at the Drama Club; and even the chapel choir engages in flirtation (4 Feb. 1888: 59).

Distinguished academic achievement by women routed the stereotype only briefly. In 1890, for example, a Newnham College resident, P.G. Fawcett, the only daughter of a deceased Cambridge don, caused a stir. As the *Times* reports, "Although it was well-known that she would attain a higher position in the class list than has ever yet been attained by a woman, it was regarded as improbable that she would obtain higher marks than the Senior Wrangler" (9 Jan. 1890: 7c). Because she was, in fact, "Seniorer to the Senior Wrangler," as *Punch* would have it, she was dubbed "Seniora Fawcett" by the *Punch* punster. Following that, Margaret Alford won a First in Classics at Girton. *Punch*'s verse response ironically mentions Tennyson's "Dream of Fair Women," a poem that celebrates those who were crossed in love:

"The Ladies' Year"

"A Dream of Fair Women"—who shine in the Schools,
The Muse should essay ere her ardour quite cools.
Come, bards, take your lyres and most carefully tune 'em,
For Girton in glory now pairs off with Newnham.
Miss FAWCETT the latter with victory wreathed,
And now, ere the males from their marvel are breathed,
Miss MARGARET ALFORD, the niece of the Dean,
As a Classical First for the former is seen.
Let Girton toast Newnham, and Newnham pledge Girton,

And—let male competitors put a brisk "spurt" on,
Lest when modern Minerva adds learning to grace,
Young Apollo should find himself out of the race! [28 June 1890: 309]


Again, *Punch* toasts "Seniora Fawcett" in sketch and poem on the occasion of the award in Paris of a doctorate to the Romanian scholar Mlle. Belesco. The poet, who claims to distinguish between the foolish demands of the New Women and the solid achievements of Belesco and Fawcett, quaintly implies the beginning of an "Old Girl" network:


"Place Aux Dames"

To Seniora FAWCETT
   The Wranglers yield first place;
And now, first of the t=Law set,
   One of another race,
Beauty, Brunette, Roumanian,
   From man takes top Degree!
In learning's race Melanion
   Is beaten, one can see,
By the new Atalanta;
   At Law School or Sorbonne,
As at our native Granta
   The girls the prize have won.
Bravo, brunette BELESCO!
   Some limner ought to draw
A quasi-classic fresco,
   O Lady of the Law!
O Mathematic Maiden!
   And show the pretty pair
With Learning's trophies laden
   And manhood in a scare.
Ah, *Portia* of Paris!
   *Urania* of the Cam!
*Punch*, whose especial care is
   To sever truth from sham,
Is no great Woman's-Rightist,
   But *this* is not clap-trap;
Of pundits the politest,

To you he lifts his cap!
*Docteur en Droit, Punch* watches
    Miss FAWCETT by the Cam;
To you she quick despatches
    A friendly telegram.
He, friend of all the Nations,
    Of Woman as of Man,
Adds *his* "felicitations."
    Well done, Roumanian!!! [21 June 1890: 289]

Felicitations were granted more easily than honors; indeed, the argument over whether women should be granted degrees persisted for a number of years. In 1893, for instance, the *Contemporary Review* supported the demand: "Why should women not take the B.A. degree? . . . Unfortunately the older Universities have resented every attempt at breaking down their cherished exclusiveness." *Punch*'s changing point of view may be seen in its shift from the epithet *Aspasia* to *Minerva*. Its position in the fray about granting degrees is ambiguous, however: it compliments serious scholarship and adopts as an issue the unfairness of turning qualified women away from full university status, yet it questions women's motivations in pursuing advanced study. In a typically equivocal piece, a *Punch* versifier adopts the title of one of Robert Browning's poems to comment on the issue in the persona of the women themselves but at the end suggests that the desire is based not so much on a request for equal treatment as on vanity:

"How it Strikes 'The Contemporary'"

Despotic Dons' dominion
    Still subjugates us all,
They scoff at our opinion,
    Our purposes miscall;
Will no deliverer appear,
And is it vainly, as we fear,
We hold our meetings every year
    Within St. James's Hall?

Our wrongs, if brought to knowledge,
    Would surely move your hearts,
Degreeless from her College

The Wrangler-ess departs;
And shall not too the maids, who can
Give all the usages of *àv*,
As well as any living man
        Be Bachelors of Arts?

Persuasive or abusive
        We fail our point to gain,
Disgracefully exclusive
        These ancient seats remain:
But yet a future we foresee
When Women will the rulers be,
And Men will beg a Pass-degree,
        Will beg, and beg in vain!
.......................................
P.S.—The pith of our petition
        Is seldom understood,
It is not all ambition,
        Though this, no doubt, is good;
But, speaking frankly, we declare
The point for which we really care
Is just to gain the right to wear
        That *most* becoming hood! [25 Mar. 1893: 133]

In March 1896, when both Cambridge and Oxford refused
to recognize the academic achievements of women, Oxford dis-
allowing women who took the examinations from receiving
the degree—*Punch* responded with "Ladies Not Admitted"
(Fig. 8), a Linley Sambourne drawing that on this occasion attacks the universities' position. The cartoon features a self-
satisfied Oxford professor straddling an entryway and saying,
"Very sorry, Miss Minerva, but perhaps you are not aware that
this is a Monastic Establishment." Minerva, with her classic
draperies, her books, and her caged owl, seems the real symbol
of knowledge left out in the cold (134). London *Truth* seems to
come to a similar conclusion. Generally inclined to scoff at the
New Woman, *Truth* takes a potshot at Alfred Austin, laureate
after Tennyson, and likens the academic controversy to the
Boer War. The versifier calls for a new British Jameson to rescue
the women from the injustice of the Germanic Oxford
"Kruger":

Fig. 8. "Ladies Not Admitted." *Punch*, 21 March 1896: 134.

"Wanted! Another 'Doctor Jim.' "

The "Boers" of cultured Oxford
    Vow they'll ignore the plea
Of these "Uitlander" damsels,
    Who pass for their degree.
"We'll take the fees," they tell them,
    "That you're compelled to pay,
But none of you, though you may pass,
And hold high places in your class,
    Shall get the prized B.A."

Where, then, is some new Jameson,
    The cause to undertake
Of these "Outlandish" ladies
    Proscribed for sex's sake?
Where is the gallant hero
    Who'll hasten to their aid,
And who, unstopped by jibes and jeers,
And hailed by Undergraduate cheers,
    Those "Boerish" Dons will raid?

'Twould be a famous foray
    Which, led by leader bold,
Would make the Oxford Kruger
    Shake in his college hold!
And doubtless our new Laureate—
    That most impulsive man—
Would glorify the episode
By straightway dashing off an ode—
    Too rapturous to scan.

So where is this new Jameson,
    To gallop down "the Hight,"
For Oxford's dark "blue-stockings"
    Prepared to do or die?
Where is the dashing leader
    To plan this gallant raid,
Nor cease the academic war
Till he has made a "Bachelor"
    Of every bookish maid? [12 Mar. 1896: 632]

From finishing schools to university education, the "academic war" pervaded the women's movement; education was

seen by its advocates as the key to personal independence, without which the home, the workplace, and even society as a whole would suffer. The comic record shows, however, that the British magazines were more likely to attack the women's movement for education than were their American counterparts. Between 1880 and 1900 in Britain, the question was frequently debated in serious publications and, as it was popularized, illustrated in verse and sketch in the humorous press. The more permissive, less class-ridden society in the United States undoubtedly influenced the earlier success of educational goals; with less history and more land, Americans pushed the frontier not only in tangible ways, as in the opening of the West, but also in intangible ways, as in changing social expectations. In consequence, the comic record in *Life*, *Puck*, and *Judge*, for instance, focuses primarily on the *results* of education, rather than on the struggle to obtain it. While the assumption on both sides of the Atlantic was that women were destined to marry, American women were less bound by the distinction of being "ladies" and were, therefore, on the whole more likely to create a new mythology than their British sisters.

For both, however, the public's fear centered on women's increasing independence. If women worked and were educated as men were, the argument seemed to go, then they were likely to blur the distinction between the genders. Not only would they lose their ability to charm and to please, but they would force men to take on their tasks and their feminine ways. Their increasing involvement outside the home in cultural and political affairs would leave the home bereft; a woman's mind, occupied with issues, clubs, and athletics, would detract from her maternal abilities and yearnings. Perhaps the major argument that women had to contend with, then, is that their "selfish" desires for education and recreation that developed their minds and talents materially jeopardized the next generation.

# FOUR

# Women's Clubs

## *"Girls Will Be Girls"*

Mothers of families would stay out late
    And walk queer circles on the parlor floor
When they came home, or noisily berate
    Their latchkeys when they wouldn't ope the door.
Mine own sweet wife a fond farewell had said,
    And blithely cantered off unto her club,
Leaving poor me to put the babe to bed,
    And after that to iron, cook and scrub—
    —Harold R. Vynne

THE EXCEPTIONAL proliferation of women's clubs during the last decades of the century testified to the growing independence not only of the woman whose education and whose work experience had given her a taste of her own capabilities but also of the woman who followed a more conventional path. Such exclusively female communities served a variety of purposes and raised a variety of alarms among the satirists. To be sure, women had always gathered for charitable work or for social reasons, and frequently for a combination of both, but the more deliberate and professional the organizational structures became, the more influence the clubs had. On the public front, critics complained that women might wrest enough political power from men to sway legislation; on the domestic front, they complained that once women fell into the male habit of club going, they would neglect their home duties. Gender transference was a short step away. Indeed, as women adopted new habits and changed the pattern of their lives, some of what the satirists wrote about came true.

Accompanied by gibes and quips, women's clubs multiplied, ranging in formality from nameless groups that met weekly in private homes or in boardinghouse sitting rooms to full-fledged educational, missionary, and philanthropic organizations that eventually achieved no small measure of influence through federation. It was indeed the case that the informal "unionization" of women was on the increase. As the *New York Times* reports on 12 May 1890, in two years the number of clubs in the Federation of Women's Clubs increased from 50 to 185, with a total of 20,000 members. By the last decade of the century, one writer mused retrospectively over the "silent but active revolution" of the women's club movement: "Where the clubs of men consist usually of luxuriously appointed apartments, with card-rooms, bars, restaurants, bowling-alleys, and billiard rooms for the comfort and enjoyment of the members only, women's clubs always have a basis of philanthropy, even when instituted for merely social purposes" (Rhine 519).

In an age in which women were the guardians of duty and moral concerns, the "basis in philanthropy" protected even loose associations of women against the charge of frivolity by giving distinct purpose to their gatherings and by allowing women sequestered in the home entrée into the public sphere in an acceptable way. The injunction to do one's duty, part of the definition of being "womanly," was simply broadened; an outgrowth of exercising certain domestic activities, from doing needlework to ministering to the sick, the club expanded and reinterpreted the home circle so that neighbor and city as well as nation might be conceived of as extended family. The sense of triumphalism that accompanied the club movement served to reinforce woman's redeeming role. As one writer notes in the 1890s, woman's "spirit of altruism . . . is urging her to bring about in so many ways a universal sisterhood of women, a reign of peace and happiness to all on earth" (Rhine 528).

This spirit of altruism was expressed in America in both formal and informal clubs, many of which were instrumental in improving social conditions for people in all walks. In "What Country Girls Can Do," for instance, a *Lippincott*'s article aimed at relieving the boredom of women rusticated from larger cities, the exhortation to avoid idle fingers hides a goodly amount of cultural and humanitarian enterprise. Women are urged to organize local talents for art, education, and embroidery; to set up libraries and classes; and, when possible, to affiliate with sister urban groups to compete for prizes or to gather clothing for the poor (Dodge 631-38).

Two important early clubs, while initially founded for nonphilanthropic reasons, eventually broadened their scope. The New England Woman's Club (1868), which counted Louisa May Alcott, Julia Ward Howe, and Mrs. Ralph Waldo Emerson among its members, was established for "intellectual and moral benefit and social enjoyment" but later added the words "social reform" to its objectives; Sorosis (New York, 1868), at first formed to provide common conversational ground for those with literary, artistic, and scientific tastes, developed influential subcommittees to explore the condition of the shop girl, to establish hospital care for orphans, and to petition Columbia University to open its classes to women. The Association for the Advancement of Women, known informally as the Women's Congress, evolved from Sorosis; the Congress met in 1889 in a general convention to set up a Federation of Women's Clubs, with 117 organizational members—clearly a small proportion of the clubs actually in existence (Rhine 519) but an influential number nonetheless. Other clubs are on record, many well known, like the WCTU (Woman's Christian Temperance Union) and the International Council of Women, organized by the suffragettes in 1888. Others are less familiar but just as socially active in their own spheres: the Woman's Alliance (Illinois, 1888), which vowed "justice to children—loyalty to women"; the nonsectarian King's Daughters, dedicated to improving education and bettering the lot of the poor; and the federated Working Girls' Societies (Rhine 524-26).

A contemporary analysis suggests that where food and land were plentiful, as in the West, social and literary clubs abounded; that where poverty was an intrusive social problem, as in the East, philanthropic clubs were numerous; and that in the South, where the almost "Oriental timidity" of the members prevented them from using the term *club*, such organizations were disguised as social occasions (Rhine 520, 523-26). Whatever the status of the organization, however, it is clear that the groups broadened women's sphere of influence and

experience. The organization of so many clubs around fur-
thering education or skills or providing service suggests that
the general satirical charge, that women were too frivolous to
cooperate with one another, was more honored in the breach.
Indeed, many clubs, where women followed parliamentary order and resolved themselves into working groups, were seen as
places of preparation for public life (Rhine 520), a reason that
the club movement was viewed with so much satirical alarm.

While many clubs were based on hobbies or personal interests, more formal organizations of women with common
professional goals helped to shape the women's workplace.
Across the Atlantic in London, a "Model Working-Girls' Club"
illustrates the other side of philanthropy; the members themselves are the beneficiaries of an institution that seems to have
many of the earmarks of a modern residential college. Founded
by Mrs. Quentin Hogg, whose husband's benevolent venture—
the Young Men's Polytechnic Institute—featured both extensive recreational facilities as well as classes, the young women's
"Poly" had game and sitting rooms, a restaurant, a library, and
classrooms. In 1890 dressmakers by far outnumbered applicants from other fields, who included clerks, teachers, telegraph operators, and needlewomen. The classes provided, for
the most part, advanced instruction in the trades the girls were
employed in, although French and German, music, art, first
aid, cooking, and elocution were also offered. As its chronicler
demonstrates, the club may be defended on utilitarian grounds;
not only does the "Poly" offer practical classes, protection from
the temptations of the streets, and lessons in frugality (medical
insurance and vacation "banks" were encouraged), but it fits
women for marriage, because it "encourages all that is best in
true womanhood" (Shaw, "A Model Working-Girls' Club" 169-
73).

While the Working-Girls' Club provided temporary aid to
women in transition between a career and marriage, other
groups were more single-mindedly dedicated to helping working women pursue their careers. The first royal charter given
to such an organization was awarded the Royal British Nurses'
Association in 1893 (Holcombe 99); others followed, including
male organizations that admitted women to equal status even

though they contributed proportionately less and drew on the union's resources more than their male counterparts. The National Amalgamated Union of Shop Assistants (1891) was one group (Holcombe 119); another, the National Union of Clerks (1889), is memorable for its furtherance of equality, its female members rejecting such preferential treatment as union-sponsored dowries, lower contributions to match their lower salaries, and a separate "women's league" (Holcombe 155).

These professional organizations exerted notable influence in education and nursing by supporting training and registration and in all fields by campaigning for better salaries and working conditions. Their energetically proposed reforms both belied and provoked satirical counterattacks that transposed the common stereotype of women's interests in fashion, gossip, and courtship into the formal settings of business meetings. This kind of transposition is illustrated by the response to the Board of Lady Managers of the World's Columbian Commission. The Board, set up to oversee women's interests at the Chicago World's Fair, quickly determined to appoint women to the state boards to ensure adequate representation and involvement. Their tasks were multifold; most importantly, perhaps, they were to investigate and record the participation of women in producing the goods on exhibit, and they were to administer the exhibits in the Women's Building (Palmer 24). Chicago *Figaro*'s "Board of Lady Damagers" (12 Sept. 1891: 582-83) by Harold Vynne parodies a business meeting; presided over by Mrs. President Charmer, it dissolves into catty comments about dress and spats about power.

Such a scenario became the humorists' commonplace. In "Correcting a Popular Prejudice," for example, *Life*'s author Harry Romaine presents an episode from a meeting of the "Advanced American Business Women's Union," in which the president objects to the popular notion that "Advanced Women" are perverting nature by mimicking men. Adjusting her collar and necktie, she reads from "a vulgar and offensive communication" that was sent to the meeting:

"She wants to wear trousers—'just like a man!'
    She's captured his vest and his coat!

She tries to play tennis as well as she can;
   To smoke cigarettes and to vote.
'Just like a man!' 'Just like a man!'
She wants to be just like a man!
      You cannot persuade her
      That nature has made her
On a wholly different plan."

Romaine's doggerel had both social and musical sources.
The first verse was based on an increasingly common sight—
"advanced women" smoking. Margaret Postgate, for instance,
active in the National Union of Clerks, is remembered by the
group's historian: "My first impression of her was of an attractive young woman taking an intelligent part in the branch
meeting while rather ostentatiously smoking a clay pipe"
(quoted in Holcombe 155). As a whole, however, the diatribe
in *Life* is reminiscent of the "Darwinian man" aria from Gilbert
and Sullivan's *Princess Ida*. As the feminist history in that
operetta is presented:

But it would not do,
   The scheme fell through—
For the Maiden fair, whom the monkey craved,
   Was a radiant Being,
   With a brain far-seeing—
While a Darwinian Man, though well-behaved,
At best is only a monkey shaved! [2: 263]

For Princess Ida, modern man is no better than the ape; for the
"Advanced Woman" in *Life*, the ape is preferable, as the Business Women's Union president says:

"Like a *man!* the idea! Why, we believe in advancement not re-
trogression! We would sooner imitate our ancestral apes than the modern members of the masculine sex.
"Apes never belonged to horrid clubs and came home at unholy
hours too inebriated to use a latch-key. Apes never forgot to mail
letters or made fun of their wives' cooking or objected to tidies and
window curtains. Apes never refused to pay household bills or lectured
about extravagance. And *Apes!*" she continued with magnificent emphasis, *"never refused women the right to vote!"* [7 Feb. 1895: 85]

For Gilbert and Sullivan, of course, man as monkey takes on comic proportions, but Romaine's double implication that feminists are Darwinians and that enfranchisement is somehow connected to liberal views about evolution is considerably more damaging to the cause.

A follow-up column the next week, also by Romaine, features another gathering of the Advanced American Business Women's Union, with members like "old Mrs. Mary T. Scolder, whose ceaselessly persistent efforts to get in her vote had drawn the eyes of the whole country upon her, and who had been nearly clubbed away from the polls in over fifty election districts" and "the scintillating Mrs. Twoanto, whose brilliant work on 'How to make up Accounts without Computing on the Fingers,' is fast making her an enviable reputation in feminine financial circles" and "Miss Sourgrapes, the lecturer, whose masterly and keenly critical discourses on 'Love, a Masculine Weakness,' never fail to draw crowded houses and shouts of unseemly laughter from flippant and weak-minded men" (14 Feb. 1895: 102). The denouement occurs when Miss Rosy Budd, *Life*'s paradigm for the young, attractive woman, thoughtlessly announces that the meeting has been held on St. Valentine's Day and is promptly read out of the society. Clearly, for Romaine, this "Weaker Sister," as he has entitled the column, is the strongest of all.

In Britain a similar attack appeared in *Punch* for 16 January 1901 as "The Ladies' Cabinet Council," a purported report from the Members of the Female Government. The Foreign Secretary gives news about ruffles and fur and the price of bonnets; when a dispatch box arrives from London, however, and the government scatters to examine its contents, "the latest fashions from across the Channel," "the council breaks up in confusion" (52).

On the whole, however, *Punch* seems to believe that women's groups fail for one major reason: lack of men. As the entire complex of both satirical and serious remarks suggests, men provide a rational approach to discussion, rescue proceedings from triviality, and, above all, are women's reason for being. *Punch*'s response to the establishment of a ladies' restaurant is typical, as this excerpt from "Diana at Dinner" shows. Here clubbiness gives way to the matrimonial instinct:

"This is sweet!" said AMANDA. "Delightful!" said JANE,
   While the rest in a chorus of "Charming!" combined.
And, declaring they cared not if dishes were plain,
   So the men remained absent, they solemnly dined.

And they toyed with their *entrées*, and sipped their Clicquot,
   And their smiles were as sweet as the wine that they drank.
But at last came a whisper—"Oh dear, this is slow!"
   "Hush, hush!" said the others. "How dreadfully frank!"

"Not slow; but there's something—I scarcely know what,
   An absence, a dulness I cannot define.
It may be the soup, which was not very hot,
   Or the roast, or the waiting, the ice, or the wine.

"But I'm sure there's a something." And so they agreed,
   And they formed a Committee to talk of the case.
And a programme was issued for all men to read,
   Bidding men (on page one) to abstain from the place.

But, since it is harder to ban than to bless,
   "For their own sakes," they said, "we will humour the men."
If you turn to the last page, you'll find this P.S.:—
   "Men allowed, by desire, from 6:30 to 10." [28 June 1890: 303]

   The clubs whose effectiveness was imperiled by the absence
of men caused little apprehension; these might be treated with
the kind of sweet patronage that demonstrated that relations
between the sexes had changed only superficially. Other
groups, however, caused serious alarm. Of all the amusements
that convinced the turn-of-the-century paterfamilias that the
feminists had destroyed the social structure, the most disturbing was the emulation of that holy of holies, the male smoking
and conversation club where serious business might be trans-
acted under the guise of entertainment. Certainly, the rise of
such organizations as the National Council of Women, for instance, fostered the growth of an "old girl network" and the
sort of personal associations prompted by the comfort and freedom of the traditional club. The existence of such successful
groups spurred a pointed reaction: "clubbiness," which forecast
the death of domesticity, threatened to alter clearly defined
lines of gender.
   The pervasive fear that women's newfound taste for inde-

pendence would emasculate their spouses is humorously illustrated by "Husbands in Waiting," which appeared in
*Punch's Almanack for 1897*; six beleaguered men, adorned with
collars and chains attached to hooks along the club building's
wall, wait outside "The Ladies Circle" for their wives and female friends to complete their business of reading the newspapers and lounging at the club. For other satirists, however,
the activities at the women's clubs were considerably more
ominous. The meeting of the Pioneer Club to discuss the
"Shortcomings of the Male Sex" evoked a *Punch* parody of Walt
Whitman suggesting that battalions of women, armed with
latchkeys and mounted on bicycles, were gathering to plan the
subjugation of men:

"A Slight Adaptation"

*Nova mulier vociferature more Whitmanico*

Come my modern women,
Follow me this evening, get your numbers ready,
Have you got your latchkeys? have you your members' axes?
    Pioneers! O Pioneers!

To the club in Bruton Street
We must march my darlings, one and all a great ensemble,
We the strenuous lady champions, all extremely up to date,
    Pioneers! O Pioneers!

Have our lords and masters halted?
Do they humbly take a back-seat, wearied out the Madame SARAH
    GRAND?
We take up the dual garments, and the eyeglass and the cycle.
    Pioneers! O Pioneers!

From North Hampstead, from South Tooting,
From far Peckham, from the suburbs and the shires we come,
All the dress of comrades noting, bonnets, fashions criticizing.
    Pioneers! O Pioneers!

We primeval fetters loosing,
We our husbands taming, vexing we and worrying Mrs. GRUNDY,
We our own lives freely living, we as bachelor-girls residing,
    Pioneers! O Pioneers!

Fig. 9. "In a Twentieth Century Club." *Life*, 13 June 1895: 395.

Fig. 10. "Girls Will Be Girls." *Life*, 8 July 1897: 30-31.

Literary dames are we,
Singers, speakers, temperance readers, artists we and journalists,
Here and there a festive actress (generally to be found in our smoking-
    room),
    Pioneers! O Pioneers! . . . [10 Nov. 1894: 228]

While the fear of the "manly woman" is expressed on both
sides of the Atlantic, the American *Life* takes more liberty in
depicting the sexual nuances of the phenomenon. The magazine, for instance, gives a prophetic peek "In a Twentieth Century Club" (Fig. 9) where dandified young women are drinking
and smoking while watching a bearded male dancer in a tutu
perform on stage. One woman is asked why she doesn't bring
her brother to the club, and she replies, "Oh, I think it's a bad
atmosphere for a young man who has been carefully brought
up." That women in a sporting club could outdo men is self-
evident to Charles Dana Gibson. In "Girls Will Be Girls," aside
from the "rational" dress of tie, shirt, and bloomers, what is
most obvious is the smoking and drinking of the members (Fig.
10). Such cartoons reveal, on the whole, more about men's clubs
than about women's. What seems to be happening is that the
male illustrators read their own somewhat doubtful activities
into their counterparts' lives and then accuse women of being
"manly."

Whether women who formed their own groups practiced
time-honored gentlemanly vices or engaged in their own mys-
terious and thereby threatening activities became a moot question in the light of a greater fear; such wives and mothers were
thought to be abandoning their natural inclinations for domestic duty. "The Husband of a Strong-Minded Woman," *Life's*
cartoon of an overbearing wife and her undersized spouse, sums
up the problem: "Where did you say the Woman's exchange
was?" asks the wife. "I've something I'd like to swap" (31 Aug.
1899: 170-71). Throughout the century the one suspicion that
changed little was that the domestic haven was being destroyed
by such women; what did change was the tenor of the satire.
While in the middle of the century the wife might see the error
of her ways, at the end of the century that resolution was un-
realistic both in Britain and in America. A comparison between

two dream sequences demonstrates this changing point of view: a lengthy satire published in *Punch's Almanack for 1853* entitled "The Ladies of the Creation: or, How I was Cured of Being a Strong-Minded Woman" and Harold Vynne's "A Dream of Fair Women. For which the Published Reports of the National Council of Women Were Probably Responsible," published in the Chicago *Figaro* on 14 May 1892. Each imagines, the first from a woman's point of view and the second from a man's, the changes that strong-minded women might make. *Punch's* version emphasizes the social and *Figaro's* the occupational, but the major difference is that the earlier work moves from the comic to the moralistic, from an amusing glimpse in word and picture of what would happen if each sex were to adopt the other's habits to a paean to domesticity as the writer repents her feminist ways. The persona of Vynne's dream, on the other hand, can only dismiss his fancies as a nightmare; the self-effacement of the young British wife in the middle of the century would not have been acceptable—or believable—to the reader at the turn of the century.

The young wife in *Punch* admits that she was "brought up a strong-minded woman" and so thoroughly educated that her "intellectual digestion became seriously impaired. . . . Before eighteen I had taken to green spectacles, and Professor Faraday's Friday night lectures," she writes. Her troubles begin after her marriage to a fellow scientific enthusiast, who, it turns out, attends Faraday's lectures not because of "a turn for science" but because of "a penchant" for her; indeed, "he wished as I was married I would not bother my head about such stuff." Their increasingly acrimonious arguments about her intellectual and feminist pursuits send him to "that abominable marital harbour of refuge, the club."

One night she reads Tennyson's poem "The Princess" and finds Ida's early arguments in favor of women's superiority more appealing than Tennyson's final synthesis, which shows a new relationship between the sexes:

Yet in the long years liker must they grow;
The man be more of woman, she of man;
He gain in sweetness and in moral height,

Nor lose the wrestling thews that throw the world;
She mental breadth, nor fail in childward care,
Nor lose the childlike in the larger mind;
Till at the last she set herself to man,
Like perfect music unto noble words. . . . [7: ll 263-70]

*Punch*'s young wife subsequently dreams that men and
women have changed places. Husbands bore themselves over
stale gossip and cooling tea while wives regale themselves with
conversation and wine, but the switch grows more distasteful
as the days pass. The "shocking" language of a female omnibus
driver convinces her that "women had no place before or behind
omnibuses"; a walk at dusk shows her that the female police
are too timorous and that "street-keeping is a coarse and brutal
employment, fit only for the other sex"; a visit with a female
admiral makes her decide that "it was an abominable thing to
condemn poor women to such hardships [at sea]," which, after
all, men are better suited for. The female fife-and-drum military
band plays polkas on guitars and pianos; her husband adopts
annoying "feminine" ways while shopping for a hat; and she
is held legally responsible for his cigar debts. Her unpleasant
experiences demonstrate that "when women attempted men's
work, they proved their own unfitness for it." Her conclusions
provide a set of textbook directions for mid-century feminine
behavior:

It is true, we are not in the House of Commons; but what, after all,
is public opinion? The opinion of men . . . is the opinion of men's
wives. Is there any field for political manoeuvre or legislation like
Home? What is a Chancellor of the Exchequer to a wife?—what the
Budget to the weekly house-bills?—what the difficulty of wringing
the supplies out of the House of Commons to that of extracting a
cheque from a hard-up hubby? . . .
     I saw that the question between the sexes was not one of superi-
ority or inferiority; that our two spheres lay apart from each other,
but that each exercised on the other a most blessed influence—man's
sphere, the world; woman's sphere, the home; the former bracing the
gentle influences of the latter by its rough, sharp lessons of effort,
endurance, and antagonism; the latter tempering the hardening effects
of the former by its self-denial, its sympathies, and its affections. And
I felt that if we are to compare these two spheres, the woman's—while

the narrower—is, in many respects, the nobler of the two, and her part in the battle of life not unfrequently the more important and dangerous one.

While the persona in *Punch* comes to the not surprising conclusion that she has no reason to leave her own fireside, the later writer in *Figaro* neither gains nor offers such "comfort"; all he can do is dismiss the idea of the strong-minded woman as nightmarish, but since the poem "A Dream of Fair Women" is subtitled "For Which the Published Reports of the National Council of Women Were Probably Responsible," the implication is that women's organizations are very much a reality. Tennyson's poem is evoked with irony, for the modern figures sketched by Vynne have other interests than the love for which Tennyson's Helen, Cleopatra, Eleanor, and Venus live. The burlesque "Dream" presents the full range of concern: that women have infiltrated all areas—politics, theology, law, the military, the arts, and sports—and that, as a result, the relations between the sexes have been turned topsy-turvy.

The poem appeared several days after the Federation of Women's Clubs held its first general delegate convention in Central Music Hall in Chicago "to discuss and compare the methods of conducting women's clubs the world over." Susan B. Anthony was present at the executive session that heard three committee reports on issues that are still relevant today: suitable business dress ("dress for success"?), equal rights for women in divorce cases, and "equal pay for equal work performed by women and men in the service of the Government" (*New York Times* 11 May 1892: 4). The next day, as accounts published in the *New York Times* record, Miss Anthony received the following encomium from Dr. Sarah Hackett Stevenson, president of the Chicago Woman's Club: " 'We have with us a delegate at large, representing clubs for women everywhere. She has, perhaps, done more clubbing and been clubbed more than any other woman in the world—Susan B. Anthony, whose head has grown stronger as the knocks have grown harder' " (12 May 1892: 1).

The presence of such delegates and the discussion of such issues, however, give Harold Vynne a bad dream in which do-

mestic life is transformed as women adopt the dress and habits
of men:

### I

I dreamed last night a most astounding dream
    That held me in its weird, uncanny spell
From midnight until morning's earliest gleam,
    And left me feeling very far from well.
I dreamed that men had ceased from framing laws,
    From bossing artisans by them employed,
From trading, keeping shop, declaring wars,
    And other pursuits hitherto enjoyed.
A mighty change had come upon the land:
    Turned topsy-turvy was the human race;
The LADIES (bless 'em!) had assumed command,
    And relegated MAN to second place.

### II

Our President was a most comely wench—
    Her Cabinet composed of maidens fair;
Sweet lady Judges sat upon the bench;
    Lawyers in skirts talked juries to despair.
The halls of Congress rang with dulcet notes
    Of members' voices—school girls in their teens—
The Army mounted guard in petticoats,
    The Navy swarmed with feminine Marines.
Grandames austere, be-spectacled and sleek,
    As Merchants posed in offices all day,
Whose male stenographers (at ten a week,)
    Be-banged and rouged, cast sheepish eyes their way.

### III

Bald-headed gentlemen the ballet graced,
    And executed kicks and pirouettes,
While comely girls, in front rows snugly placed,
    Gazed at their caperings through big lornettes.
Proud, dashing dames drove tandem to the track
    To view the races—that most royal sport!—
And swore devoutly when the nags they'd back
    Failed to win quite as often as they ought.
While younger beauties—saucy little sparks—
    From their club-windows ogled passers-by,

Chewing their canes and passing pert remarks
    Upon such chaps as chanced to meet their eyes.

### IV

But in my dream I saw still stranger sights:
    A lovely maid, as dazzling as a star,
Had called on her young man too many nights
    To suit the object of her love's mamma;
And that stern matron, careful of her boy,
    Had loosed the household dog—a tawny brute—
And now beheld, with mild parental joy,
    The timid lover from the mansion scoot:
Too late, alas! Her flight was much too slow
    To balk the beast of his delicious prey,
For, with a growl, he wreaked his work of woe,
    And bit her bustle almost quite away.

### V

The wives at breakfast read the paper through,
    Or loudly grumbled at the bill-of-fare;
And, if their husbands begged a V. or two,
    Their better-halves would groan, or stamp or swear.
When tailors' bills came in, the awful wrath
    Of plundered wives was horrible to see;
The hubbies, awed, vamoosed from out their path,
    Swearing no more extravagant to be.
At balls, the gentlemen, in serried rows,
    Sat wielding fans and gossiping with zest,
Whilst ladies smote each other on the nose
    In rivalry for him they loved the best.

### VI

Mothers of families would stay out late
    And walk queer circles on the parlor floor
When they came home, or noisily berate
    Their latchkeys when they wouldn't ope the door.
Mine own sweet wife a fond farewell had said,
    And blithely cantered off unto her club,
Leaving poor me to put the babe to bed,
    And after that to iron, cook and scrub—
. . . . . . . . . . . . . . . . . . . . . . . . . . . . . . . . . . . . . . . . . . . . . . . .
Just then I woke. By dint of many rubs

My eyes were opened, and I saw it all:
'Twas at the meeting of the Women's Clubs—
   I'd gone to sleep in Central Music Hall. [14 May 1892: 187]

This kind of role reversal is also highlighted by turn-of-the-century *Punch*, which presented "The New Man" as an effeminate creation of his club-going wife. Seated with the children's toys and cold, disregarded dinner, he watches time pass and waits for his wife, remembering the joy of his honeymoon and the way it faded into commonplace reality:

He recollected the anxiety of ALICE to get back to town, to be off into the City. Of course he could not follow his wife into her business haunts; it would be immodest—nay, even improper. Still, he had been treated kindly, in a rough, condescending sort of way. He had had a Brougham, and had been allowed to visit his gentlemen friends. He had plenty of chats, and occasionally ALICE had accompanied him round the park. Then he had seen a good deal of his children. His daughter, however, had now gone to school, and his sons were always with their nursery tutor.

As the clock strikes three, he tries to amuse himself by reading a novel called *Bobby*: " 'How can men write of men like this?' he murmured. 'I am not surprised that women think badly of us when we thus paint ourselves. Visiting a music-hall with his female cousin! Going to the Zoological Gardens unattended! Oh, BOBBY, BOBBY, what a creation!' " When Alice finally staggers in from her club revels, he sadly goes to bed: " 'Oh wife,' murmured the aggrieved husband, as he mounted the stairs, 'you cannot help bringing woe to man, for unless you did so you would not be a woe-man' " (6 Oct. 1894: 167).

In such commentary the humor resides in sexual ambiguity. Sometimes, however, the tables are turned and the old order restored, as in George Rugg's *The New Woman: A Farcical Sketch, with One Act, One Scene, and One Purpose*. The skit features Darius Simpkins, his wife Maria, an attorney, and her two friends Mrs. High-Mind and Miss Betty Boston (named as if they were personified vices in a modern *Pilgrim's Progress*). Darius, who cares for the children and house, is discovered doing the washing, while Maria prepares to begin her day, which includes the Monday Morning Club, office work, dinner (prepared by Darius), bicycling, a political class, presentation of a lecture—the "Rights of Married Men"—at the Women's College of Law, a boxing round at the gymnasium, and a "smoke-talk at the Emerson Club [about] 'Degeneration of Man.' " Maria and her two friends practice their boxing, versifying, and oratory until Darius, poking behind the stove, discovers a mouse, with which he blackmails his terrified wife: "Peace be to his ashes, for he has been the means of showing up you three women in your true light. Henceforth the 'Old Man' will divide honors with the 'New Woman' in this household." [6]

Another farcical skit by Edyth M. Wormwood entitled *The New Woman in Mother Goose Land* makes the opposite point, although the characters are similar. Based on the child's verse about Peter, the Pumpkin Eater, the skit features Mrs. Peter, who is entrapped by her husband in a huge crepe paper pumpkin to prevent her from going to her club. Bachelor, one of Peter's friends, arrives to complain: "Wifey's off to the Club, and to Charity 'Fairs; / She's simply determined to vote. / She has no time to spend with her husband at home, / Or to mend up his trousers and coat." Jack, Jill, Mary, Simon, Willie Winkie, the children of other club-going wives, appear crying for food and attention. Promising submission, Mrs. Peter is freed from the pumpkin but then entraps her husband and announces her demands:

*Mrs. Peter—*
No use, darling. 'Twas so yesterday
You served me. It's our turn now. We'll have our say.
You've granted we're equals, the women and men,
You gave us the vote, now stay in that pen.
You're to give us some money to use as we please.
We don't like for every penny to tease.
*Peter—*
But then you'll all do as you did yesterday.
Leave your homes and your children to us every day.

*Mrs. Bachelor—*
No, you'll find, since you gave us the vote, as you should,
That every woman will quickly make good.
There'll be no need of working for these things, you see,
And now they are ours, as you'll surely agree,
Our homes and our children, with pride we will tend,
And protect them, as well. Come, agree now, my friend [21]

As a frivolous version of Aristophanes' *Lysistrata*, then, the skit suggests that women's power resides in their withholding domestic services; it goes further, however, and perhaps short-sightedly suggests that once women are granted financial and political equality, they will have no reason to leave house and home to devote time to social action groups.

Clearly, the question of women's clubs had many ramifications. Exaggerated by the satirical pen, the possibilities were endless: women enjoying their postprandial cigars and liqueurs; wives escaping to their clubs for newspapers and risqué entertainment. The drawings and commentary that connect such experimentation to defeminization manifest a worried recognition not so much that women had their own clubs, as they always had had, but that they were recreating the pattern of their lives. Interestingly enough, the only pattern most of the satirists could imagine was the already-established masculine one; yet the versifiers, in lambasting liberated females (as Harold Vynne does, for example) for dissipating their lives in gambling and flirting or bearishly growling at wives and children, are actually assailing accepted masculine behavior itself.

It is not surprising, then, that social habits became a gauge of the degree of liberation from old ideas. One of the profound changes that can be traced through the pages of the comic magazines is the shifting point of view about women smoking. The adoption of a male habit seemed, to some, to suggest that women's search for independence had created a new gender, the "manly woman"; consequently, the question of smoking became a sign of "advanced" views. Today's Virginia Slims advertisements present a fictive history of women's smoking; scandalized husbands, boyfriends, and neighbors parade through magazine pages in sepia tones. The real record, however, is much more complex. The new woman either smoked or made smokers on trains and buses her new purview; indeed, at times, she was encouraged to smoke for her health, although the antitobacconists' leagues resoundingly declared the habit distasteful for social, rather than for medical, reasons.

Quips and cartoons of a general nature abound in *Punch.* One joke about old and new expectations regularly reappears. In an early version, when an indignant old lady asks a guard if smoking is allowed in her compartment, he answers, "Haw, weel, if nane o' the Gentlemen object, ye can tak' a bit draw o' the pipe" (23 Sept. 1871: 121). Almost thirty years later, when a similar question is asked, the answer is, "No, Mum. 'Igher up!" (21 Nov. 1900: 370). Such holdovers from a day when women were scandalized by smoking are, however, increasingly replaced by jokes about the New Woman. When a straitlaced young man is shocked to discover Miss Lucy smoking, she replies, "It's classical and correct. 'Ex Lucy dare fumum' " (25 Apr. 1900: 292). Presumably, the Latin is an attempted pun on the idea that without smoke there is no fire and hence no *luce,* or light, but the Latin is as questionable as the young lady's actions must have been to some of her contemporaries.

More focused commentary appears as well. When, for example, the antitobacconists announced a meeting at the Paris Exhibition to examine the question of female smoking, one *Punch* poetaster suggested that love can conquer, or at least ignore, cigarette smoke:

"To Phyllis Who Smokes"

PHYLLIS, you a magic chain
    Weave about my heart so tight,
That, despite its constant pain
    At your conduct light,
Frivolous though your behaviour be,
From your toils, alas! I can't get free.

But a hope I have in view
    That your sway I need not fear now,
Since of girls who smoke—like you—
    (So at least we hear now)

They can prove, by force of logic rightful,
That they are not really so delightful.

Then to Paris I will wend—
    When the anti-smoking mission
Meets in congress I'll attend
    At the Exhibition;
So their doctrines when they there explain,
Haply I may find your influence wane.

Ah! how foolish to rebel
    At a tyranny so sweet,
And to strive to break your spell,
    Since, when we shall meet
And I once again to you am near,
I'll forget their arguments—I fear. [21 Mar. 1900: 213]


Another versifier objects strongly to cigarettes—*because* of
love:

            "A Personal Answer"
            (By a Prejudiced Party.)

    Why should not Ladies smoke
        The fragrant cigarette?
Ah! surely that is asked in joke,
        My sweet-lipped pet!

    I know the practice grows,
        Like others that are baneful;
But see a "weed" beneath *your* nose?
        The thought's too painful!

    Personal? Why, of course!
        Yet 'tis "most relative."
Answer of more conclusive force
        How could I give?

    Let females coarse and plain,
        With lips none care to kiss,
Puff what is womanhood's worst bane,
        Though manhood's bliss.

    But *you*, with birdlike lips,
        And breath like briars in June?

No! Take my earnestest of tips—
    'Tis not in tune.

    Take no foul cigarette
    Beneath that dainty nose.
Heavens! Who would fuming Tophet set
    Too near the Rose? [16 Feb. 1889: 81]

The more modern connection between smoking and sexual attractiveness surfaces in *Judy* in 1880, in a verse whose final stanza illustrates the theme: "A winsome, clever, cool coquette— / Who flouts all Grundian decrees— / A pretty, pouting, piquant pet, / Who loves to smoke a cigarette!" (14 Jan. 1880: 21). While most periodicals represent a variety of views, *Pick-Me-Up* moves from disapproval to mild teasing. Oscar Wilson's cover sketch of a woman lolling seductively in a cloud of smoke (28 Apr. 1894), for instance, is a considerable distance from the readers' consensus in the 1880 prize competition for answers to the question "Should women be permitted to smoke?" The winners in the competition, who received works by Washington Irving and Lord Byron and a copy of *Half Hours with the Best Authors*, replied in dactylic negatives: "Now aid me, Saint Grundy, with just indignation, / To thunder a "NO!" to a question like this; / Should the lips of fair woman thus court desecration, / Be she grandam or spinster, a mistress or miss?" (23 Mar. 1889: 362-63). As the wide divergence of answers shows, opinions were mixed about women smoking. Social pressure was not the only discouragement; learning to smoke was potentially unpleasant, as the artist in "New Gallery Novelties" suggests (17 May 1890: 238). "No. 141. Il Cigaretto; or, Should Women Smoke? After her first attempt" shows a bilious young lady leaning weakly into a cloud of smoke. Almost to a man, however, the satirists reacted negatively to the attempts of women to invade the private purlieus of the railroad smoker. If, on the one hand, women themselves sought to smoke, they upset the conservative tenor of the smoker, which was then no longer a male haven; if, on the other hand, they sought to "liberate" a male retreat for mischievous or political reasons, they were likely to demand the curtailment of smoking. *Punch* complains in a mock pastoral:

"The Invasion of Woman"

When STREPHON shuts the ledger to,
   Relinquishing his duties,
And takes the train from Waterloo
   For Clapham's rural beauties
He dearly loves *en route*, we read,
To smoke the solitary weed.

His hopes, alas, are quickly dashed,
   For CHLOË, maid provoking!
Alertly enters, unabashed,
   The carriage labelled "Smoking";
His frown, his powerful cigar,
His match—all unavailing are.

Yes, CHLOË comes, and brings no doubt,
   A friend to talk of fashions,
While STREPHON lets his weed go out,
   A prey to angry passions,
Which, later on, released will be
Within the excellent D.T.

Yet grieve not so, ungallant swain,
   Nor curse this innovation,
Or, even if you do, refrain
   From words like "frequentation,"
But really, you should do no less
Than cease to curse, and wholly bless.

For if the charm this female band
   Finds in you so immense is,
That they contentedly can stand
   The smell your weed dispenses,
A compliment they pay you then
You will not gain from fellow-men! [29 Sept. 1894: 145]

Women who wanted to adopt male habits but refused to smoke posed a different problem. In a recommendation to male riders to accept the inevitable "invasion," this time on the public bus, a *Punch* versifier suggests that, rather than complaining about the lack of fresh air, the New Women who feel free to sit anywhere should themselves light up:

"Smoked Off!"
(An Appeal from the Knife-board of a City Omnibus)

[The latest complaint of "the Ladies" is that they are being "smoked
    off" the tops of the omnibuses.]
The "knife-board," sacred once to broad male feet,
    The "Happy Garden Seat,"
Invaded now by the non-smoking sex,
    Virginal scruples vex,
And matronly anathemas assail.
    Alas! and what avail
Man's immunities of time or place?
    The sweet she-creatures chase
From all old coigns of vantage harried man.
    In vain, how vain to ban
Beauty from billiard-room or—Morning Bus
    What use to fume or fuss?
And yet, and yet indeed it is no joke!
    Where *shall* one get a smoke
Without annoying Shes with our cheroots,
    And being badged as "brutes"?
If a poor fellow may not snatch a whiff
    (Without the feminine sniff)
Upon the "Bus-roof," where in thunder's name
    *Shall* he draw that same!
The ladies, climb, sit, suffocate, and scoff,
    Declare *they* are "smoked off."
Is there no room inside? If smoke means Hades,
    We, "to oblige the ladies,"
Have taken outside seats this many a year,
    Cold, but with weeds to cheer
Our mackintosh-enswathed umbrella'd bodies;
    Now we are called churl-noddies
Because we puff the humble briar-root.
    Is man indeed a "brute"
Because he may upon the knife-board's rack owe
    Some solace to Tobacco?
If so it be, then man's last, only chance,
    Is in the full advance
Of the "emancipated" sex. Sweet elves,
    *Pray learn to smoke yourselves!*
Don't crowd us out, don't snub, and sneer, and sniff,
    But—join us in a whiff! [25 July 1891: 45]

The doggerel seems innocent enough, but from the accompanying sketch of a cheerful briar-pipe smoker and the mention of a cheroot earlier in the poem, it is actually an invitation for women to smoke either pipes or cigars. Such an invitation is one that the conservative apologist Eliza Lynn Linton would see as ironically appropriate, since she compares the "Wild Woman" with her cigarette to the rustic harridan with her briar pipe ("Wild Women as Social Insurgents" 597).

Some women smoked because the cigarette was a stylish and comparatively harmless way to flout convention; others heeded medical advice and acquired the habit as a way of relieving tension. In one *Punch* poem, for instance, the versifier writes a paean in response to a medical endorsement of smoking:

"My Cigarette"

["The cigarette, which was banned for so many years by the faculty, is now upheld by the *Hospital* as 'a panacea against many of the smaller ills of life,' and women are urged to seek the solace of tobacco when troubled by domestic or other worries."—*Daily Graphic*]

Time was they boded woes untold
Whene'er thy snowy length I rolled,
Croaking with raven voice that Death
Lurked in thine all too fragrant breath.
I heeded nothing what they said,
Nor marked the wisely-wagging head,
But, blindly loving, lingered yet
O'er thy sweet joys, my Cigarette!

And as I watched with dreaming eyes
Thine inter-wreathèd fancies rise,
Lo! at thy magic softly stole
A peace divine upon my soul.
My troubles vanished. Filled with thee,
What was the weary world to me?
Sorrow and care I would forget
In thy sweet joys, my Cigarette!

But now thy dark eclipse is past,
Thine hour of triumph dawns at last;
While Slander, dumb and put to shame,

No longer dares besmirch thy name.
The sick and sorrowful shall flee,
All trustful confidence, to thee,
To find a cure for care and fret
In thy sweet joys, my Cigarette! [21 May 1898: 237]

The question of smoking, then, had serious ramifications for the woman who wished to establish a new identity. For the satirists, this and other habits are traced to the kind of gender-destroying independence fostered by club going. Middle-class women began to demand the keys to their own front doors and to organize their days around their own schedules, reserving time for private endeavors and appointments that were not necessarily service oriented. They began to wear clothing that freed them from the restrictions of corsets and allowed them to climb astride bicycles. Such women, some implied, were endangering their own marital prospects, if not the special status of womankind as a whole. If "Slander" became "dumb," as "My Cigarette" hopefully suggests, the new, manly habits made chivalry dumb likewise. A writer in *Truth* complains in "The Age of Rudeness" that women had forfeited all right to polite treatment. The accompanying double-page spread entitled "Ancient and Modern Courtesy" depicts on the left a 1793 scene in which a young swain kneels to his beloved in a pastoral landscape and on the right an 1893 scene in which a girl casually perching with crossed legs is chatting to a man lounging in a chair and smoking. The writer says:

He treats her as "one of the boys." His talk is of poker parties and skirt dancers. He veils a few phrases and uses an occasional circumlocution. Otherwise, he might be chatting with his crony at the club. . . . Do you think that gentle folk of other days could find delight in a performance of vulgar songs and indecent dances. Do you think that a man of position who loved a woman in bygone times would take her to drink Vermouth cocktails in an atmosphere of tobacco smoke and in the company of fast men? . . .
    It is the fault of the women. They sighed for "emancipation," and they have it, with all its attendant disadvantages. They have lost the respect of the men, even if the men refuse to believe it; and they will

never regain that respect until they return to the simple modesty which used to be the glory of their sex. [18 Mar. 1893: 6]

Rose Thorne, whose assertions as well as curiously apt name suggest that the author may indeed be male, writes about "The War of the Sexes" in the *Idler*, September 1900, and agrees. For her, "the party which has most to lose and nothing to gain, the weaker in brain and muscle," is putting chivalry to a "sore trial" by slandering those who provide shelter, music, art, and religion. "No female writer has ever made anybody laugh," she writes; and "even the sister of charity, who has been so often quoted as the type of self-sacrificing womanhood, owes her existence to Saint François de Sales." Referring to Tennyson, the author concludes that "for a thousand natural and social reasons, man must defend the hearth and woman must keep it clean": "We women really seem to want all the privileges of strength and frailty combined. We want to be alternately the equal and the superior of man, to be fellow-workers, queens and angels, and we ignore the self-evident fact that a fellow-worker can never seem an angel" (29).

While the *Idler* generally uses whimsy to deplore the advent of the New Woman, the more vituperative essays and letters of Eliza Lynn Linton are deliberately provocative. In "Is Chivalry Dead?" for instance, the *Punch* cartoonist attacks both Miss Linton and the vanity of faded beauty. In the sketch, an elderly woman sits in front of her 1834 portrait:

*Miss Letitia Cox (reading Mrs. Lynn Linton's Letter in the Daily Telegraph).* "If Chivalry has died out, is it not that Women themselves have won away from their own best selves?" Ah, how true!
[*Miss L.C. has—vide her Portrait.*]
[6 Apr. 1889: 159]

A longer, more complex reference to the question of the death of chivalry appears on 13 April 1889 in " 'Arry on Chivalry," a reply to the Scottish poet Robert Buchanan's *Daily Telegraph* remarks in which he attacks the "modern young man" who has forgotten the chivalrous behavior of his grandfather. 'Arry, writing a versified letter to his friend Charlie, rails against the idea of returning to outmoded courtesy, when social standing and wealth rule the day: "Sech hantydeluvian kibosh may cosset up kittens or kids," he says, but it is no match for what really counts—"Class and the quids." Women are conveniences for 'Arry until they become impediments, and chivalry is simply a waste of time:

Wot this Chivalry wos, mate, fust off, BOB BUCHANAN may know—
    or he mayn't—
But if it meant making the Woman a speeches of gingerbread Saint
And a bobbin' around her with billy-doos, big battle-haxes, and such,
Like a lot of tin-kettles with trimmings, it won't work to-day, mate,
    not much.

BUCHANAN's a poet, they tell me, and poets don't nick me, nohow,
Kind o' long-winded loonatics, mostly, dead-nuts on the biggest bow-
    wow;
Sort of gushing G.O.M.'s in metre; and Chivalry, if you arsk *me*,
Seems a stror-stuffed poetical "property," all bloomin' fiddle-de-
    dee. . . .

But Woman! Well, Woman's all right enough, not arf a bad sort of
    thing
When a fellow is young and permiskus. And when he has 'ad his fair
    fling,
And wants quiet diggings or nussing, she do come in 'andy no doubt;
In fack, taking Woman all round, she's good goods the world carn't
    do without.

But washup 'er, CHARLIE? Wot bunkum—! as Mrs. LYNN LINTON re-
    marks.
To watch *her* wire into 'er sex like Jemimer, old man, is rare larks.
She do let 'em 'ave it to-rights. 'Ow I larf as she lays on the lash!
It must rile 'er to know she's a She, but I do like 'er devil and dash.

While 'Arry admires Linton for her energetic attack on the advanced woman, he vociferously objects to Buchanan's recommendation that the modern young man should mend his ways. Men are alike no matter what their social class, 'Arry says; the *real* modern young man, like him, cares only for fun, money, and his own well-being.

ROBERT's down on the Modern Young Man, who's a 'ARRY sez he ('ang
    his cheek!)
*With* a H.! Now that give me the needle, old man. I ain't mealy or
    meek,
Nor yet one of yer rhym-pumping milksops wot look on a gal as a
    saint,
But I *do* know the petticoats, yus, and I'm fly to palaver and paint. . . .

The Modern Young Man? Wy, that's *Me*, CHARLIE! 'Arry's the model
    and type,
But no more like BUCHANAN's stuffed dummy than prime *pully sowty's*
    like tripe.
At the Pubs or the Clubs it's all one; it is me sets the fashion, old pal;
And we're all of a mind to a hinch about togs, lotion, larks, or a gal.

This here Chivalry ain't in our *maynoo*; we ain't sech blind mugs as
    all that.
The Modern Young Man must be wide-oh! He's never a spoon or a
    flat;
Takes nothink on trust, don't "part" easy, is orkurd to nobble or spoof;
And there's only three things he believes in—hisself, a prime lark,
    and the oof.

There you 'ave it, BUCHANAN, my buffer, put neat in a nutshell, old
    man.
We *don't* dream, or kotow to the petticoats; no Sir, that isn't our plan;
And you arsk wot we're coming to? Well, you may arsk and arsk on
    till all's blue,
But one thing we *ain't* coming to, BOB, that's to learn of a poet—like
    you! . . .

Woman washup's good fun in its way; I can fake it myself, dontcher
    know—
With a jolly clear heye to wot's wot, and a sense of the true *quid* for
    *quo*—
But be a mere moke to the Feminines, mugged up to kneel, fetch, and
    carry?
That may do for Chivalry-BOB, but I'm blowed if it will for
                                     Yours,       'ARRY [177]

What 'Arry is writing about, of course, is more than the death
of chivalry; it is the rise of the "me generation," the glorifi-
cation of the acquisitive urge, the worship of social status.

While exaggerated by the versifier, 'Arry's approach seems to suggest that men are as much to blame for shifting societal expectations as women. Women at the turn of the century found themselves affected by 'Arryism in a number of ways. Their growing independence, as witnessed by their interest in activities outside the home, took them beyond the pale of the old protective assumptions about their physical frailty and mental incapacity. New terms were needed, and 'Arry presents one set of unlooked-for possibilities.

Better educated, with more knowledge of the world and with more independence that came not only from earning her own living but from establishing new "families" outside of the domestic sphere, the New Woman was well on her way to learning a new set of rules. "Ladies first" meant not only protection from danger but confronting it. The woman who wanted to be independent also had to learn to be first, as the *Punch* cartoonists make clear. In "Vive La Politesse! Ladies First!" an elderly gentleman whose hat is festooned over the horn of an enraged bull uses his corpulent lady companion as a buffer (1 May 1897: 26); in "So Polite!" two riding to hunt approach a barrier, and a slim, nervous man says, "Hold hard, you Brute! 'Ladies first!' " (2 Dec. 1893: 262). Just as the old phrases took on new meanings and the New Woman was negotiating her identity—and with it, her relationships with her male counterparts—she began to take on a new appearance. Her increased intellectual development and involvement in social and worldly affairs manifested themselves in changed manners and changed costume. New wine could not be contained in old bottles; the time for "rational dress" had arrived.

# FIVE

# Women's Fashions

## The Shape of Things to Come

" 'New Woman' Number Three adopts a not unusual plan,
As a man-woman she affects a milksop woman-man."
    —*Truth* 25 Dec. 1894: 36

THE WOMAN who worked or went to college might persistently and inaccurately be seen as an anomaly; indeed, her more conservative sisters might dismiss her activities and continue living cheerfully as the Mrs. Notions of the nineteenth century. When fashions began to mirror and express the new way in which women perceived themselves, however, everyone took notice. Perhaps satirists have always made fun of the seemingly irrational developments in women's fashions, just as some women themselves have made a fetish of studying and following the fillips of frills and flounces. Even so, the new change to "rational dress," the change that eliminated tight corsets and long, heavy petticoats and skirts, was almost immediately seen as a threat not only to the female image but to male status. The simplified clothing adopted by the New Woman reaffirmed the public fear that reform meant the rise of a hybrid, the "manly woman" who advertised her abandonment of her God-given domestic role by dividing her skirts and taking to the streets as career woman, club woman, and student.

Not surprisingly, then, magazine writers and illustrators, supported in many cases by medical experts, attacked "mannish fashions." Perhaps they forgot that in the history of fashion women had made use of tailoring techniques to transmogrify male accessories into frilly gewgaws; perhaps they were subconsciously aware of the equation between titillation and clothing inversion (in New York *Truth*, for instance, many of the centerfolds featured female dancers in top hat and coattails). What may have been most disturbing for the opponents of rational dress, however, was the missing element of play in such fashions; rather than an expression of female frivolity, the New Woman's dress was, for the most part, a representation of the ideas she stood for. The outfit that announced subliminally that a man was in control carried the same message when a woman wore it.

The argument that raged about the healthfulness of corsets and lacing, petticoats and "trowsers" was, then, actually an argument about woman's identity and sphere. Freed from heavy, clinging skirts and constrictive whalebone undervests and wearing stout boots instead of slippers, the New Woman increased her physical movement both in and out of the home. She did so at the risk of violating received opinion, however. Lacing was held to support the back, and multilayered petticoats were said to provide modest covering more suitable than drawers, which mimicked an article of male dress. More importantly, however, traditional female clothing signaled that the wearer was in her proper place on the Victorian chain of being. A writer in the *Lancet*, the leading medical journal of the day, credits Amelia Bloomer and her innovative trousers with an understanding of the impact of "dress for success": "Mrs. Bloomer rightly appreciated the importance of external decorations for subjugating the intellect of mankind. The petticoat is the garment that is the most in harmony with the mental qualities that Nature has implanted in the female sex" (quoted in Duffin 40).

More advanced medical practitioners and reformers argued that drawers were warmer and less cumbersome than petticoats which, when worn in the rain and mud, could almost double in weight. Some advocated supporting the heavy skirts from the shoulders in an effort to remove the weight from the pelvis, but that solution merely made woman into a new kind of Atlas, carrying the weight of her own world. The mid-century crinoline was considerably lighter than petticoats, but it, like the enormous festooned sleeves of the 1830s and 1890s, made physical closeness and easy movement impossible. Indeed, as fashion progressed from the revealing, Grecian lines of the early 1800s to the imprisoning carapace of high Victorianism, one can see a graphic denial of the female form. Here, then, would seem to be the conceptual source of the scandalized reaction to bloomers. The woman who denied her body by dressing conventionally was a living affirmation that the female principle was the locus of purity and redemption, while the woman who made a radical change in her clothing forced a redefinition of virtue.

It was precisely this question of modesty that led to the popularity of a masculine article of dress; drawers became mandatory when the crinoline proved to be swayed by every passing breeze. As one writer to the *London Times* put it, "No man of ordinary feelings of delicacy can pass an hour in the streets without seeing much to startle, if not to shock him" (quoted in Crow 123). The relative freedom from heavy skirts that the crinoline provided had, besides voyeurism, other drawbacks, including the difficulties of traveling and horseback riding, danger from fire, inconvenience in public places, and drafts. Most were ignored by the determined woman of fashion, who all unknowingly in both drawers and skirt is emblematic of a middle stage of gender development.

Despite the strength and prevalence of conservative views, then, fashion seemed to be conspiring with reform in demanding modest undergarments. Encased in light hoops, a growing number of Victorian women agreed with such writers as Dr. Edward John Tilt, who argues in his *Elements of Health and Principles of Female Hygiene* that the flannel or cambric drawers that young girls wore should be modified for adult women to protect them from the climate. Like the writer in the *Lancet*, though, Dr. Tilt insists on the importance of womanly dress. Women should not wear "trowsers" exclusively, he says, for "in assuming our costume, there would be a great likelihood of women assuming our masculine manners, which would not enhance their charms. It is, therefore, important that there should be a different costume for the girl and the woman, in order that on quitting one for the other, girls should feel that they were promoted in Society and that therefore more is expected of them" (quoted in Crow 126-27).

The paradox at the heart of the clothing controversy was that the conservative woman who carefully maintained this distinction in dress throughout the century publicly wore the emblem of her own sexuality. At the end of the century, when the crinoline had been collapsed into the bustle and fashionable women were again swathing themselves in clothing that drew attention to their lineaments, as Gibbs-Smith's collection of plates from the Victoria and Albert Museum shows, the conflict between philosophy and dress was exacerbated. The New Woman's adoption of "rational dress," the costume that allowed her to engage in sports and climb omnibus stairs, must thus be seen in the context of her less liberated sister's overt flaunting of sexuality that suggested even to some male commentators a new form of entrapment, not freedom. During the discussion that raged over business shirtwaists and divided skirts, the argument about the connection between modes of dress and gender identification was reinterpreted. As one writer explains, since men and women differ, so should their dress, but since their activities are becoming more alike, "so [women's] dress should permit equal freedom of movement and equal health." Most modern men prefer simpler fashions, he goes on to say; in fact, most would prefer "a bachelor's grave . . . to taking a chance in that lottery where the diamonds and the booby-prizes, the Venuses and the viragoes, have all been concealed in a maze of crinoline and whalebone, cotton, powder and paint" (Crandall 252).

*Punch* agrees with this moderate point of view. In "The English Wife," for instance, a versifier contemplates the corseting and stuffing and false hair that produces a typical English bride:

And once again I see that brow—
    No bridal wreath is there—
A ring of curl-papers conceals
    What's left of her scant hair.
She sits on one side of the hearth,
    Her spouse, poor man, sits near.
And wonders how that scarecrow thing
    Could once to him be dear! [2 Nov. 1895: 207]

Similarly, *Judy*, which inveighs against hair dye and wigs in
" 'Silken Tresses': Some Remarkable Revelations" (5 Nov.
1884: 218), exclaims in verse, "Away with the Powder-Puff":

From damask cheeks it takes the bloom,
And gives the pallor of the tomb;
It makes you look like spectres wan,
Like Beauty's ghost, whose beauty's gone.
Your powdered faces, white as dough,
Resemble uncooked pasties, so
That men might think you're going straight
To get them baked at baker's grate. . . . [21 Nov. 1883: 242]

The views that were publicized about women's dress varied
widely; indeed, because both barbed attacks and lighthearted
quips are directed at conventional and reform dress alike, the
record might seem one of personal whim. On the whole, however, the satirists did seem to focus on whatever seemed exaggerated, whether it was cosmetics, skirts, trousers, or hats.
The "old woman" thus came in for her share of commentary,
although the New Woman was exposed to more obloquy. When
the former erred, she was forgiven or patronized for her exces-
sive desire to be feminine, and the humor was gentler; when
the latter erred, she was seen as threatening, and the humor
was correspondingly more biting.

One example of the attack on fashion was the long-running
series of cartoons and commentary about the Gainsborough or
theater hat. *Life*, for instance, ran a concerted campaign against
the edifice of feathers and ruching that society women wore to
matinees. In "Revenge is Sweet: Some of the Troubles in Store
for the New Woman," three men wearing outrageous hats are
depicted blocking the view of those behind (25 Mar. 1897: 228);
in a reversal of the idea in "Is This to be the Bald-Headed Row
of the Future?" women in the front row of a theater are shown
in fancy dresses and shaved heads (15 Apr. 1897: 301). Such
comic commentary was minor, however, when compared to
the four-page illustrated poem by Carolyn Wells entitled "The
Tragedy of the Theatre Hat" (4 Mar. 1897: 168-71). The devil,
"in a spirit of mirth," decides one day to attend a matinee,
where he is seated behind "a society queen":

Her shoulders were broad, and supported a cape
Which gave you no clue to her possible shape,
    'Twas so plaited and quilled,
    And ruffled and frilled,
And it tinkled with bugles that never were stilled;
    And wide epaulettes
    All covered with jets,
Caught up here and there with enormous rosettes,
And further adorned with gold-spangled aigrettes.
Encircling her neck was a boa of gauze,
Accordion-plaited and trimmed with gew-gaws;
And perched on the top of her haughty, blonde head
Was a HAT! Now, of course, you have all of you read
    Of the theatre hats
    That are seen at the mats.,
That are higher than steeples and broader than flats;
But this one as far outshone all of the others
As young Joseph's dream-sheaves exceeded his brothers'.
'Twas a wide-rolling brim, and a high-peakèd crown,
And black feathers stood up and black feathers hung down
Without any visible scheme of connection.
'Twas decked with rare flowers of a marvelous size,
And colors that seemed to bedazzle the eyes.
    And each vacant space
    Was filled in with ace,
And twenty-three birds in the ribbons found place.

"The devil was nonplussed," Wells continues, and asks her to remove her hat:

. . . many fair ladies, as gorgeously gowned,
    Held their hats in their laps,
    Or, still better, perhaps,
Had left them outside in the room with their wraps.

When she haughtily refuses, the devil curses her to wear it wherever she goes:

She wore it at dinners, she wore it at balls;
She wore it at home when receiving her calls;
  . . . In summer or winter, the hat was still there,
And 'twas *so* in the way when she shampooed her hair.

Her lover would fain his sweetheart caress,
But who to his bosom could tenderly press
Twelve black, waving feathers and twenty-three birds?

Her engagement broken, she discovers that even a convent refuses to take her: "She carried that ill-fated hat to her grave."

Playgoers in Britain were just as disturbed by the millinery
fad as their American counterparts. One versified *Punch* review
of *The Beauty Stone*, with music by Sir Arthur Sullivan and
libretto by Comyns Carr and Arthur Wing Pinero, concentrated
less on the romantic plot of the talisman that grants both
beauty and despair than on the difficulty of seeing the performance:

> "Madder Matinee Hats"
>
> Oh! ladies with towering hats,
>     I am a diminutive man,
> I see your fine feathers, and that's
>     The utmost I possibly can.
>
> I go very rarely, it's true,
>     To *matinees* anywhere; though
> I might enjoy looking at you,
>     I don't care to see your *chapeaux*.
>
> But Messrs. PINERO and CARR
>     Have started quite lately a play
> With head-dresses towering far
>     Above the small things of to-day.
>
> *The Beauty Stone*, there you will see
>     Some types of the *matinee* hat.
> Green with envy you'll certainly be,
>     Compared with them yours are quite flat.
>
> Good gracious! suppose you should try
>     To follow that fashion as well!
> We give you some inches, then why
>     Not measure your hats by the ell?
>
> Your headgear is mad anyhow;
>     I've already explained that I'm small,
> I cannot see much even now,
>     I then should see nothing at all. [25 June 1898: 291]

Other feminine follies of the day found their way into comic expression. The two ends of a long feather boa, *Punch* recommends in a sketch entitled "Happy Thought," may be twined around the necks of two admirers during a stroll, both enrapturing and warming them (5 Mar. 1887: 111). The high-heeled boot, which restricted movement, is the subject of another versifier's complaint; his beloved's footsteps sound like those of the Norwegian Arctic explorer Fridtjof Nansen, and, he is sure, the tightness of the boot not only distracts her from her prayers but prevents pleasurable rambles in the countryside.

"Sportive Songs"

*A long-time lover expresses his intense dislike*
*to the high-heeled tight Boots of his Lady, who*
*professes to enjoy the wearing of the same.*

Your heels of brass make pit-a-pat,
    Like NANSEN's feet about the Pole;
Upon an india-rubber mat
    You'd make the substance pay its toll,
In order to attention draw
    To those twin props on which you walk!
I think upon a street of straw
    You'd demonstrate your pedal talk!

The instep arched is fair to view,
    The little *brodequin* fine and neat,
But when I love to look at you,
    Must I be always at your feet?
May not my eyes be sometimes raised
    To meet those orbs of liquid glow
Shot with pure gold that, half amazed,
    Have kindred tints with boots below?

I never have quite understood
    The glory of the cobbler's art;
The last, I know, is made of wood,
    And only lasts that we may "part"!
But in your shoon of tightest fit,
    Such as you wore at church to-day,

I'm sure you said a little bit
    That could not fitly rhyme with "pray"! . . . [15 May 1897: 237]


The faddishness of the "womanly woman" was generally
treated with comic distress, underlaid with the assumption that
frivolity was a mark of femininity. While one might speculate
that it is simply the act of wearing clothing at all—the curse
of the fig leaf—that inspires the humorists, extravagant frivolity was taken to be an acceptable expression of women's
lesser powers of intellect and concentration. A *Punch* takeoff
on Shakespeare illustrates this point:


"The Seven Ages of Woman"
*By a Cantankerous Old Curmudgeon.*

All the world's a Wardrobe,
And all the girls and women merely wearers:
They have their fashions and their fantasies,
And one she in her time wears many garments
Throughout her Seven Stages. First, the baby,
Befrilled and broidered, in her nurse's arms.
And then the trim-hosed schoolgirl, with her flounces
And small-boy-scorning face, tripping, skirt-waggling,
Coquettishly to school. And then the flirt,
Ogling like Circe, with a business *oeillade*
Kept on her low-cut corset. Then a bride
Full of strange finery, vestured like an angel,
Veiled vaporously, yet vigilant of glance,
Seeking the Woman's heaven, Admiration,
Even at the Altar's steps. And then the matron,
In fair rich velvet with suave satin line,
With eyes severe, and skirts of youthful cut
Full of dress-saws and modish instances,
To teach her girls *their* part. The sixth age shifts
Into the grey yet gorgeous grandmamma
With gold *pince-nez* on nose and fan at side,
Her youthful tastes still strong, and worldly wise
In sumptuary law, her quavering voice
Prosing of Fashion and *Le Follet*, pipes
Of robes and bargains rare. Last scene of all,
That ends the Sex's *Mode*-swayed history,

Is second childishness and sheer oblivion
Of youth, taste, passion, all—save love of Dress! [20 May 1882: 230]


A similar attitude was held with regard to woman's crown-
ing glory. Implicit in the satirists' resistance to new hairstyles
was the idea that it was, nonetheless, feminine to experiment
with them. In *Punch*'s "Lover's Complaint," the versifier objects to the "back interest" created by new ways of coiling and
looping the hair:


When I was yours and you were mine,
    Your hair, I thought, was most delightful,
But now, through Fashion's last design,
    It looks, to my taste, simply frightful!
Though why this should be I don't know,
    For I can think of nothing madder
Than hair decked out in coils that go
    To make what seems to be a ladder. . . .

Again—you will not take it ill—
    You are, my dear, distinctly dumpy:
A flowing cape it's certain will
    Well—*not* become one short and stumpy.
Yet since, although you are not tall,
    You wear a cape, you may take my word
That in the mouths of one and all
    You have become a very byword. . . . [15 Aug. 1891: 81]


"Back interest" was not all that bemused the poetasters;
"banging" the hair, perhaps an initial step to the shorthaired
bob of the 1920s, caused a loud outcry in the 1880s. One popular
humorist speculates "scientifically" in *Chic* that according to
the experiments of Professor Huxley, bangs are popular because
the "purpose [of the style] is to conceal the ravages of picnics
and tête-à-têtes in the back parlor. The banged girl can do with
impunity what would lead to the immediate detection of the
unbanged girl" (15 Dec. 1880: 2). One versifier in *Chic* complains that he lost an inheritance because of his wife's new
hairdo:

I've an uncle, rich, old, gouty—
    A most gluttonous gourmet,
Big-paunched, purple-faced and gouty,
    Who invited us one day
To a most récherché dinner
    Of Delmonico's best fare:
We were late, as I am a sinner!
    *For my wife would bang her hair.*

It would not sit to please her,
    So she singed, and fumed and curled;
Said she wished I would not teaze her,
    As my hat and cane I twirled.
Then our cab was slow, got blocked out,
    And two hours late we were.
From his will my name was knocked out,
    *While she stopped to bang her hair!*

He concludes:

For though her love's past rating,
    Feel certain *ma belle chère*
Would keep my funeral waiting
    *While she stopped to bang her hair.* [15 Sept. 1880: 7]

One of *Punch*'s responses to the style, a parody of Henry Kendall's poem "Astarte" in *Bookman*, veils class consciousness in an attack on fashion. A red-haired cockney, a female version of " 'Arry," has banged her hair in imitation of her better-born sisters; she wears jet-black bugles, or glass beads, on her cloak, and she both uses perfume and dyes her hair. The verse does show that certain styles and practices were popular enough to be adopted by several classes at once:

    " 'Arriet. A Realistic Rhapsody"

Across the wind-blown bridges,
    O look, lugubrious Night!
She comes, the red-haired beauty
    Illumined by gaslight!
    By London's dim gaslight!
    So hush, ye cads, your roar!

Behind her plumes are waving
　　Her oil'd fringe flaps before.

O 'ARRIET, Cockney sister,
　　Your face is writhed with jeers;
How awful is the angle
　　Of those protuberant ears!
　　Those red, protuberant ears!
　　And your splay feet—O lor!!!
My loud, my Cockney sister,
　　Where oil'd fringe flops before.

Ah, 'ARRIET! Gracious 'eavens!
　　How your greased locks do glow!
I swoon! The "hodoration"
　　(I heard you call it so)
　　Sickens my senses so;
　　'Tis "Citronel"—no more,
That scents, like a cheap barber's,
　　That oil'd fringe hung before.

'ARRIET, my knowing darling,
　　Your eyes a cross-watch keep.
You're togged in shop-girl's fashion,
　　Your cloak is bugled deep,
　　Black-bugled broad and deep,
　　With buttons dappled o'er,
Good gr-racious! how it's grown, too—
　　That oil'd fringe flopped before!

That "bang" is awfully trying,
　　That odour maddens me.
By Jingo! you've been dyeing
　　Those rufous locks, I see,
　　Those sandy locks, I see,
　　They're darker than of yore.
Avaunt! I'd be forgetting
　　That oil'd fringe flopped before. [20 Aug. 1892: 73]

Dyeing the hair and choosing to cut, coil, or frizzle it in
elaborate ways were symptomatic of the new technology that
not only provided electric light for the home but changed personal habits as well. In a whimsical scene from a music room,

for instance, *Punch* depicts well-dressed women and their es-
corts equipped with paper umbrellas; the "Happy Thought" is
that "the electric light, so favourable to' furniture, wall papers,
pictures, screens, &c., is not always becoming to the female
complexion. Light Japanese sunshades will be found invaluable" (20 July 1889: 30). Perhaps more to the point, however,
is a cartoon entitled "Abominations of Modern Science" in
which a long-haired, banged beauty stands forlornly holding
her curling iron and contemplating an electric light bulb:
"Mariana arrives at the Moated Grange (after a long, damp
Journey) just in time to dress for Dinner, and finds, to her sorrow, that her Room is warmed by Hot Water Pipes and lighted
by Electricity" (30 Jan. 1892: 53).

The technology that provided the "modern" comforts of
heat, hot water, and light on demand went hand in hand with
the newly utilitarian movement in dress. At the same time
that the mechanics of caring for clothing and hair became easier, styles were simplified, and the movement toward "rational
dress" was intensified. Two factors helped to popularize the
revolution: an increased number of women working and an
increased number of middle-class families that could not afford
a full panoply of servants to provide personal care. Both working
women and housewives, who lived in a world far removed from
tight boots and theater hats, were likely to sympathize with a
movement that sought to correlate the responsible woman's
dress with her life-style.

Indeed, in a symposium on "Women: How Shall They
Dress?" in the January 1885 *North American Review*, only one
writer, the journalist and novelist Charles Dudley Warner, pos-
tulates that the progress of civilization entails increasing differentiation in men's and women's dress, an argument based
on Herbert Spencer's contention that the disparate nature of
men's and women's activities is one mark of civilization. Warner's conclusion, that "beauty is a duty women owe to society,"
mirrors the attitude of earlier decades (563). Others, like William Hammond, argue from history in favor of trousers (565-
68); Kate Jackson makes a plea for simplicity and maintains
that "evidently the first requisite to physical culture is physio-

logical dress" (570); and E.M. King gives six characteristics of the ideal, lightweight dress and notes, "Indeed, we are poor creatures, with cramped minds in cramped bodies" (557-60).

Some of the "cramped minds," however, devised a way to popularize dress reform. Lady Harberton, who created the divided skirt and established the Rational Dress Society, herself wore bloomers in the 1880s (Crow 129), and before meeting at the World's Fair in Chicago, the dress reform committee of the National Council of Women issued a call to all women to inaugurate a new outfit "suitable for business hours, for shopping, for marketing, house work and other forms of exercise." Women were encouraged to wear their rational dress en masse at the fair; in fact, the chair of the dress reform committee, Frances E. Russell, believed that bloomers failed because of their oddity, not because of their ugliness, and so sought to persuade those unburdened by work and family that it was their duty to help their more timid sisters ("Dress Reform" 312-15).

Russell, who emphasized the practicality of the new outfit, was perhaps somewhat simplistic. Whereas writers generally viewed fashionable foibles with condescension, for many satirists as well as many women, "rational dress" was not simply a convenience but an expression of a philosophical stance about the relationship between the sexes and about women's role in worldly affairs. Women who were willing to undertake such a graphic statement of belief seemed, for the most part, to be from the middle and upper classes, even though many cartoons suggested that the discussion raged at all levels of society. Such periodicals as *Judy* and *Pick-Me-Up* used figures from other walks primarily to increase the humor, as in a 13 October 1895 cover for *Pick-Me-Up*, in which a ruffian gives "The Retort Provocative" to a British sailor who, accompanied by his sweetheart, is dressed in the uniform's wide pants: "Bin an' borrered 'er di-vi-ded skirt, ain't yer?" Likewise, *Judy* shows a plump housewife dressed in modified bloomers, conversing with a friend, while laundry flaps in the wind behind her: "My 'Usband he say, 'Take them things off,' he say. 'And wear them 'orrid Skirts again,' says I? 'Not me!' " (6 June 1883: 276). Indeed, while the concern for tradition made British satire more critical and less whimsical than American, there was little *éclat* at any level of society in wearing an outfit made popular in the United States.

Typical of the American approach, one of the contributors to the short-lived New York *Chic*, greeted the new fad for masculine clothing with quiet nonsense, maintaining that for a woman to return to back-buttoned waists would eradicate "all that the sex has gained in the last three centuries of independence and individuality" by making her depend on someone else for the state of her dress (13 Oct. 1880: 2). In addition, he lays the penchant for toothpicks and trousers to a jealousy over masculine habits: "Our young ladies, having taken to dressing so much like our young men that the sexes above the waist present an identical appearance, wish to complete their toilet with cigars. They know, however, that the public is not yet educated up to beholding with complacency a young lady with a cigar projecting from her mouth. They have, therefore, resolved to accustom us to the sight of the projecting toothpick, feeling confident that when we have become accustomed to this, even a cigar will not shock us" (22 Nov. 1881: 2).

The toothpick "boom" is followed by the matches craze; as one *Chic* writer contends, what the sex needs is not "minor matters" like suffrage or an entrée into medicine or law but a place to scratch matches, an "invaluable privilege" that she lacks and that "conclusively show[s] her inferiority to man." Thus, "the whole secret of the trousers-wearing movement among strong-minded women" lies in their desire to place themselves on an equality with men in point of matches because "to man alone is given the ability to scratch matches on his trousers"; he is "the king of creation" (5 Apr. 1881).

Such a lighthearted approach generally characterizes the American magazines that deal with the "rational dress" movement. While the columns and comments do indicate that the new dress is recognized as a statement of life-style, on the whole it is treated with amusement as yet another expression of womanly frivolity. For *Life*, both clubs and dress are an accepted fact. On the cover for 25 March 1897, for example, William Walker draws two New Women, the first replete with bowler, bulldog, and bloomers, the second with cane, spats, top hat, and overcoat:

Fig. 11. "In the New Age." *Life*, 11 June 1896: 480.

"Where Duty Called"

"Hello, Mary, old girl! Didn't see you at the Culture Club last night."

"No, there was an important meeting of the House Committee at the Pants Club."

More pointed is "In the New Age," P. Leonard's assessment of times to come, when a reversal in roles changes the family structure. The accompanying illustration by Walker (Fig. 11), which shows a careworn father quietly talking to his mild-mannered son while his two daughters in knickers rollick merrily in the background, carries the perhaps unspoken lesson of the vignette, which is that woman's lot is hardly to be envied:

The man of the future sat patiently darning the family socks. From time to time his mild blue eyes glanced wearily at the pile of mending at his elbow, and he sighed as he thought of the raw Irishman in the kitchen, who needed incessant instruction in the simplest details of culinary art. Two noisy, sturdy girls, as aggressive as became their sex, romped merrily about the sewing-room, aggravating his headache; while their gentle little brother sat quietly by his father's side, studying the pictures in an old book of bygone fashions which he had found, and which appealed, of course, to the instincts of the miniature man.

"Look, father!" he said, pointing to an old print of the year 1890— "see what queer clothes that man has on! What are they? Did men really wear them then?"

"Yes, dear," said his father, laying down his needle for a moment and bending over the page—"I never saw any; but father once told me that grandfather wore them when he was a boy. They called them pantaloons." [11 June 1896: 480]

Like *Life*, New York *Truth* could be critical at times, as a short story in the 1895 Christmas number shows. The heroine, "A Modern Diana" (presumably a parody of George Meredith's *Diana of the Crossways*), is initially mistaken for "a young fellow" as she takes part in a fox hunt: "the most striking note in her costume was her bloomers and leggings." The denouement is that she receives a proposal at the fox hunt ball but only *after* she has changed into the long dress that befits an old-fashioned Diana (14 Dec. 1895: 28-29).

The British reaction was much harsher, especially as it appeared in London *Truth*, which was almost uniformly antagonistic to the new movement in dress, seeing in it a breakdown of old values. One contributor suggests that women are not only less charming in the new fashions but also more duplicitous. Men should be wary of the new styles; the bachelor pleased to rid himself of a "maze of crinoline" might be fooled after all:

"The True Reason for 'Rational Dress' "

[The makers of artificial sinews and muscles are said to be unusually busy just now, owing to the demand for padded calves which has arisen amongst lady cyclists who have adopted the so-called "rational" dress.—*Daily Telegraph*]

This piece of news, alas! confirms—
And in a manner most dismaying—

What we, in well-considered terms,
    About New Women have been saying.
We've always been inclined to doubt,
    And more than once have plainly said it,
Whether despite the way they shout,
    They were deserving of much credit.

We've always urged—and, as it seems,
    Our words were evidently sure ones—
That for their ill-considered schemes
    Their motives were not wholly pure ones.
And now, those critics to confuse,
    Who vowed we did but idly vapour,
There comes the aforesaid piece of news,
    Reported in a leading paper.

We'd tried to hope, O Women New!
    When 'gainst convention you wore kickers,
And when with such a zeal undue
    You fearlessly went in for knickers,
There was good reason why you'd link'd
    The thought of petticoats with loathing,
And why, in "cylinders distinct,"
    Your nether limbs you had been clothing.

We'd tried to think, in your defense,
    Your *penchant* strong for garments novel
Was only meant to show your sense
    Which in old grooves no more would grovel;
We'd even hoped that you at last,
    Weary of fussy declamation,
From artificial fads had past,
    Fired by a natural inspiration.

But we have been deceived again,
    Again our hope's met with re-buffing,
For you, to shapely legs obtain,
    Have flown to wadding and mill-puffing.
Yes, Women New, you have been led
    By the old Eve that still is in you,
For you "improve" your legs, 'tis said,
    With pads of artificial sinew!

In other words, you make it plain,
    That when you ape our male humanity
Your only object is to gain
    Fresh scope for your excessive vanity;
And clearly demonstrate once more
    That your unwise, persistent fadding
(Which all true friends so much deplore)
    A pretext is for puff and padding! [11 Oct. 1894: 811]

Along with the philosophical and social changes suggested
by the new mode of dress, what *Truth* most objects to is the
publicity and vociferousness attached to the demand for reform. Its versifier recommends that if women wish to dress like
men they should do so without fanfare:

    "The 'New Woman' Again"

That appalling "New Woman!"—she's at it again,
All attempts to repress her once more have proved vain.
Yes, again, with assurance which does not grow less,
She's discussing the question of "Rational Dress."
Again, as the season called "Silly" comes round,
She is making the press with her shrieking resound,
And attracting attention, which seems half ironical,
By what she declares and demands in the *Chronicle*.

More outspoken than ever she loudly parades
The skirt as a garment that woman degrades;
Henceforth, she proclaims, all her sex must be stickers
For that new "Magna Charta" of Woman—"cloth knickers"!
Yes, each leg, she asserts, in a manner succinct,
Must be "clothed in a cylinder wholly distinct,"
And she calls on all women to act on this plan,
And thus prove they are "bipeds exactly like man."

Then men, in their turn, blithely join in the fray,
And pick up the gauntlet thrown down day by day.
"What! woman wear knickers!" cries one. "That's too strong,
Why, the fact is, her two nether limbs are all wrong!"
"A woman in cylinders!" echoes a second;
"Is *that*, then, a rational dress to be reckoned?"
Whilst comments not fit for these columns are heard
From the plain-speaking tongue of a much-aggrieved third.

And what does *TRUTH* say? Why, she utters once more
The remarks that with reason she's uttered before;
If "New Woman" 's resolved she will "cylinders" don,
Then let her by all means put "cylinders" on;
But there's not the least need, though her legs she'd array so,
To rush to a paper of platform to say so;
And her fondness for "knickers" affords her no reason
For becoming the butt of the new "Silly Season."

When men want to change their attire—why, they change it,
And without any fuss with their tailors arrange it;
They do not hold meetings, and write to the papers,
And publicly cut most ridiculous capers.
And so, too, "New Woman," if it's your plan,
To pose as a "biped exactly like man,"
Your exuberance frank you must certainly fetter,
And the sooner you do it, "New Woman," the better!
[23 Aug. 1894: 412]

Such a complaint is inconsiderable, however, in light of the
elaborate and vituperative satire that appears in the Christmas
number for 1894, in which *Truth* categorizes, in rhyme and
illustration, the kinds of women who adopt freer modes of
dress. These New Women, *Truth* maintains, are "new" not
necessarily because they are liberated but because they adopt
shock tactics to differentiate themselves from their predecessors. In each case, their dress represents their frame of mind;
indeed, what *Truth* seems to be suggesting is that advanced
women are mere poseurs, living up to a set of faddish conventions that make them unattractive. In "Our Girls *Have* Altered," four kinds of New Women are made to cavort through
*Truth*'s poem. The first is the "Beardsley Woman," the second
a cousin to Mrs. Grundy (the dictator of conservative social
mores), the third a mannish dresser, and the fourth a bluestocking (Fig. 12).

Like the "Inner Sanctum" columns in *Life* in which the
mascot cherub interviews notables of the day and like the ob-
servations that Mr. Punch makes as an antic figure dressed in
cap, bells, and motley, *Truth* invokes the spirit of Baron Mun-

Fig. 12. "Our Girls *Have* Altered." London *Truth*, 25 December 1894: 34. Courtesy of the General Research Division, New York Public Library, Astor, Lenox and Tilden foundations.

chausen, who has returned after a century to survey the changes. He notes that the "most charming" girls seem to have changed; *Truth* replies sadly, "I fear, Munchausen, you are right; the change which you surmise / Has most undoubtedly gone on for years beneath my eyes. / Our girls *have* altered; and, to this, the fact, no doubt is due, / That many English women, too, are now so very 'New.' " The "first loathsome figure, so indelicately fat," has been "Bowdlerised" by the artist, who "add[ed] a frill and put some gauze where all before was bare." *Truth* gives a "recipe" for her creation, reminiscent of the Chorus of Dragoons in Act I of Gilbert and Sullivan's aesthetic spoof *Patience*. Instead of "If you want a receipt for that popular mystery, / Known to the world as a Heavy Dragoon, / Take all the remarkable people in history, / Rattle them off to a popular tune," *Truth* creates a potpourri in which the combination of poisonous herbs, unpalatable ingredients, and

aesthetic references is emblematic of the loathing for the unconventional behavior and ambiguous sexuality of the Wilde
decade:

Take of Swinburne's ballads three—
    Choose the most erotic—
Let them simmer in a pan,
    Steeped in some narcotic;
Stew some sketches by de Groux—
    *Primitif* sensations—
Chop in little bits, and add,
    Several green carnations.
In this mixture, when a scum,
    Thick and green, is on it,
Throw a scene from Maeterlinck,
    And one hot Richepin sonnet;
Lard some *chansons* by Verlaine,
    Grill until they're greasy,
Pepper with obscenity,
    Franco-Japanesy,
Boil a "Yellow Book" well down
    In broth of burnt sienna,
Add a "Minor Poet" stewed
    In hasheesh dashed with henna;
Spice *ad lib.* with morbid taste
    (Give the steam no egress);
Put in whole the unctuous lips
    Of a Cuban negress;
Grate some cankered Dead-Sea fruit,
    And withered flowers of passion,
Drench with *sauce* à Schopenhauer
    Mixed in latest fashion;
Add a paradox or two
    (See they're Oscar Wilde-ish);
Sprinkle in some draughtsmanship,
    Absolutely childish;
Equal parts of venom take,
    Slime, and impudicity,
Belladona, sewer-gas,
    Laudanum, and lubricity.
And, when all these things you've mixed
    In a hotch-potch baleful,

Chinese white and ivory black
   Dash in by the pail-ful.
Take the mixture off the fire
   When it is well heated,
Put it in the sink to stand
   Till it grows quite fetid.
Pour it in a tainted mould,
   Like to nothing human,
Shut your eyes and hold your nose,
                    And serve
                THE BEARDSLEY WOMAN!

The versifier leaves no doubt that he finds the first New Woman unattractive; she is a compound of many of the aesthetic tendencies that the poet Robert Buchanan sums up when he includes Algernon Swinburne and his followers in what he calls "the fleshly school of poetry." With its numerous references to the French symbolists, to Oscar Wilde, and to publications like the *Green Carnation* by Robert Hichens and the *Yellow Book*, in which Aubrey Beardsley's drawings were published, the verse seems directed primarily against the aesthetes themselves; the New Woman is treated as the concoction of a movement even more dangerous than feminism.

The other sections are different, in that they pillory the women themselves. The second version of the New Woman, sketched with corkscrew curls, a prudish pucker, and a pince-nez, is a moral "Vigilant" of the Mrs. Grundy type, perpetually on the lookout for *roués*. By other satirists Mrs. Grundy is evoked as a convenient moral foil to the New Woman; here she appears in very different garb, a New Woman by virtue of her professed antagonism to men. As the writer explains to Baron Munchausen:

"She also is convinced that man is very, very bad,
And that most women go about far too sparsely
   clad;
She holds 'the times are out of joint,' but deems it
   'cruel spite'
That she's been born (or thinks she has) to quickly set
   them right;

And to the Decalogue, which now we say at church on
    Sunday,
Would add this new commandment—'Serve no God but Mrs.
    Grundy!' "


As a New Woman, the third type is perhaps the most telling,
for her costume indicates an effort to take control of her life.
Dressed in an outfit that frees her not only from skirts but from
the old-fashioned, submissive stereotype, she is possessed of
an important accessory—the latchkey, which allows her to
come and go as she pleases:

" 'New Woman' Number Three affects the ways of man to
    ape,
Her collars have a mannish cut, her vests a mannish
    shape;
Vulgar and slangy, she goes in for cigarettes and
    'spats,'
And marks her spirit of revolt by how she cocks her
    hats.
Her eye-glass, necktie, skirts curtailed, and latchkey in her
    pocket,
Don't prove she knows the world, but show how pleased
    she is to shock it.
In short, disgusted by her style, which 'Dodo' doubtless
    taught her,
Good taste instinctively revolts at this 'revolting
    daughter.' "


The argument here is less explicitly the same as the argument
about sexual ambiguity in the Beardsley woman, but the focus
is more upon undefined good taste; the veiled reference at the
end to one of Eliza Lynn Linton's phrases seems to make Mrs.
Linton and her injunctions against the "shrieking sisterhood"
into a new Mrs. Grundy, the old being pilloried as a New
Woman type.

Finally, following the New Woman with cigarette, monocle,
and bowler hat is the bluestocking college girl, wearing spectacles, jacket, and simple dress. *Truth*'s complaint is that her
knowledge is irrelevant to her sphere; classical subjects are no

help in homemaking or in developing charming social manners:

" 'New Woman' Number Four who now our libraries is
    blocking,
Is but a brand-new darn upon the well-known old 'blue
    stocking.'
She wastes a lot of midnight-oil at some new-fangled
    college;
She stores her hydrocephalic head with loads of useless
    knowledge;
She's up on Greek antiquities, but can't be called good-
    looking;
She's great at conic sections, but quite ignorant of
    cooking;
She tackles metaphysics, and some subjects even tougher;
But at housekeeping and the like distinctly proves a
    duffer.
She's many fads, but not one charm; no vice, but many
    views;
Which, in the dreariest novels, she is eager to diffuse.
Her code is quite impossible, for, though with learning
    fraught,
Of life and human nature she knows positively nought.
She reads and masters all the books which fill her study
    shelf,
But she never looks in her own heart and tries to read
    herself." [25 Dec. 1894: 34-37]

*Truth*'s objections are similar to those framed in a less abrasive manner by *Life*; the college girl, overeducated in matters of the head, is ignorant in ways of the heart. The versifier concludes that, matrimonially speaking, each New Woman meets her match by attracting her opposite ("The New Women's Men," Fig. 13). The first marries a Beardsley Man (sketched as an overweight, effeminate Wildean); the second, a younger, fashionable profligate; the third, "As a man-woman . . . affects a milksop woman-man"; and the fourth, a "brainless military man."

Overall, then, the love of dress was taken in a contradictory way. An affirmation of empty-mindedness, it nonetheless was

Fig. 13. "The New Women's Men." London *Truth*, 25 December 1894: 35. Courtesy of the General Research Division, New York Public Library, Astor, Lenox and Tilden foundations.

an acceptable way for a woman to exercise some control over her personal environment. In many cases, however, fashion, no matter how outrageous, was a response to masculine values for women. Long skirts were domestic; high-heeled boots, although condemned for their frivolity, nonetheless also restricted movement and, thus, exploration; the bustle and the corset emphasized portions of the female anatomy that many writers thought "charming." Once fashion became a response to women's changing values about themselves, however, it became a more threatening expression of control and evoked more seriously condemnatory responses. While such "rational" dress became widely accepted only in the twentieth century, it was accompanied by the democratization of transportation and the popularity of the bicycle and so eventually ceased to be treated as a phenomenon in its own right. The connection between simplified dress and increased exercise, an apparently utilitarian movement, actually represented a shift in both status and control. In restrictive, ornate clothing, woman was an aesthetic object, inspiring others by her symbolic value; in rational dress, the work of art became an artist and seized direct control of the world, influencing others by direct action. As a matter of physical and intellectual expansion and health, then, the new modes of dress coupled with the growing popularity of athletics loosened hidebound stereotypes and encouraged feminine independence and individual well-being.

# SIX

# Women's Athletics
## *A Bicycle Built for One*

Here's a nice position for a man. I've got to scrub the floor and do all the housework, just because my wife wants to go out riding on her bike. Oh! This is what I get for marrying a new woman.
   —Frank Dumont

THE WOMAN who put on divided skirts and took to the roads on her "safety" gained not only independence but also a measure of health and a sense of well-being that her neurasthenic sister of earlier decades might have envied. As angel in the home, woman was symbol and ideal; she participated in a well-recognized tradition. As New Woman on a bicycle, however, she exercised power more fundamentally, changing the conventions of courtship and chaperonage, of marriage and travel. As her sphere of influence broadened and her physical stamina increased, the focus of the satire and caricature that recorded her development also changed. Rather than depicting women as fragile beings to be patronized for frivolous tastes, humorists joked about the Amazonian physique exercise produced and warned in mock horror about the inevitable submission of men. More serious writers, versed in Spencerian theory, feared that such progress was really regress to a more primitive state; the more activities and interests men and women shared, the less differentiated and less civilized they purportedly grew. Even female doctors argued against exercise, believing that strenuous physical exertion would redirect vital energy needed to produce healthy children. Engaging in so mild a sport as riding a bicycle, then, was no mere matter of amusement; the very act of pedaling might counteract the evolution, if not the very existence, of the human race.

Hindsight shows, of course, that the naysayers were right in warning that change would come, but few of the negative predictions came true. Shedding tight corsets, women became more vigorous and gave birth to larger babies; achieving some measure of physical independence, they conceptualized themselves as capable of handling intellectual and emotional independence. The feminist movement at the end of the century, which can be traced, in part, to the superfluity of women, may take as its emblem the two-wheeler. The contrast between the woman in the earlier *Punch* cartoon labeled "No Reasonable Offer Refused" and the woman on bicycle is instructive. On the one hand, the woman standing in front of the sign is a passive commodity, waiting for someone male to purchase her; she has no choice, no option to be selective, and her position, although respectable, suggests that she has become close kin to her sisters of the streets. On the other hand, the woman on a bicycle represents both activity and options; the woman on wheels may decide where she wishes to go and what she plans to do when she gets there, regardless of a male companion, or lack of one. Her influence upon the world is more immediate; no longer confined to the home or hoping to escape from the vicissitudes of earning a living, she actively seeks new experience and intends to have some impact on the world around her.

The path to change was not an easy one, however; the experts themselves were hagridden by gender stereotypes. The evolutionary argument against exercise was posed, for instance, as late as 1899. Indeed, a published discussion between Arabella Kenealy, a physician, and her respondent, Mrs. L. Ormiston Chant, reveals how authoritative medical opinion could be. Beginning with the postulate that the human body is a finely balanced "instrument" in which varying degrees of physical qualities (such as mind, emotion, or muscle) determine personality, Kenealy goes on to suggest that the development of muscle detracts from feminine sensitivity. "It is . . . the subordination of muscle power to express idea, emotional, intellectual, or moral, which is man's especial forte," she says; in woman, the development of muscle means a loss of charm, of mysteriousness, of gentleness. The woman who exercises becomes "brusque," and her voice becomes "assertive": "She says everything—leaves nothing to the imagination" (365-66).

Since unselfishness, domestic skill, and taste require "as much nerve output as do the movements of mere muscles," Kenealy opts for the old system: "I am inclined to doubt if it really was so pernicious in its physiological results or so subversive of domestic happiness and the welfare of the race as is the present system which sets our mothers bicycling all day and dancing all night and our grandmothers playing golf" (369). Her final contention is that while women's emancipation was a ploy on the part of Nature to prepare a more educated motherhood, "[Nature] knows it is the laboriously evolved potentiality of the race they are expending on their muscles" (368). Interestingly, Kenealy does not phrase the more commonplace argument, that intellectual endeavor also detracts from the "potentiality of the race." Many doctors cautioned mothers of prepubescent teens not to allow their daughters to dissipate their "feminine" energies by such unnatural acts as reading and studying.

Kenealy's arguments are answered point for point by Mrs. Chant, a female reader who apparently speaks from experience; importantly, it is the presumably less educated of the two who points out that Nature favors the physically strong mother and that the victims of the old system are the ones who produce unhealthy children (800), the "spectacled, knock-kneed" offspring that Kenealy warns against ("Rejoinder" 209). While Chant's tone is commonsensical and her recommendations for moderate exercise reasonable, Kenealy is, by virtue of her training, more authoritative. Indeed, her final word combines the evolutionary argument and the bicycle in a monitory way: "The Wheel of Evolution is a wheel which never stands still, except in that terrible moment when it slackens, halts, and finally whirls down the fearsome way of Devolution" (212).

Many satirists took Kenealy's "Devolution" argument one step further to show that the masculinization of women entailed the feminization of men. As in the record of complaints about women's education, careers, and clubs, gender transference was the root fear behind complaints about women's athleticism. Both serious and humorous writers viewed the sports-minded female as a "manly woman," a term that seemed to fulfill neo-Spencerian fears. When women developed a taste for masculine interests like horse trading, boxing, and hunting, men were said to become unwilling household drudges, wearing aprons and rearing children.

The popular mythology that flourished around the belief that muscle and femininity were in a delicate mathematical balance was reflected and abetted in comic and serious responses. In *Punch*'s "Our Girls, What to Give Them?" a parody letter by "One of the Weaker Sex," for instance, the male persona has adopted female ways: "When my sisters went off to the cricket-field on a fine summer morning, and left me at home to darn the socks and overhaul the washing, I used to feel the bitterness of things and to blame Fate that had made me a man." He goes on to suggest timely gifts for his sisters: "a hundred cigarettes"; a "cane-spliced bat and a pair of pads"; "a pair of boxing gloves"; and "the loudest and best bicycle bell in the market" for Nellie, "who is something of a scorcher, [and who] used to complain that her road-racing records were always being spoilt by stupid deaf old gentlemen, who *would* keep getting knocked down" (22 Jan. 1898: 25).

More seriously, in *Blackwood's* "Modern Mannish Maidens," the writer argues that a woman forfeits charm when she engages in the ungainly positions active sports require. Some activities, like rowing and skating, are appropriate because they are graceful; others, like riding and walking, have their limitations. For the first, the writer exclaims, "May our Cynthias of the future rest content with the side-saddle and riding whip, nor ever be persuaded by radical reformers to adopt mannish modes of sitting a horse"; for the second, he suggests that woman may walk and "scale as many mountain-sides as she pleases, with her nearest and dearest." Sports that entail competition and publicity are discouraged; even "enterprising . . . females" avoid cycling, he says, and as far as cricket and football are concerned, "mannishness, burlesque, and incongruity can no further go" (253-60).

Again, *Saturday Review*'s diatribe against "Manly Women" bewails the transformation of the domestic goddess into the huntress who rides with hare and hound. That kind of activity, the writer complains, drives women not only to the "imitation of men's clothes by men tailors" but also to the use of racing slang and argot that detracts from the tone of society; furthermore, such women are likely to gamble seriously and to frequent music halls, there mixing with the demimonde. *Punch*'s "Modern Types: No. XXII.—The Manly Maiden" seems to echo many of *Saturday Review*'s complaints:

The Manly Maiden may be defined as the feminine exaggeration of those rougher qualities which men display in their intercourse with one another, or in the pursuit of those sports in which courage, strength, and endurance play a part. In a fatal moment she conceives the idea that she can earn the proud title of "a good fellow" by emulating the fashions and the habits of the robuster sex. . . . In spite of what the crazy theorists of the perfect equality school may say, men still continue to expect and to admire in women precisely those qualities in which they feel themselves to be chiefly deficient. . . . Of slang, and of slaps upon the back, of strength, whether of language or of body, they get enough and to spare amongst themselves. [6 Dec. 1890: 265]

*Punch*'s "manly woman" rides and shoots (much to the distaste of her male companions), drinks brandy in the field, and picks up the language of sportsmanship. She is, in short, a version of *Saturday Review*'s later type, the "V.W."—or "varmity woman," for whom "the mating of horses, hounds, and cattle is the only form of lovemaking in which she takes the slightest interest" (15 Aug. 1891: 193). Like the critics who attack the clubwoman for aping masculine habits, those who satirize the sportswoman make comments that redound upon themselves by choosing the objectionable qualities as definitive of masculinity. In so doing, they miss the point that many feminists, while adopting male manners and clothing as an expression of philosophy, really sought for the less tangible rewards of independence and equal treatment. Such women did, indeed, enter a man's world with gusto and, perhaps, with mischief, yet the attacks on them are motivated by more than that. In ceasing to play the courtship game, they gave up flirtation for a chase of a different kind—the joy of competition in and of itself.

While the recurrent fear of masculine effacement reappears

as a motif in many bicycling cartoons in which diminutive
men seek to teach their buxom wives and sweethearts how to
ride, the satirical reaction to women's improved muscle tone
was not all negative, nor was it confined to cycling. Even fashionable chitchat about ladylike exercise welcomed the idea,
prescribing a course energetic enough to satisfy the modern
woman: "Then exercise! How abused and neglected! Three
miles a day of walking is enough, and not too much, or a horseback gallop of six or eight miles. To be out in the air twice a
day is well, but never, never, to overfatigue oneself. Once is
too much. Once has broken a constitution" (Gordon 467). Indeed, the barbs were sometimes directed against the compound
of delicacy and nerves that made up the "old" woman as well
as against those who criticized the new. In one *Punch* column,
for instance, Mrs. Grundy, the Victorian bugbear of manners,
is taken to task for frowning at "a natural waist, or absence
of corsets, . . . [or] tailor-made attire or accepted bathing-cos-
tume." She is described in high Victorian style, the better to
increase the irony, as "a portly, florid, and high-nosed elderly
dame, of pompous demeanour, and flamboyant raiment, elabo-
rately and obviously cosmetiqued, and arrayed in a startlingly
low-cut garment" (13 Oct. 1894: 178). That such an artificial
figure loses ground to physiology becomes clear as early as 1879
when *Punch* gives tongue-in-cheek treatment to the commonly
accepted equation between "lady" and "elaborate clothing."
The drawing, unexceptional to modern eyes but unusual for its
time, shows four attractive women posing with tennis rackets,
their dresses unstructured, their figures rounded, and their arms
muscular (Fig. 14). The caption warns of a new style ahead:

"Hygienic Excess"

The O'Farrell-Mackenzie Girls have gone in so extensively for Early
Rising, Fresh Air, Cold Water, Farinaceous Food, Rowing, Riding,
Rinking, Lawn-Tennis, Gymnastics, and what not, that they have dis-
torted their Figures into the likeness of so many Greek Statues, and
have no more waist to speak of than that quite too horrid Venus at
the Louvre; indeed they have given up stays altogether as a bad job.
As they are all engaged to marry Dukes, Mr. Punch fears they will set
the fashion; and as he holds that a long and wasp-like Waist is as

Fig. 14. "Hygienic Excess." *Punch*, 18 October 1879: 174.

essential to a Lady as a—well, as a Hump between the Shoulders, a prominent Nose and Chin, and a protuberant Abdomen are to a Gentleman, he hopes that the above Caricature may serve as an Example and a Warning. [18 Oct. 1879: 174]

Mr. Punch's mock support of an obviously vanishing silhouette is part of the general reassessment of what a lady is. Despite this cartoon, however, the Americans were somewhat quicker than the British to recognize that a woman might still be a lady, even if she chose to be athletic; hand in hand with the proverbial social freedom of the American girl—the Daisy Miller of her time—went her proverbial health. *Figaro*, for instance, in publishing a series on "Types of Womankind," treats "The Muscular Beauty" with a mixture of awe and reserved approval. As long as she eschews "starched high collars," the Amazonian woman can charm her onlookers with "freshness and honesty"; she is given as generous and spirited, eager to argue dogs and football. The writer is nevertheless insistent upon the idea that opposites attract and quietly reverts to the theme of gender transference; the "Muscular Beauty's" favorite beaux are said to be "of delicate mould and quiet tastes, some of whom might even be called effeminate" (12 Mar. 1892: 36).

How such a turn-of-the-century Amazon maintains her physique is explored in New York *Truth's* "The One I Know," W.A. Stotesbury's breath-stopping catalog of the New Woman's athletic endeavors:

The *fin de siècle* maiden that I know is up to date.
She has given up all balls and plays, and never stops out late;
Pays attention to her diet, has a fine contempt for sweets,
Isn't training for the ballet, but is bent on gymnast feats.

She takes a pair of dumb bells, and she works them in the Gym;
The Indian club she twirls about with an aggressive vim,
All pulley weights she handles, and she jumps the bar of course,
Then she turns a double somersault, and vaults across the horse.

She runs around the tan bark, twenty laps there make a mile,
Her bloomers let her do this, but that need not make you smile;
For she's very much in earnest as she fences, drills and spars;
She knows her arm is bigger and her—well, she jumps the bars.

She strikes a sparring attitude, and gives herself a twist;
Then says "Now look at me and see the muscles on my wrist. . . ."
[25 May 1895: 5]

The question of whether the New Woman was manly or womanly was considerably more than a social concern; in fact, the same arguments were applied to athletics as to formal education. Both mental and physical exertion were believed to detract from womanly functions. Just as the educated girl was expected to unbalance her resources so that she would be unable, for example, to nurse her children successfully, the athletic girl was expected to grow either spare and thin or overmuscular, but in any case misshapen. Disagreement with received opinion grew more persistent as the century progressed and as women became personally healthier under the new regimen. The babies' pictures displayed in the Woman's Building at the Chicago World's Fair, for instance, went some way to dispel the argument about adverse genetic effects; all offspring of women with advanced degrees, they were reported to be "cuddlesome, happy-looking, intelligent, and buxom" (Chant 799). Similarly, women trained in the values of fair play were sometimes said to be promising spouses. Honnor Morten records a conversation between two instructors watching a high school gymnasium class in which girls were, "to the tune of the 'Harmonious Blacksmith,' . . . clanging their dumb-bells":

"Awful young Amazons!" said one. "Aren't you sorry for their husbands that are to be?"

"No," replied the other. "I played hockey against them last winter, and they never lost their tempers, and they never played offside. I think they will make rather nice wives." [23]

That competitive sports might inculcate a sense of fair play and team spirit as well as self-confidence was argued only after athletic programs were incorporated into the curriculum in female schools. Indeed, the difference between drill and games was partly a class difference. In the 1870s military drill was mandated in British schools; the utilitarian argument was that lower-class boys trained in the values of discipline and health would make not only a better labor force but a more law-abiding one. Exclusive prep schools, graced with expansive playing fields and proper equipment, trained their students for the exigencies of foreign, political, and military service through competitive sports (Atkinson 94). Women, who were not expected to enter the public sphere, were thought, like the lower classes, to profit from a regimented life-style—hence the popularity of drill. Calisthenics, the grandparent of today's aerobics, was introduced into women's schools as "Swedish exercises," a system of synchronized movements publicized as a therapeutic cure for the debilitation that was said to follow too much study. Madame Bergman-Osterberg, hired by the London School Board to set up training sessions in physical education for teachers, herself exemplified the somewhat paradoxical mixture of the old and the new woman that became evident at the end of the century. Just as Mrs. L. Ormiston Chant ends her rejoinder to Dr. Arabella Kenealy with a paean to old-fashioned virtues— "So let us modern women take heart of grace, and go on doing the best we can to develop muscular vigor, along with a sneaking fondness for frills and pleatings, and an openly avowed adhesion to the Eternal Baby, and its father" (806)—so Madame Bergman-Osterberg enunciates the evolutionary plea, although in more formal terms: "I try to train my girls to help raise their own sex, and to accelerate the progress of the race; for unless the women are strong, healthy, pure and true how can the race progress?" (quoted in Atkinson 99).

The "awful young Amazons," then, were a product of a system that began with lockstep exercise, but exercise that provided a welcome diversion not only from the routine of needlework and reading current in many schools but also from the conventional attitude about women's capabilities. The role of physical education in making women's intellectual education acceptable can hardly be overemphasized. Questioned in its own right, exercise was nonetheless posed as the way to strengthen women's health. Its positive results were, moreover, documentable; weight gain, increased motor skills, endurance—these could be measured "scientifically," while matters of charm, female subtlety, and gentleness, all traditional values, were assessed subjectively. Indeed, when Claës Enebuske published data gathered at the Boston Normal School of Gymnastics, he was able to conclude that "the susceptibility of American women to gymnastic training is considerable. . . . [B]y seven months' training the mere physical working capacity of these women, such as manifests itself in gymnasium work, has grown from the 10 per cent grade to the 50 per cent grade, and from the 50 per cent grade to the 80 or 90 per cent grade" (609).

The original argument, then, that calisthenics inculcated discipline in the lower classes, became reinterpreted in regard to women. Initially seen as a way to develop coordination and discipline, synchronous exercise came to be thought of as a way to counteract the deleterious effects of intellectual endeavors. The result was that study, thought to be unwomanly, became validated by athletics, another unwomanly activity. The importance of competitive athletic events also became reinterpreted but more slowly; the first field day for women was not held in Britain until 1890, when it was organized under the aegis of Frances Buss (Atkinson 113). The same virtues of fair play and team spirit thought necessary for upper-class boys who would be entering a life of corporate action could be given a domestic cast, for running a household was similar to running a business, except that the hearth was expected to be the moral center of the family. Indeed, some apologists even held that exercise and morality were inseparable. D.A. Sargent, for example, in discussing the "Physical Development of Women," interprets Spencer and the argument about conservation of biological energy to suggest not only that exercise helps women realize "the full perfection of their being" but that it makes them healthy enough to undertake their responsibilities for "the higher evolution of mind and body" in others (184).

The schoolgirl of the 1890s, then, had gained license to cast off whalebone and buckram and stretch both mind and body, but her sisters in other walks had considerably less leeway. Many other sports, like riding or golf, required expensive clothing and equipment and were strongly class related. The one activity that was inexpensive and available to almost all was cycling; no other individual sport seemed to further the women's movement so radically. It could be ladylike or daring, depending on whether its rider pedaled demurely, petticoats and all, on a tricycle or donned bloomers, tie, and waistcoat and "scorched" down the streets on a two-wheeler. This revolutionary traveling machine changed patterns of courtship, marriage, and work, to say nothing of transportation; it altered dress styles and language, exercise and education. The very proliferation of satirical verses, comments, and cartoons might suggest merely a craze rather than a revolution, for humorists are quick to lampoon a fad, yet the progress of the satire, developing as it does from reaction to a social phenomenon to reflection on a social fact, suggests otherwise. Early commentary, often moral aspersion in the guise of humor, debates the usual questions of femininity in terms of pantaloons and wheels and predictably intimates that woman's broadening interests will destroy the domestic circle. Later, when simple quips become rife and the bicycle appears as a hobbyhorse for old jokes, the fad is accepted as an unthreatening commonplace. Certainly, the direct efforts for women's emancipation received

an unexpected boost from what is apparently only a recreational device.

The history of cycling as seen in cartoon and satire runs the
gamut from early machines that women could ride without
shocking Mrs. Grundy to vehicles predictive of widespread
changes. The tricycle velocipede was the version believed to
be most appropriate for women; one of the earliest was built
in the 1850s (Ritchie 45), but its weight—eighty-six pounds—
coupled with the weight of the ordinary walking costume must
have considerably hampered the rider. On the other hand,
comic illustrations featured both women in minidresses and
women riding bicycles shaped like men (in one political cartoon, the figures of Britain and France are astride the Prince
Regent and Napoleon, respectively). These are omens not only
of the change in fashion but of the very real fear that the liberated woman would become less chaste.

As the bicycle evolved, it became more and more unsuitable
for women. Aside from unstable steering and bone-shaking
rides caused by irregular wheels (frequently made of wood), the
very construction of the machine made riding dangerous for
anyone in petticoats. To improve speed, manufacturers produced ever-larger front wheels, where the pedals were attached;
if a woman could mount the "Ordinary," as it came to be called,
she would likely be tumbled head foremost as her long skirts
caught in the spokes. Not until the development of the "safety"
bicycle and pneumatic tire, and the revival of the tricycle and
its concomitant fad of "sociable" cycling, did the exercise become truly available to women, attracting those of the most
conservative persuasion. The lone sport of "Ordinary" riding
gave way to family expeditions and a new easy-going relationship between the sexes. *The Tricyclist*, the devotee's magazine,
praised the tricycle and tandem as the bachelor's best friends.
Even evangelists recommended "sociable" riding for health of
body and spirit (Ritchie 117-18), an idea that *Life* expands on
in a double-page spread entitled "For the Souls of Wheelers,"
showing a peripatetic church service, with parishioners and
choir on wheels and the minister riding backward on a tandem
(6 Feb. 1896: 98-99).

Cycling, then, allowed for a new kind of camaraderie and opened an inexpensive form of exercise to those who did not keep horses, either from choice or because of expense. Women who rode bicycles faced problems similar to those of their wealthier sisters, as the journalistic record suggests; discussion prevailed in both cases about appropriate riding costumes and the use of the sidesaddle. Indeed, the increasingly vocal complaints about dress by accomplished equestriennes suggest that in this case middle-class women who took to bloomers or modified skirts had vaulted over the economic barrier; they had gained the *éclat* and independence of riding without the expense and trouble of maintaining a stable.

The case for the sidesaddle, argued vehemently by antifeminists, surfaced in the discussion of whether—and how—women should cycle. Manufacturers did their best; the sidesaddle velocipede appeared in the 1870s (Ritchie 151). When the *New York Sun* made a serious suggestion—"With a proper teacher of their own sex, and with suitable dresses for the preliminary practice, ladies can obtain such a command over the velocipedes in one week's practice, of an hour daily, that they can ride side-saddle-wise with the utmost ease"—*Punch* spoofed the idea in a 15 May 1869 cartoon of a wasp-waisted lady perched uncomfortably to one side of a two-wheeler (205).

Obviously, the compromise proved impractical for cycling; for horseback riding, where sidesaddles were common and women's costumes made to accommodate the posture, the case was not so clear. Both theory and practice are given by C. Pelham Clinton and Margherita Arlina Hamm in New York *Truth*. Clinton, who comes up with the novel idea of a one-sided skirt ("Mounting and dismounting," he says, "could be performed in private") to reduce the bulk of the sidesaddle costume, is loath to give up the uncomfortable contrivance altogether. His arguments against rational riding dress are familiar, mirroring those against the general masculinity of fashion. He appeals to the innate physiological differences between men and women as a bar to the regular saddle: "Women who are by nature so formed as to have any control or grip of a horse when riding in the fashion of men are very rare." And he appeals not only to aesthetics as an argument against boots and breeches—"Variety is always charming, and it is this variety that the women in their riding habits give to the hunting field"—but also to the politics of sexual power: "It is probable that in some cases breeches and boots might give a woman increased control over her steed, but it would scarcely heighten her power and influence over men, for it is admitted that the latter are nearly always influenced a great deal by pretty petticoats worn by pretty women. . . . Imitation may be the sincerest form of flattery in many instances, but not in this, and the more the women try to imitate the dress of the men the less they are likely to be respected and admired by them" (6 Feb. 1892: 14).

Hamm, however, in "Her Private Opinion," inveighs against not only the riding habit and trousers and boots but also the sidesaddle:

To demonstrate that she is man's equal she dons his characteristic nether garments. . . . When fully equipped for the road she is very much like a warrior of old in his unwieldy armor, she can neither walk, run, jump, climb, dance, float or swim. She can't even get up into her perch without the ignominy of being "boosted." Nature indicates that the human being should emulate the domestic clothespin in sitting upon four-legged animals; but no clothes-pin for lovely woman! Either she, some fiendish man, or Satan in person, invented the side-saddle, which isn't a saddle, a chair, a seat, or anything except an instrument of the Spanish Inquisition. It is so constructed as to shrivel and ruin the muscles of one limb and stretch and mal-form those of the other.

She concludes wryly, "The only civilized women who ride well and sensibly in these days are the Sandwich Islanders, and it is not likely that their peculiar costume will become suddenly popular in our large cities" (16 Mar. 1895: 4).

In terms of recreation, and eventually of transportation, the answer for many women was the bicycle, but the question of which "peculiar costume" was appropriate remained. Certainly, the call for looser clothing necessitated by women's participation in active sports spurred dress reform overall. On the whole, though, British satirists took a dimmer view of the new riding costumes than the Americans did. Responses varied from, for instance, the series of wry biking tales that appeared in *Judy* ("An Extraordinary Elopement on a Double-Tricycle: A Briefless Barrister's Tale" was published on 21 July 1886) to drawings of tricyclists in frilly, short skirts on the cover of *Pick-Me-Up* (20 Sept. 1890). Convinced that trousered women were freakish, New York *Truth* published a monody to Amelia Bloomer:

"A Suggested Epitaph"

Here lies
(Quite safe at last from reckless rumors)
The erst well-known
and
Well-abused
Miss Bloomer
Living too long,
She saw her once bold coup
Rendered old-fashioned by the Woman New.

By noisy imitators vexed and piqued,
Her fads out-fadded
and
Her freaks out-freaked,
She did not die till she had seen and heard
All her absurdities made more absurd.

In short,
She found Dame Fortune but ill-humored,
And passed away
In every point out-Bloomered. [17 Jan. 1895]

The "freakishness" of rational dress was complemented by its practicality, but, as many writers pointed out, while it allowed freedom of movement and answered medical objections to tight lacing, it considerably altered the way in which men regarded women. Where once the glimpse of a well-turned ankle provided a pleasurable fillip, the glimpse of an entire leg was viewed either as immoral lure or as political warning that male power was being usurped. As *Punch* suggests, bloomers destroy the mystery of the female form:

"Rational Dress"
(A Reformer's Note to a Current Controversy.)

Oh, ungallant must be the man indeed
Who calls "nine women out of ten" "knock-kneed"!
And he should not remain in peace for long,
Who says "the nether limbs of women" are "all wrong."
Such are the arguments designed to prove
That Woman's ill-advised to make a move
To mannish clothes. These arguments are such
As to be of the kind that prove too much.
If Woman's limbs in truth unshapely grow,
The present style of dress just makes them so! [1 Sept. 1894: 101]

For the satirists, dress is important because of the frame of mind it reveals. By the end of the century, complaints were fading, although even then *Punch* presents a deliberately unflattering picture of cycling clothes. In "Fashion à la Shakspeare [*sic*]," a female "scorcher" illustrates the *Othello* line "I have a Suit wherein I mean to touch your Love indeed"; a young woman jauntily clad in checkered long coat, knee-length pants, and cap gives a come-hither look to a conservatively dressed beau in a monocle who, sucking his cane, eyes her askance (Fig. 15). *Punch*'s clever 1895 Valentine to a cyclist is a more veiled attack, phrased as it is in Chaucerian patois; the mock archaisms deploring "reckless scorchers," breeches and rational dress, and the death of chivalry imply that by 1895 so outspoken an objection against the modern woman need be discreetly clothed:

"A Valentyne"
(*And a Remonstrance.*)

This day to yow, dere ladye, wol I schowe
Myn hertes wissche—*cum privilegio.*
Of alle seintes nis ther more benigne
To man and mayden noon thanne Valentyne;
Sith everych yeer on that swete seintes day
Man can to mayden al his herte displaie
(Bye Cupid arwes smit in sory plighte—
One grote al pleyn and twayn ypeinted brighte).

Then wol I mak my playnte, so maist ye knowe
Yon whele, dere ladye, don me mochel wo.
Algates I greve, whanne that scorchours I mete
That riden reccheles adoun the strete:
I praie, bethynke yow, swiche diversioun
Ben weel for mayde of mene condicioun,
But lady fayre in brekes al ydighte
Certes meseems ne verray semelye sighte.
Swiche gere, yclept "raccionale," parde,
Righte sone wol be the dethe of chivalrye;
And we schal heren, whanne that it be dede,
The verdite, "Dethe by—Newe Womman-hede."
Heede then theffect and end of my prayere,
Upyeve thy whele, ne mannissche brekes were,
Contente in graces maydenlye to schyne,
So mote ye be myn owen Valentyne. [16 Feb. 1895: 81]

Unlike their British counterparts, who persistently objected to the change in life-style created by the bicycle, American humorists were more likely to co-opt the new style by treating it whimsically and by adopting the cycling argot as the basis for their jokes. Serious discussion proliferated as well. *Figaro* reprinted "Bicycling for Ladies" from the *Home Maker*, in which the writer gives instructions on "proper pedaling" and correct breathing, both of which, she maintains, are conducive to mental and physical well-being; yet, while recognizing the discomfort of skirts, she recommends instep-long riding costumes, for "skirtless freedom . . . is not to be had, at least in this generation, outside the opera-bouffe stage" (16 July 1891: 400). In 1895, however, the same year that *Punch* nostalgically called for a return to "graces maydenlye," *Scribner's* published an issue almost entirely devoted to bicycling for women, in which Marguerite Merington could say with some confidence that the variety of clothing worn for bicycling no longer attracted remark, whether it was the "uniform" of sailor hat and serge skirt, knickerbockers, bloomers, or a "cloth walking-dress [over] silk trousers" (Apr. 1885: 703).

While the *Scribner's* article is both serious and liberal, even a more lighthearted and conservative periodical like New York *Truth*, for example, agreed that rational dress was an established fact. Its mock history of the divided skirt suggested that the dress fad was hardly an innovation (Fig. 16). After showing the Bloomer Girl of '32 and '50, "Half a Century of Bloomers" continues:

The Bloomer Girl of '58 with righteous anger frowns,
To see Amelia Bloomer in her pair of hand-me-downs.
"Am I awake," she loudly cries, "or am I in a trance?
O is it true that 'gents' are not alone in wearing pants."

And then Amelia Bloomer hides behind her "umberell"
The day her startled optics see the modern Daisy Bell;
"Alas![''] she cries, "Put up your wheel, you really had'nt oughter
Until you've coaxed 'em down a bit, my brave, misguided daughter."

But Daisy Bell is not abashed and merely cries "For shame,
To criticise the bloomerloons that bear your honored name!
We're pushing on, and when at last we women get our rights
I'll be surprised if men object to see us ride in tights!"
        [13 Apr. 1895:12]

Unlike *Truth*, which appealed to the man-about-town, the American *Life* represented the middle-class reader with a variety of interests in art, music, drama, and politics; its audience was generally well read and *au courant*. Its mixed reaction, then, to the New Woman on wheels is a reasonably good barometer of public opinion in America. Initially, *Life* seems to agree with *Punch* that "mannish clothes" were beyond the pale; yet, at the same time, its cartoonists and quipsters provide the readers with a proliferation of one-line jokes and charming drawings that suggest more appreciation for the new style than disapproval. *Life*'s mildly schizophrenic reaction is, however, reasonably indicative of its readership's mixed state of mind, and so it is of special interest as a cultural reflector. It inveighs, for instance, against the "conspirators" Lady Henry Somerset and Miss Frances Willard, "whose heads are forever getting together over some plot for curtailing the privileges of men, or amplifying the dimensions of woman's sphere" and who organized, as *Life* dubs it, the "Women's Bicycle Trowsers Union." It is less the fashion than the threat of gender reversal

Fig. 15. "Fashion à la Shakspeare." *Punch*, 11 September 1897: 110

that bothers the writer, who reiterates some of *Punch*'s complaints:

It is a newly discovered fact that women who are entirely satisfied with skirts for ordinary uses, no sooner get upon bicycles than they begin to long for knickerbockers. . . .

Now, there is no sound objection to women riding bicycles in the most suitable costume that can be devised. . . . On the right sort of women knickerbockers are a joyous sight, and no wise person objects to them. There is just one disquieting thought about the adopting of them by women, which is that it should strike such promoters as Lady Henry and Miss Frances as a move of such importance. Why these ladies should yearn so earnestly to get trowsers on other women is a mystery, unless, as seems too probable, their ultimate purpose is to turn all womankind upside down, to which consummation trowsers would of course be indispensable. [23 Aug. 1884: 116]

In the final analysis, however, *Life* adopts the "bicycle girl" just as it does the "summer girl," whose swimming outfit is considerably more revealing than the bloomers that were fashionable for cycling (Fig. 17). *Life*'s approval transforms the "bicycle girl" into an acceptable icon of the American *fin de siècle* woman: "Be it recorded that a large proportion of the bicycle girls look exceedingly well in the bicycle clothes. Whether they wear stockings or leggings, whether they wear divided skirts . . . they adorn creation. . . . Not the least good thing that the bicycle has done has been to demonstrate publicly that women have legs. Their legs are unquestionably becoming to them. So are their shirt-waists. Long may they wave!" (17 June 1897: 512).

Aside from dress, learning to ride a bicycle also created controversy, partly because it precluded private training. Like the new day schools, then, lessons at specially equipped rinks expanded women's social sphere. Such lessons, however, exposed women to more than the "dangers" cited at day or boarding schools, for not only did different classes mix, but also different sexes. The trainers were male and provided a more direct physical contact than the ritualized and decorous movement that, for instance, instruction in ballroom dancing involved; indeed, the trainers had the onerous job of steering and supporting both

The Bloomer Girl of '32, who
wore athletic dress,
Beholds the 1850 girl and. cries
in deep distress:
"She's wearing pantaloons I see,
with brazen, shameless ease,
And mercy! how the horrid things
are bagging at the knees."

The Bloomer Girl of '50 then is greatly shocked to see
2 Her prototype of '58, and says "Oh! Can it be?
The horrid, horrid, horrid thing, to wear so bold a suit,
It's like a pair of pantaloons below a parachute!"

The Bloomer Girl of '58 with
righteous 'anger frowns,
To see Amelia Bloomer in her
pair of hand-me-downs.
"Am I awake," she loudly cries,
"or am I in a trance?
O is it true that 'gents' are not
alone in wearing pants."

And then Amelia Bloomer hides behind her "umberell'"
The day her startled optics see the
modern Daisy Bell,
"Alas! she cries, "Put up your wheel,
you really had'nt oughter
Until you've cussed 'em down a bit, my
brave, misguided daughter."

But Daisy Bell is not abashed and merely cries " For shame,
To criticise the bloomerloons that bear your honored name!
We're pushing on, and when at last we women get our rights
I'll be surprised if men object to see us ride in tights!"

Fig. 16. "Half a Century of Bloomers." New York *Truth*, 13 April
1895: 12.

rider and bicycle at the same time. While the cartoonists and versifiers found humor in the problems faced by novice and trainer, Lawrence Reamer's column on "Bicycling" in New York *Truth* gives a more serious and extended glimpse in photo, sketch, and word into the professional lessons the wobblers might undertake:

She was moving laboriously around the room, with an expression of ineffable self-consciousness on her face. She varied this look, occasionally, by a deprecatory simper that broadened into a smile when she reached the end of the room where her friend sat. . . . Three times around the rink she had rolled her one hundred and eighty pounds. She had gotten red in the face, very red. Her hair was coming down and her hat was badly listed to port. Perspiration was streaming down her cheeks. . . . The instructor pushed the bicycle, Mary's legs involuntarily responded to the revolution of the pedals while he held her up, and in this way the first lesson was a success. She had done all she could to send the bicycle over to one side or the other, and she clutched the handle-bars in a desperate grip; but the man managed to keep her upright. He did it bravely through the half-hour, pushing against her with all his force when the wheel started to fall toward him, and clinging to it, as desperately as a drowning man, when it fell to the other side. [26 Oct. 1895: 5-7]

As Reamer also notes, much transpires at the rink besides teaching: the more attractive the learner, the longer the lesson and the larger the tip. He suggests that exhibitionism motivates many neophytes to emulate the "scorcher," the publicity-hungry trickster who, racing around in checkered pants and jaunty cap (the 1890s version of the motorcyclist, perhaps), can gain an audience at the rink for fifty cents an hour.

Reamer makes another, less obvious point as well; his unstated assumption that any woman riding a bicycle does so for male attention indicates one of the hidden social pressures braved by the New Woman. As he writes, "The woman who has the courage of her convictions can put on a pair of bloomers and mount her wheel secure in the conviction that every man she passes will turn around and look at her." Many women undoubtedly felt ill at ease at the novel costumes and exercise, particularly when they had been reared to believe in the myth

Fig. 17. "The Voice of Modesty." *Life*, 29 August 1895: cover.

of their own fragility; to attribute their sometimes tentative desire to learn to ride to exhibitionism posed an unspoken threat to the feminist movement as a whole.

On the other hand, the humorists backhandedly helped the New Woman by making fun of her ungainliness. The idea that the new athleticism fostered gigantic women coupled with the very real physical problems of learning to ride a bicycle together helped to destroy the myth of the delicate, sickly woman that had for so long been a deterrent to endeavor. Periodicals ricocheted wildly between showing women as they really looked while wobbling on unmanageable wheels and creating a new myth of femininity: the elegant, streamlined woman decked out in a charming array of buttons and bows, demurely intent on her travels. The spate of cartoons of undersized men endeavoring to support their portly girlfriends and spouses on two-wheelers certainly is, in one sense, another facet of the complaint that women's liberation emasculated the male; but, for the most part, the cartoons really seem to suggest more about the women than the men. That it was a struggle is shown in such drawings as *Punch*'s "Things are not Always What They Seem," a sketch of an apparent mugging, which, as the caption says, "is not a cowardly attack upon an unprotected Lady Cyclist, but merely Tom giving his Heart's Idol her First Lesson" (15 Aug. 1896: 75). Again, in a back lot turned into a rink an exhausted instructor of jockey weight struggles to maintain Miss Heavytopp's balance on her first lesson and mutters, "I only hope it won't be my *last!*" (Fig. 18).

To show the average woman in unattractive postures was indeed a departure for most of the illustrators, for while the more rabid New Woman might be caricatured, her less political sisters were, at most, made fun of for vanity or ignorance. The latter kind of humor was perpetuated in a running joke about believing the bicycle to be alive. The invention cartoon, like that of the horse/bicycle, a "new patent spring-heeled 'bike' for the hunting field" that had retractable springed hoofs for leaping over barriers (*Punch* 12 Oct. 1895: 171), was less prevalent than the transference of equestrian habits to cycling. "The Force of Habit," a *Punch* cartoon in which Miss Diana and her beau are cycling down a country road, is typical. She exclaims:

Fig. 18. Miss Heavytopp's Bicycle Lesson. *Punch*, 13 September 1899: 129.

"Oh, Jack, I'm certain this Thing is going to shy at those horrid Pigs! Do you mind leading it past?" (3 Aug. 1895: 59).

Once the bloomer girl became a commonplace, another kind of joke illustrating women's ignorance about mechanical matters arose. At its extreme, the idea is given in *Punch's Almanack for 1897*, where a disheveled young woman is sprawled on the floor clutching her bicycle, while her "three bosom Friends (all experts— who have run round to see the Christmas gift)" ask in alarm what she is doing. She replies: "Oh—you see—it was awfully kind of the Pater to give it to me—but I have to look after it myself—and I knew I should *never have Breath enough to blow the Tyres out!*" On the other hand, cartoons like Du Maurier's "Division of Labor" prepared the public for the idea that women could take care of their own machinery. Du Maurier's drawing in *Punch* shows two young women equipped with rags, pail, and stained aprons, while the impeccably turned-out servants supervise: "It is not the business of Ducal Footmen to Clean the Family Bicycles. The Ladies Ermyntrude and Adelgitha have to do it themselves" (4 Jan. 1896: 6).

Just as the popular response to the bicycle changed the definition of femininity, removing from it the twin plagues of helplessness and physical infirmity, it also helped to redefine the relationship between the sexes. Perhaps one of the bicycle's most far-reaching effects was freedom from chaperons, one of the earliest requests of the "revolting daughters" who found the constant presence of a bored lady's maid both onerous and demeaning. The newfound freedom gave rise to such verses in *Life* as W.J. Lampton's "A Warning," in which Paulina argues that her cyclometer is an adequate chaperon:

Her mother frowned. "My dear," she said,
    "Last night I chanced to see
Your beau and you absorbed in talk
    Beneath a spreading tree."

"And as you talked, he whirled your wheel
    Until the figures showed
That you had traveled twenty miles
    Or more along the road."

L'Envoi
Oh maidens fair and lovers true,
If you would win your fight,
Don't play your cyclometric game
Unless you're out of sight. [20 Aug. 1898: 140]

Similar verses about elopement also appeared in *Life*, showing that the bicycle had become a standard fixture in the humorist's panoply. "Sportive Songs: A Coward Cyclist to his
Companion in Elopement," for instance, might almost be a
paradigm for the coming of the twentieth century; it ends when
the bicyclists are overtaken by a new form of transportation—
the motorcycle.

. . . Your father is a grave J.P.,
    And rules with iron sway;
Your uncle is a grim C.C.—
    They shall not stop our way!
They may not catch the fleetest pair
    That ever "bikes" bestrode.
I'd like to know the man who'd dare
    Dispute our right of road!

Ha! Ha! The wheels are whirling round!
    The goal's no longer far!
Ha! Ha! The end will soon be found!
    I laugh like *Lochinvar!*
What ho? A locomotor's sound!
    Your father's latest fad?
Together we must not be found.
    Farewell to you and dad!

    Too bad! 'Tis sad!
    Did you say "cad"?
Well, still I must to treadles trust.
    Farewell to you and dad! [7 Mar. 1896: 113]

On the other hand, the end of such "cyclometry" might be,
as *Life*'s E.F. Comins shows, "The Bicycler's Bride," clad in a
long veil that trails well behind her frilly bloomer outfit (22
Nov. 1894: 339). "A Brooklyn Tandem" (24 Dec. 1896: 516)

gives the next step: a wicker baby carriage suspended on the center bar of a bicycle built for two. A non-Brooklyn version appeared on the cover of the 8 October 1896 issue, in which a *grande dame* is seated regally on a filigreed ironwork coach chair labeled "magnus Americanus," her coach boy behind her; the whole contraption is propelled by two grooms on a four-wheeled tandem.

Once references to the bicycle begin to be standard in light verse, cartoons, and quips, it becomes clear that men and women have altered their perceptions of each other. The informality that developed was probably one of the most significant innovations, and while some commentators certainly implied that companionable cycling was simply an excuse for the old, old story of love and marriage, it was, as well, pursued for its own sake. It did, after all, touch many areas of a woman's life, providing both transportation and entertainment and encouraging exercise and good health. Importantly, it extended her sphere across the threshold, for in loosening her stays and dividing her skirts, the New Woman took possession of her own movements and achieved a measure of self-confidence that carried her into the twentieth century.

The commentary of *Punch*'s 'Arry, transformed into a cockney scorcher who takes the lisping Lil Johnson to Battersea Park to teach her how to cycle, provides a fitting summation of the humorous view of the New Woman and her effect on the social scene. What 'Arry sees at Battersea is high society on wheels. Indeed, as he writes to his friend, he is much taken by "them beauties on bikes":

One young piece in grey knicks and cream cloth, and a sort of soft
    tile called a *toke*,
Took my fancy perdigious, dear boy. I'd ha' blued arf-a-bull to 'ave
    spoke,
But a stiff-bristled swell in a dog-cart 'ad got a sharp eye upon 'er;
And *I* couldn't ha' done the perlite without raising a bit of a stir.

If I could ha' got rid o' LIL, I'd ha' mounted my wheel, and wired in,
Balloon-tyred smart safety, old man! *I*'d ha' showed Miss Grey Knicks
    'ow to spin.

One tasty young thing wos in tears, 'cos the bike she bespoke wosn't
    there.
I hoffered 'er mine, but the arnser I got wos a freeze-me-stiff stare.

In the face of such fashion, Lil grows shy about pedaling in her
cotton dress. 'Arry is angry, for he knows not only that he can
hold his own with the best but also that the lower classes are
more conventional than the "toffs." He sees, moreover, that
the New Woman will win the day:

"They borrow their barnies from *hus*, arterall, LIL. Toffs want a new
    lark,
So they straddle the bike *ah lah* Brixton, and tumble to Battersea Park.
'Divideds' and 'Knickers,' my dysy, are sniffed at out Hislington way,
But when countesses mount 'em at Chelsea, they're trotty and puffeck
    OK!"

World shifts it, old man, that's a moral! We'll soon 'ave some duchess,
    on wheels,
A-cuttin' all records, and showing young ZIMMY a clean pair of 'eels.
Hadvanced Women? Jimminy-Whizz! With the spars and the sails they
    now carry
They'll race us all round, pooty soon, and romp in heasy winners.
                                                            Yours,
[15 June 1895: 265]                                          'ARRY

Whether a woman would dare sit astride a bicycle or show
an expanse of stocking may seem trivial questions in modern
times; yet Victorian prudery was not the only motivating factor
in the seeming reluctance to move into the twentieth century.
All forms of exercise, whether supervised, like Swedish drill,
or unsupervised, like cycling, were forceable reminders that a
woman's body was her own to control. Emblematic of a tradition that defined femininity in terms of physical weakness
and moral strength, the average woman was called upon to
make few autonomous decisions. Moving within the relative
freedom of the gymnasium or playing field, or more indepen-
dently wheeling down the road, however, she was responsible
for her own health and well-being. That synchronous exercise
was performed under supervision undoubtedly made it attractive, for it could be understood as providing controlled activity,

a liberating design that the woman herself did not have to fabricate. The bicycle, however, was a different story, granting as it did not only recreation or exercise but transportation. As such, to ride a bicycle meant to change one's life-style in irrevocable fashion. Clothing was the most noticeable manifestation of change and one that the satirists seized upon immediately. Less obviously, perhaps, even the proposition that a woman should care for her own machine (and as all bicycle riders know, tire inflation and oiling can become personal manifestos) meant a radical reinterpretation of the division of labor. The woman who traveled on her own wheels, then, whether she did so for a lark or for serious transportation, expanded her boundaries well beyond the home circle. She became, as 'Arry predicted, a citizen of the world.

# CONCLUSION

# The New Woman

How can I further encourage you to go about the business of life? Young women, I would say, and please attend, for the peroration is beginning. . . . For my belief is that if we live another century or so— I am talking of the common life which is the real life and not of the little separate lives which we live as individuals—and have five hundred a year each of us and rooms of our own; if we have the habit of freedom and the courage to write exactly what we think; if we escape a little from the common sitting-room and see human beings not always in their relation to each other but in relation to reality; . . . if we face the fact, for it is a fact, that there is no arm to cling to, but that we go alone and that our relation is to the world of reality and not only to the world of men and women . . .

[Virginia Woolf, *A Room of One's Own*]

LONG BEFORE Queen Victoria died, she had ceased to represent the new, fresh hope of the nation that she had become when, as a girl of eighteen, she woke up one morning to find herself queen of England. Indeed, once she put on her mourning gown for Albert in 1861, she fixed herself forever in the imagination of the world as an emblem of a set of values that many came to consider hidebound. Yet there is no question that during her reign England and its sister country America grew in all ways—socially, industrially, intellectually—in an unprecedented manner. If the stout, ultimately bourgeois Victoria is taken as a model for one tendency of the age, then at the end of the century we see her opposite: shedding traditional clothing as she sheds traditional modes of thought and manners of living, the New Woman, who is both a product of the Victorian frame of mind and an antagonist to it.

That a woman, seen traditionally as being delicate and feminine and as having great moral power within her limited sphere, should end up not only defining the direction of a country but a frame of mind is one of the ironies of the century; even more so, that the same woman, so staunchly vocal about family values and woman's place, should be the cultural grandmother of the New Woman. Thomas Carlyle, glimpsing the young queen after her coronation, may be said to define the tension from which the *fin de siècle* woman comes. "Poor little Queen," he remarks: "she is at an age at which a girl can hardly be trusted to choose a bonnet for herself; yet a task is laid upon her from which an archangel might shrink" (quoted in Longford 83). If the nineteenth century is seen, as Walter Houghton maintains, to be one of transition and dialectic, then the New Woman is arguably the necessary manifestation of a century dominated by a queen who sought to coordinate leadership and domesticity in her own life. The progress of the New Woman, the woman who wanted a kingdom different from the home and a sphere of power broader than the domestic, the woman who asked for equality of education, jobs, and personal habits, is in its essence a truly Victorian phenomenon, forged as it is out of the tension between male and female, submissiveness and power, and domestic and public fronts.

The figure that is presented to public view by the periodicals is, as all caricature and satire are, an exaggeration. In her everyday garb, the New Woman is neither the "scorcher" nor the "screaming sister," neither the clubwoman in monocle and spats nor the "varmity woman"; rather, she is the soberly dressed woman who seeks to make the most of her intellectual capabilities, to receive adequate training so that she may contribute actively to society and, in return, maintain her life in independence. What the comic periodicals show, however, in linecut and verse, is the embodiment of multifold fears about change itself. Much of the pressure that was exerted upon the so-called superfluous woman to find a means of supporting herself without violating her traditional role characterized by submissiveness and by moral, rather than intellectual, suasion was transferred to the social sphere as women, out of a combination of necessity and choice, carved out a wider niche. The result was that more traditional demands for, say, husband, children, home, and clothing became transformed into demands for education and employment, and woman was seen as "New," a hitherto unmeasured force.

The caricatures and satires that appeared, then, exaggerated as they might be, tried to represent the unthinkable, the phenomenon that had not yet appeared; and in so doing, the illustrators and writers chose to invert the characteristics by which women were superficially identified. If women were no longer *acting* like women, then they must be their opposites; hence, many of the attributes given to them were male. They are shown smoking cigarettes, setting up their own "old girl network," and becoming brusque, muscular, and independent; they are lambasted for demanding the keys to their own front doors, engaging in social and political action, and mastering analytical subjects. The list is endless, as are the fears. Men are warned that they will have to darn their own socks, diaper the baby, and scrub the floors; they are depicted by the illustrators and satirists as smaller, more timid, and less aggressive.

Intellectually speaking, this kind of inversion has its own kind of satiric logic; emotionally, however, it taps a deep fear of gender transference. To judge by the immediate reaction of the comic press, many of the changes must have been morally and aesthetically unpleasant to the average reader schooled in the traditions of his parents. The long skirts and frilly accessories pared down into "rational dress" changed women's silhouettes and quietly suggested that by mimicking men's tailoring women might mimic competitiveness as well. Liberation from restrictive dress, from laces that interfered with breathing, and from hoops that needed managing suggested liberation of another sort. The newfound freedom to breathe and walk encouraged movement out of the house; exercise became the rage. For the average reader, then, women were no longer fixed in a definable locus but were as liable to be out on the playing field or in the office as they were in the home. Less concerned with dress or with social graces, the New Woman perhaps seemed more serious, more concerned with the business of life. What the comic periodicals threatened, then, was that the New Woman, in expanding her field of interest, would irrevocably change the relationship between the sexes.

Certainly, she did change that relationship, as men and women began to study, work, and exercise side by side. With the loss of the "mystique" came a new sense of camaraderie that persists to the present day. Whether these changes were attacked or welcomed by those editors who both mirrored and redefined the preconceptions of their readers depended largely on the social climate. In America, the popular press displayed the insouciance of a new republic determined to set its own standards and create its own mythology. *Life*, especially, turned its lampoons of dress and behavior into a series of charming drawings that immortalized the New Woman, whose grace outshone her garments and whose air of independence expressed the democracy she was born into. An American woman was presumed to be safe wherever she went, preserved not only by the natural chivalry of her male counterpart, but by her own innate virtue; hence, to picture her actively engaged in the world was a commonplace. The attitude, however, was not always proud recognition and support for change; frequently, it took the form of patronizing acceptance. The readjustment caused by woman's egalitarian drive for education and career was, for instance, often taken to be another manifestation of feminine whim, and her presence in the classroom and office was considered to be an attempt at marital head-hunting. Nonetheless, she is sometimes used as a vehicle for reformist diatribes against a variety of problems, among them the inadequacy of women's education, marriage settlements and property rights, medical problems entailed by fashionable lacing, and factory abuses.

In Britain the comic record shows a somewhat less permissive society, one that, while changing, is still very aware of the status quo. The Victorians displayed a thoroughgoing social sense; and although the wealthy were often attacked, as they are today, for ignoring the plight of the poor, nonetheless major social critics like Mill and Carlyle and novelists like Dickens and Thackeray were quick to point out the interdependence of all classes. Such integral connection depended to a great degree upon the class system, which itself was under attack. Given the ferment, the possibility that the one thing that seemed stable—a man's home and family—should change in structure was unsettling. The reaction of the British press mirrors, then, a greater paranoia about the adverse effects of women's emancipation than the American press. The verse was more bitter, and even the cartoons in *Punch*, for instance, which for many years refused on principle to show a woman in an unattractive pose, were harsher. Coupled with the attack on the New Woman, however, was a strong social awareness of abuses. The shop girl's and the prostitute's condition, the paucity of education, the annoying and unhealthful aspects of fashion: all of these found their way into comic commentary. The double mind-set that blames the universities for excluding qualified women but condemns women who wished to be educated and that congratulates female academic achievement but is dismayed by the career woman is perhaps indicative of the chaotic responses not only of the women themselves but of the readership as a whole.

If British and American cartoonists and writers had one attitude in common, however, it was that immoderation characterized the movement as a whole. The New Woman as a figure who had simply followed a new dress fad was ultimately acceptable, because her frivolity was expected. The New Woman whose dress indicated a real change in life-style was considerably more threatening, not only because once she shifted her place in society everyone else had to make accommodation, but because she held the physiological key to the next generation. Her choices affected not only herself and her immediate relations but also the shape of the coming era. The New Woman who stridently proclaimed her differences was, in the final analysis, the figure that all of the periodicals attacked most heartily. And when they did so they fell into proclaiming the virtues of the quiet, "feminine" woman.

In a very real sense, then, Queen Victoria was responsible for the New Woman. In her own role as ruler and wife, she embodied the tensions of the age and, despite her public avowal of family values, was considerably more modern than many of her nineteenth-century sisters in terms of undertaking work and family at once. After Prince Albert's death, however, she seemed to abrogate that role, becoming instead an emblem of a pattern of thought that seemed outworn. A static figure, she remains in the center of the age in her black dress, unmoved through all of the social, intellectual, and political ferment that surrounded her. Her choice to stop, as it were, was an inadequate solution to the dialectic; other women, if they were to survive, could not make the same choice. Hence, the distance between the wide black skirts and widow's cap of Queen Victoria and the New Woman, no longer an angel in the home but rather an angel in tights and gaiters wielding a latchkey, is not that surprising.

The paradox—that a woman who stood for family values should for part of her life be considerably more than a figurehead monarch—was one that perhaps Victoria never came to terms with. Seen in this way, her life, an avowal of both traditional family relationships and monarchical strength, seems to foster the kind of emasculation with which magazine writers charged the New Woman. Her stubbornness in dealing with affairs of state, her persistence in a mode of dress seen to be distinctly unfashionable and politically unwise, her interest in the political affairs of other nations, inextricably tied to the family intermarriages that she so carefully supervised: much of this mixture can be traced in her cultural granddaughter, the New Woman.

# WORKS CITED

Arling, Nat. "What Is the Role of the 'New Woman'?" *Westminster Review*, Nov. 1898: 576-87.

Atkinson, Paul. "Fitness, Feminism and Schooling." In Delamont and Duffin, *Nineteenth-Century Woman*, 92-133.

Auerbach, Nina. *Woman and the Demon: The Life of a Victorian Myth*. Cambridge: Harvard Univ. Press, 1982.

Besant, Walter. "The Endowment of the Daughter." *Longman's*, Apr. 1888: 604-15.

Boswell, John. "Badly Treated by All Her Sons." Review of *Eve: History of an Idea*, by John A. Phillips. *New York Times Book Review*, 15 July 1984: 7, 9.

Browne, Junius Henri. "Are Women Companionable to Men?" *Cosmopolitan*, Feb. 1888: 450-55.

Caird, Mona. "A Defence of the So-Called 'Wild Women.' " *Nineteenth Century*, May 1892: 811-29.

Chant, Mrs. Ormiston. "Woman as Athlete: A Reply to Dr. Arabella Kenealy." *Living Age* 3 (1899): 799-806.

Crackanthorpe, B.A. "The Revolt of the Daughters: I. A Last Word on 'The Revolt.' " *Nineteenth Century*, Mar. 1894: 424-29.

Crandall, C.H. "What Men Think of Women's Dress." *North American Review*, Aug. 1895: 251-53.

Crow, Duncan. *The Victorian Woman*. New York: Stein and Day, 1971.

Cuffe, Kathleen. "A Reply from the Daughters." *Nineteenth Century*, Mar. 1894: 437-42.

Dare, Shirley. "Brighter Hope for Women." *Cosmopolitan*, Nov. 1887: 195-99.

Delamont, Sara, and Lorna Duffin, eds. *The Nineteenth-Century Woman: Her Cultural and Physical World*. London: Croom Helm, 1978.

Dodge, Grace H. "What Country Girls Can Do." *Lippincott's*, 47 (1891): 631-38.

Douglas, Emily. *Remember the Ladies: The Story of Great Women Who Helped America*. New York: Putnam, 1966.

"Dress Reform at the Chicago Exposition." *Review of Reviews*, Apr. 1893: 312-16.

Duffin, Lorna. "The Conspicuous Consumptive: Woman as Invalid." In Delamont and Duffin, *Nineteenth-Century Woman*, 26-55.

Dumont, Frank. *The New Woman's Husband*. Philadelphia: Penn, 1912.

Enebuske, Claës J. "Gymnastic Training of Women." *American Statistical Association* 3 (1893): 600-610.

Gibbs-Smith, Charles. *The Fashionable Lady in the Nineteenth Century*. London: Her Majesty's Stationery Office, 1960.

Gilbert, W.S., and Arthur Sullivan. *The Annotated Gilbert and Sullivan*. Ed. Ian Bradley. 2 vols. New York: Penguin, 1984.

Girvin, Ernest A. *Domestic Duels: Evening Talks on the Woman Question*. San Francisco: Bronson, 1898.

Gordon, Julien. "Healthy Heroines." *Lippincott's* 48 (1891): 466-68.

Gorham, Deborah. *The Victorian Girl and the Feminine Ideal*. Bloomington: Indiana Univ. Press, 1982.

Grundy, Sydney. *The New Woman: An Original Comedy, in Four Acts*. London: Chiswick Press, 1894.

Hall, E.B. "Novissima." *Cornhill* 70 (1894): 365-68.

Hammerton, A. James. "Feminism and Female Emigration, 1861-1886." In Vicinus, *Widening Sphere*, 52-71.

Haweis, M.E. "The Revolt of the Daughters: II. Daughters and Mothers." *Nineteenth Century*, Mar. 1894: 430-36.

Hawthorne, Nathaniel. *The Marble Faun: Or, the Romance of Monte Beni*. Vol. 4 of Centenary Edition of the Works of Nathaniel Hawthorne. Ed. Roy Harvey Pearce et al. Columbus: Ohio State Univ. Press, 1968.

Hellerstein, Erna Olafson, Leslie Parker Hume, and Karen M. Offen, eds. *Victorian Women: A Documentary Account of Women's Lives in Nineteenth-Century England, France, and the United States*. Stanford: Stanford Univ. Press, 1981.

Helsinger, Elizabeth K., Robin Lauterbach Sheets, and William Veeder. *The Woman Question: Defining Voices, 1837-1883*. 3 vols. New York: Garland, 1983.

Holcombe, Lee. *Victorian Ladies at Work: Middle-Class Working Women in England and Wales, 1850-1914*. Newton Abbot: David & Charles, 1973.

Hollis, Patricia. *Women in Public, 1850-1900: Documents of the Victorian Women's Movement*. London: Allen & Unwin, 1979.

Houghton, Walter. *The Victorian Frame of Mind, 1830-1870*. New Haven: Yale Univ. Press, 1957.

"How to Court the 'Advanced Woman.'" *Idler*, Sept. 1894: 192-211.

Hughes, Molly V. *A Victorian Family*. 3 vols. 1946; rpt. Oxford: Oxford Univ. Press, 1980.

Johansson, Sheila Ryan. "Sex and Death in Victorian England: An Examination of Age- and Sex-Specific Death Rates, 1840-1910." In Vicinus, *Widening Sphere*, 163-81.

Jordan, Ellen. "The Christening of the New Woman: May 1894." *Victorian Newsletter*, no. 63 (1983): 19-21.

Kaplan, Fred. *Sacred Tears: Sentimentality in Victorian Literature*. Princeton: Princeton Univ. Press, 1987.

Kenealy, Arabella. "Woman as an Athlete." *Living Age* 3 (1899): 363-70.

———. "Woman as Athlete: A Rejoinder." *Living Age* 4 (1899): 201-13.

Kraditor, Aileen S. *Up from the Pedestal: Selected Writings in the History of Feminism*. Baton Rouge: Louisiana State Univ. Press, 1981.

Linton, E. Lynn. "The Partisans of the Wild Women." *Nineteenth Century*, Mar. 1892: 455-64.

———. "The Wild Women as Social Insurgents." *Nineteenth Century*, Oct. 1891: 596-605.

"Live Questions: Is Marriage a Failure?" *Cosmopolitan*, Nov. 1888-Apr. 1889: 196-203.

Longford, Elizabeth. *Queen Victoria: Born to Succeed*. New York: Harper, 1964.

McWilliams-Tullberg, Rita. "Women and Degrees at Cambridge University, 1862-1897." In Vicinus, *Widening Sphere*, 117-45.

"Manly Women." *Saturday Review*, 22 June 1889: 756-57.

Merington, Marguerite. "Woman and the Bicycle." *Scribner's*, Apr. 1895: 702-4.

Mitchell, Sally. *Dinah Mulock Craik*. Boston: Twayne, 1983.

"Modern Mannish Maidens." *Blackwood's*, Feb. 1890: 252-64.

Morten, Honnor. *Questions for Women (and Men)*. London: Black, 1899.

Mott, Frank Luther. *A History of American Magazines*. 5 vols. Cambridge: Harvard Univ. Press, 1957.

Palmer, Mrs. Potter. "The Board of Lady Managers: Its Aims, Objects and Achievements Thus Far." *Figaro*, 12 Mar. 1892: 24-25.

Parrish, C.S. "Womanly Women." *Independent*, 4 Apr. 1901: 775-78.

Peck, Harry Thurston. "For Maids and Mothers: The Woman of To-Day and of To-Morrow." *Cosmopolitan*, June 1899: 149-62.

Peterson, M. Jeanne. "The Victorian Governess: Status Incongruence in Family and Society." In Vicinus, *Suffer and Be Still*, 3-19.

Prager, Arthur. *The Mahogany Tree: An Informal History of "Punch."* New York: Hawthorne Books, 1975.

Reamer, Lawrence. "Bicycling." New York *Truth*, 26 Oct. 1895: 5-7.

Rhine, Alice Hyneman. "Work of Women's Clubs." *Forum*, Sept. 1891- Feb. 1892: 519-28.

Ritchie, Andrew. *King of the Road: An Illustrated History of Cycling.* London: Wildwood, 1975.

Romanes, G.J. "Mental Differences of Women and Men." *Popular Science Monthly*, Aug. 1887: 383-401.

Roosevelt, J. West. "A Doctor's View of Bicycling." *Scribner's*, Apr. 1895: 708-13.

Rugg, George. *The New Woman: A Farcical Sketch, with One Act, One Scene, and One Purpose.* Boston: Baker, 1896.

Sanks, Samuel Q. *Descriptive History of Woman.* Baltimore: J. Young, 1880.

Sargent, D.A. "Physical Development of Women." *Scribner's*, Feb. 1889: 172-85.

Shaw, Albert. "A Model Working-Girls' Club." *Scribner's*, Jan.–June 1892: 169-77.

Shaw, George Bernard. *Man and Superman. Complete Plays with Prefaces.* 6 vols. New York: Dodd, Mead, 1963. 3: 483-743.

Sigsworth, E.M., and T.J. Wyke. "A Study of Victorian Prostitution and Venereal Disease." In Vicinus, *Suffer and Be Still*, 77-99.

Simcox, Edith. "The Capacity of Women." *Nineteenth Century*, Sept. 1887: 391-402.

Smith, Alys W. Pearsall. "A Reply from the Daughters." *Nineteenth Century*, Mar. 1894: 443-50.

Sothern, Winifred. "The Truth About the Bachelor Girl." *Munsey's Magazine*, May 1901: 282-83.

Spielmann, M.H. *The History of* Punch. 1895; rpt. New York: Greenwood Press, 1969.

Stewart, Edna Seass. "Some Ancient New Women." *Arena*, Nov. 1901: 513-18.

Tennyson, Arthur. "The Princess." *Poems*. Ed. Jerome Hamilton Buckley. Boston: Houghton Mifflin, 1958.

Thorne, Rose. "The War of the Sexes." *Idler*, Sept. 1900: 24-32.

*Too Many Women. And What Comes of It. By One of 'Em.* New York: Clark & Zugalla, 1888.

Unite, Pleasaunce. "Disillusioned Daughters." *Fortnightly Review*, July 1900: 850-58.

Vicinus, Martha. *Independent Women: Work & Community for Single Women, 1850-1920.* Chicago: Univ. of Chicago Press, 1985.

———, ed. *Suffer and Be Still: Women in the Victorian Age.* Bloomington: Indiana Univ. Press, 1973.

———, ed. *A Widening Sphere: Changing Roles of Victorian Women.* Bloomington: Indiana Univ. Press, 1980.

"V.W., The." *Saturday Review*, 15 Aug. 1891: 192-93.

Winchester, Boyd. "The Eternal Feminine: I. The New Woman." *Arena*, Apr. 1902: 367-73.

"Women: How Shall They Dress?" *North American Review*, Jan. 1885: 557-71.

Woolf, Virginia. *A Room of One's Own.* New York: Harcourt, 1929.

Wordsworth, William. "She Was a Phantom of Delight." *William Wordsworth: The Poems.* Ed. John O. Hayden. Vol. 1. New Haven: Yale Univ. Press, 1977.

Wormwood, Edyth M. *The New Woman in Mother Goose Land.* Franklin and Denver: Eldridge, n.d.

# INDEX

Abbott, Angus Evan, 37
abortion, 60
Adams, Abigail, 6
Adams, John, 6
advanced women, 5, 14, 15, 37, 121, 122
aerobics. *See* calisthenics
Alcott, Louisa May, 119
Alford, Margaret, 110
Amazonian women, 174, 180, 181, 182, 183
American magazines, attitudes of, 2, 18, 22, 45, 116, 207, 208
*Angel in the House* (Patmore), 4
annuities, deferred, 31-32
Anthony, Susan B., 62-63, 130
Antioch College, 91
antitobacconists, 136-38. *See also* smoking
*Arena*, 6
Aristophanes, 135
Arling, Nat, 6-7, 87
'Arriet, 157-58
'Arry, 24, 34, 51, 52-54, 90, 143-45, 157, 201-2
Aspasia, 108-9, 112
Association for the Advancement of Women, 119
athletics. *See* sports
Attwood, Francis, 22
Auerbach, Nina, 10, 62
Austin, Alfred, 113
Australia, emigration to, 29, 30
authors, women as, 80-84

bachelor girl, 89
banging, of the hair, 156-57, 159
Bangs, John Kendrick, 21, 161
barbers, women as, 87
bathing beauties, 19
bathing costumes, 193
Beardsley, Aubrey, 37, 169
Beecher, Catherine, 91
Beecher, Henry Ward, 98

Belesco, Mlle., 111
Bell, James, 48, 51
Bergman-Osterberg, Madame, 182-83
Besant, Walter, 31
bicycle girl, 193
bicycles, 2, 22, 125, 134, 142, 172, 185. *See also* cycling
Blackwell, Elizabeth, 72
Blackwell, Emily, 73
*Blackwood's*, 177
Blake, Sophia Jex, 74
Bloomer, Amelia, 148, 188, 191
bloomer girls, 6, 191, 199
bloomers, 2, 20, 21, 22, 23, 87, 88, 127, 148, 149, 160, 163, 181, 188-89, 190, 195. *See also* clothing
bluestockings, 20, 22, 37, 80, 81, 98, 100, 170
Board of Lady Managers of the World's Columbian Commission, 121
bobbing, of the hair, 156
Bodichon, Barbara, 28, 59
boots, 148, 154, 159, 172, 186-87
Boyd, A.S., 95
Braddon, Mary Elizabeth, 83
Brainard, Harriet C., 99
brain capacity, and intellect, 103
breeches, 186-87, 189
British magazines, attitudes of, 2, 18, 22, 116, 207-8
*British Medical Journal*, 47
Brontë, Charlotte, 57
Brontë, Emily, 57
Brown, Antoinette, 77
Browne, Sir James Crichton, 12
Browning, Robert, 112
Bryn Mawr College, 91
Buchanan, Robert, 143, 144, 169
*Buffalo Democracy*, 76
Buss, Frances Mary, 56-57, 59, 100, 183
bustles, 150, 172
Byron, George Gordon (Lord), 138

Caird, Mona, 8-9, 43, 51
calisthenics, 182-83
Cambridge University, 92, 104, 109, 113
Canada, emigration to, 28
careers, for women, 2, 24, 59, 70, 74, 88, 120. *See also* work, for women
Carlyle, Thomas, 205, 207
Carr, Comyns, 153
*Century* dictionary, 4, 9
Chant, Mrs. L. Ormiston, 175, 176, 182
charity, 66-67
charwomen, 58-59
*Chic* (New York): on clothing for women, 161; on hairstyles, 156; opposition to New Woman in, 21-22; opposition to women as theologians, 79
Chicago Woman's Club, 130
childbearing, as correct role for women, 6, 8, 15, 41, 43, 56, 80, 90, 174, 175, 181-82. *See also* fertility
chivalry, death of, 142, 143-45, 189
*Chronicle*, 58
cigarettes. *See* smoking
cigars. *See* smoking
class. *See* social distinctions
Cleaves, Reginald, 95
clerks, women as, 120, 121
Clinton, C. Pelham, 186
clothing: and covert changes in women, 35; mannish, 15, 16, 19, 121, 131, 147, 161, 170, 187, 191, 206; and modesty, 149, 188; "rational," 2, 127, 146, 147, 148, 150, 159, 160, 161, 163, 165, 172, 188, 189, 190-91, 206; as symbolic of changes in women's roles, 95, 142, 146, 147, 148, 160, 172-73; for success, 130, 148; women's control over, 171-72. *See also* bloomers; cycling: clothing for
clubs, for women: and independence for women, 117; philanthropy by, 118-19; power of, 117, 118, 119-20; professionalism in, 120-21, 122; proliferation of, 117-18; smoking in, 124, 135
Cobb, Frances Power, 97, 98
Coe, Emma R., 75
Columbia University, 119

Comins, E.F., 200
Comstock, Anthony, 20
Contagious Diseases Act of 1864 (British), 62-63
Contagious Diseases Act of 1867 (American), 62-63
*Contemporary Review*, 112
Corelli, Marie, 83
*Cornhill*, 5-6
corsets, 142, 147, 148, 172, 175, 179
cosmetics, 151, 179
*Cosmopolitan*, 51
courtship: and cycling, 188, 193, 199-201; difficulties of, 32-33; new modes for, 34, 35, 37, 38-41
"cow-women" (household drudges), 11
Cox, Harriet Caryl, 105
Crackanthorpe, B.A., 9
crinolines, 148, 149, 150
Cuffe, Kathleen, 9
cycling: clothing for, 163, 186, 187-93, 203; and exhibitionism, 195-97; and independence, 174, 184-85, 186; lessons and training for, 193-95, 197, 201; and modesty, 185, 186-87, 193, 202; as symbolic of independence for women, 174, 175, 184, 202-3. *See also* bicycles

*Daily News*, 69
*Daily Telegraph*, 51-52, 143
Dall, Caroline, 62
Dalziel, Davison, 19
Darwin, Charles, 103
Darwinian man, 122
David, Jacques-Louis, 82
Davies, Emily, 109-10
Dickens, Charles, 56, 60, 68, 70, 74, 207
disease, 26, 47-48, 62, 65. *See also* health; marriage: "hygienic"
divided skirts, 147, 150, 160, 174, 191, 193
divorce, 3, 47, 51, 130
doctors. *See* physicians
*Domestic Duels: Evening Talks on the Woman Question* (1898), 41, 42-43
domesticity, of women, 2, 7, 10, 11, 14, 16, 17, 41-44, 55, 77, 80, 92,

99, 100, 117, 124, 127, 129, 130-31, 135, 184

domestic science, 42-43

domestic servants: and marriage, 32; reduction in numbers of, 159; as suitable employment for women, 28

*dot*, 31-32

dowries, 121

drawers, 148, 149

dress. *See* clothing

dressmakers. *See* seamstresses

drinking, by women, 127, 135, 178

Du Maurier, George, 22, 98, 199

Dumont, Frank, 174

Dunn, Mary Chevalita, 37

education, for men/boys, 90, 91, 92

education, for women/girls: in America, 91, 95, 104, 108; curriculum for, 96-98, 99-100, 102, 120, 182; demanded by New Woman, 2, 6, 7, 9, 10, 15, 19, 22; and demise of romance, 40-41, 98-99; in England, 91-92, 95, 99, 104, 108; expense of, 90, 97; and granting of degrees, 112-13; and preparation for independence, 55-57, 59, 85, 89, 91, 93-95, 97-98, 116, 146, 170-71; proper (womanly), 7, 55-56; and sapping of womanliness, 12, 90, 98-99, 100, 102, 176; and sexual misconduct, 109-10. *See also* intellect, of women

Egerton, George (pseud. Mary Chevalita Dunn), 37

Eliot, George, 56, 80

elopement, 188, 200

Emerson, Lydia Jackson (Mrs. Ralph Waldo Emerson), 119

emigration, 22, 28-31

Enebuske, Claës, 183

*English Woman's Journal*, 28

equal pay, 130. *See also* work, for women: and salaries

eugenics, 26-27, 28

Eve, 9

evolution: feminists and, 123; and gender differentiation, 8, 103, 122, 174; as responsibility of women, 116, 184, 208; and selection of

most fit women as mothers, 26-27, 175-76

exercise. *See* calisthetics; cycling; sports

factory work, by women, 26, 58, 60, 62, 67, 88

family size, limits on, 9

fashions. *See* clothing

Fawcett, P.G., 110

feather boas, 154

Federation of Women's Clubs, 118, 119, 130

female, definition of, 4-5, 92. *See also* womanliness

feminism, 2, 10, 21, 26, 28, 38, 42, 43, 56, 79, 88, 93, 106, 123, 124, 128, 169, 175, 178

fertility, 26. *See also* childbearing

fidelity, 14

*Figaro* (Chicago): and athletic women, 180; on cycling, 190; and education for women, 99; and women as writers, 81; and women's clubs, 121, 128, 130

finishing schools, 90, 91, 92, 95, 97-98, 115

footwear, 148. *See also* boots

Furniss, Harry, 60, 109

Gaiety girl, 61, 63

Gainsborough hats, 151

Garrett, Elizabeth, 74

gender roles: and evolution, 8; and new type, 3; reversal (transference) of, 2-3, 13, 38-40, 85, 98, 116, 117, 121, 124, 128-29, 130, 131-33, 162-63, 176-77, 178-79, 180-81, 191, 206. *See also* clothing: mannish

Gibbs-Smith, Charles, 150

Gibson, Charles Dana, 79, 87, 105, 127

Gilbert, William Schwenck, 80, 90, 122, 123, 167

Girton College, 104, 109, 110

governesses, 24, 57, 61, 67-70, 88, 90, 91-92

Governesses' Benevolent Association, 68

Grand, Sarah, 10-11, 37

Greg, W.R., 31, 59

Grundy, Sydney, 3

hair: cutting of, 3, 156-57, 158, 159; styles of, 150, 151, 156-58
Hall, Blakely, 19
Hall, E.B., 5-6
Hall, Ruth, 19
Hambridge, Jay, 40
Hamm, Margherita Arlina, 186, 187
Hammond, William, 159
Harberton, Lady, 160
Harvard College, 91
hats, 151-53, 159
Haweis, M.E., 9
Hawthorne, Nathaniel, 80
health, of women, 26, 27-28, 47-48; and athletics, 174, 175-76, 179, 180, 185, 190, 197, 199, 206; and clothing, 148, 149, 206, 207, 208. See also disease
Hemans, Felicia, 83
Hemingway, Clara, 81
Henry, O., 63
Herbert, Sir Sidney, 29
Hichens, Robert, 169
Hill, Raven, 88
Hogg, Mrs. Quentin, 120
Holcombe, Lee, 67
home and hearth. See domesticity
Home Maker, 190
Hood, Thomas, 58
Hope, Anthony, 83
Hopkins, Evard, 44, 81
Houghton, Walter, 205
housework, 45, 55-56. See also domesticity
Howe, Julia Ward, 119
Hughes, Molly, 10, 33, 57, 100
hunting: as unwomanly, 8; by women, 163
hysteria, 10, 65

Ibsen, Henrik, 12, 44, 50, 100, 101
Idler, 15-16, 37, 143
independence, for women, 8, 9, 28, 34, 35, 55, 56-57, 67-68, 89, 91, 104, 116, 117, 124-25, 142, 146, 173, 199, 201
Independent Women (Vicinus), 71
intellect, of women, 2, 7, 12, 15, 16, 38, 43, 45, 49, 90, 95, 97, 100, 102-4, 105-6, 128, 146, 155, 175, 183, 197-99. See also education, for women

International Council of Women, 119
Irving, Washington, 138

Jackson, Kate, 159
James, Alice, 22
Jerome, Jerome K., 15
Jerrold, Douglas, 83
Jordan, Ellen, 10
journalism, women in, 67, 84-87
Judge, 20, 116
Judy, 103, 138, 151, 160, 188

Kaplan, Fred, 66
Keene, Charles, 109
Kendall, Henry, 157
Kenealy, Arabella, 175-76, 182
King, E.M., 160
King's Daughters, 119
Kipling, Rudyard, 83

ladies, 2, 4-5, 8, 14, 59, 69, 85, 92-93, 104, 116, 179, 180
Lady's Own Paper, 74
Lampton, W.J., 199
Lancet, 148, 149
latchkeys, for women, 117, 122, 125, 132, 142, 170, 206, 209
lawyers, women as, 74-76, 105, 131
Leonard, P., 162
Life, 2, 166, 191; advanced woman lampooned in, 121-22, 123, 207; on age of New Woman concept, 6; on clothing for women, 151, 161-62, 191; on cycling, 185, 191-93, 199-201; on education for women, 95, 98-99, 105-8, 109, 116, 171; on gender transference, 121-22, 127; opposition to New Woman in, 20-21; women as manipulators in, 38; on women in military service, 87; on women theologians, 79; on women writers, 84-85; on working women, 88
Lilith, 9
Linton, Eliza Lynn, 7-8, 17, 37, 141, 143, 144, 170
Lippincott, 118
Lockwood, Belva, 51
London Girl of the 1880's, A (Hughes), 10

*London Home of the 1890's, A* (Hughes), 100
London University, 108
Lorne, Lord, 28
Lowell, Massachusetts, employment in factories at, 60
Luks, George B., 3
*Lysistrata* (Aristophanes), 135

male superiority: based on economics, 38; based on physical strength, 3-4, 6, 73
*Man and Superman* (Shaw), 27, 56
manipulation, by women, 10, 38, 39, 44, 129, 135
manliness, definition of, 4, 6-7, 92. *See also* manly men
manly men, 7. *see also* manliness
manly women, 2-3, 9, 127, 135, 147, 177-78. *See also* clothing, mannish
marriage: age at, 51; ambiguity of advantages in, 50-54; desirability of, 32, 60, 80, 90, 105; discord in, 41-42; expense of, 33-34, 54; failure of, 24, 50-53; "hygienic," 27, 47-48; and natural selection, 26-27; timing of, 9; withheld from manly women, 3, 6; withheld from redundant women, 24, 26, 28, 29-31; women's responsibilities within, 35, 55-56. *See also* courtship; elopement; weddings
Married Woman's Property Act of 1882, 48-49, 50
matches, women's use of, 161
maternity leave, 60
Mayhew, Henry, 62
Maynard, Constance, 100
Mays, Phil, 5
men: numbers of, 26; subjugated by women, 125-27; as women's reason for being, 123. *See also* gender roles; male superiority; manliness
Mendel's law, 104
Meredith, George, 20, 163
Merington, Marguerite, 190
military, women in, 87-88, 131
Mill, John Stuart, 207
Milliken, E.J., 52
mining, by women, 26
ministry, women in. *See* theologians, women as

Mitchell, John Ames, 20
Montague, Lady Mary, 6
mortality rates, 26
Morten, Honnor, 43-44, 74, 182
Moses, Montrose J., 106
motherhood, *See* childbearing
Mother Nature, 9
motorcycles, 200
Mt. Holyoke College, 91
Murray, David Christie, 82
Murray, Lindley, 82
mutual respect, in marriage, 42
mythologizing, of women, 1, 2, 9-10, 22, 89, 108, 116, 197

Nansen, Fridtjof, 154
National Amalgamated Union of Shop Assistants, 121
National Council of Women, 124, 128, 160
*National Review*, 59
National Union of Clerks, 121, 122
National Union of Shop Assistants, 67
Needlewoman Emigration Society, 29
needlewomen: charity for, 67; clubs for, 120; emigration by, 29-30; redundancy among, 28-29. *See also* needlework
needlework, 57. *See also* needlewomen
neurasthenia, 9, 22, 26, 174
New Adam, 11
New England Woman's Club, 119
New Man, 39-40, 133
Newnham College, 104, 109, 110
New Woman: demands of, 1-2, 205; use of the term, 5-6, 10-11, 93
*New Woman: A Farcical Sketch, with One Act, One Scene, and One Purpose, The* (Rugg), 133-34
*New Woman: An Original Comedy, in Four Acts, The* (Grundy), 3
*New Woman in Mother Goose Land, The* (Wormwood), 134
*New York Herald*, 26
*New York Sun*, 186
*New York Times*, 51, 52, 118, 130
Nightingale, Florence, 71
*Nineteenth Century*, 8

*North American Review*: on cloth-
ing for women, 159; use of term
*New Woman* in, 10-11
North London Collegiate School for
Girls, 56, 57, 100
Norton, Caroline Sheridan, 49
Norton, George, 49
nursing, 24, 61, 67, 70-72, 74, 120,
121
nutrition, 26, 181

Oberlin College, 91
old girl network, 124, 206
Old Woman, 15, 16-17, 23, 151
Ouida (pseud. Marie Louise de la Ra-
mée), 11, 83
Oxford University, 92, 104, 113

*Pall Mall Gazette*, 47
Parkes, Bessie, 28, 59
Parliament, and women, 6, 129
Partridge, Bernard, 81
Patmore, Coventry, 4
Pearse, F. Mabelle, 15
Peck, Harry Thurston, 3-4
petticoats, 148, 164, 185, 187
Phillips, H.W., 20
physicians, women as, 70, 72-74,
174
physiology, and women's role, 43.
*See also* health; women, physical
stamina of; women, physical
weakness of
*Pick-Me-Up*: on clothing for
women, 160; on cycling, 188; on
education for women, 100; on
New Man, 39; poll on failure of
marriage, 51; and science of marriage, 27; on smoking, 138; on unwomanliness of New Woman, 12-
13; on womanly New Woman, 7;
on working women, 88
Pinero, Arthur Wing, 153
Pioneer Club, 125
pneumatic tires, 185
Pope, Alexander, 77
*Popular Science Monthly*, 103
Postgate, Margaret, 122
procreation. *See* childbearing
prostitution, 11, 22, 26, 30, 31, 61-
63, 65, 66, 67, 79, 120, 208. *See
also* Gaiety girl
*Puck*, 2, 20, 45, 116

*Punch*, 2, 166; on athletics for
women, 177, 178, 179; changing
opinion of New Woman reflected
in, 44-45; on clothing for women,
95, 150, 153, 154, 155, 188-89,
190; on clubs for women, 123;
courtship depicted in, 40; on cycling, 186, 189-90, 197-99, 201-2;
distinction between "lady" and
"female" in, 4-5, 92; on domesticity, 41, 129-30; on education for
women, 95, 96-97, 98, 100-101,
108-9, 110, 111-13; on emigration
schemes, 28-30; on exploitation of
women workers, 58, 60, 67, 68-70;
on hairstyles, 156, 157; on independence for women, 125, 128-30;
on lighting and women's complex-
ions, 159; marriage depicted in, 24,
32, 33-38, 44, 45, 47-48, 50, 51, 52;
and married woman's property
rights, 49-50; on New Man, 133;
on nursing, 71; opposition to New
Woman in, 11-12, 16-17, 136, 143-
45, 208; on prostitution, 61-62, 63,
66; on smoking by women, 136,
138-41; valentines in, 13-15, 95-96,
189; on women writers, 80, 81, 82,
83, 84; on working women, 59-60,
72-74, 75, 79-80, 87, 88

Q (pseud. Douglas Jerrold), 83

Ramée, Marie Louise de la, 11, 83
Rational Dress Society, 160
Reamer, Lawrence, 195
redundancy, of women, 24-26, 28,
29, 30-31, 41, 43, 54, 56-57, 60, 62,
89. *See also* spinsterhood
Report of the Lady Commissioners
on Women's Labour, 75
restaurants, for women only, 123-24
revolt of the daughters, 7, 9, 170,
199
Richards, E.T., 20
Romaine, Harry, 121-22, 123
romance, destruction of, 40-41, 48
Romanes, George J., 103
Royal British Nurses' Association,
120
Ruggs, George, 133
Russell, Frances E., 160
Russell, Lillian, 20

*Sacred Tears* (Kaplan), 67
safety bicycles, 185
Sambourne, Linley, 109, 113
Sargent, D.A., 184
Sargent, John Singer, 10
*Saturday Review*, 177, 178
scorchers, 189, 195, 205
*Scotsman*, 73
screaming sister, 205
scribbling women, 22
*Scribner's*, 190
"scum-women" (prostitutes), 11
seamstresses, 26, 58, 61, 72, 88, 120
sentiment, as feminine, 7, 43, 98
sex roles. *See* gender roles
sexuality: and education, 109-10; and smoking, 138. *See also* clothing; and modesty
Shakespeare, William, 11-12, 19, 83, 155-56, 189
Shaw, George Bernard, 27, 56
shirtwaists, 150, 193
shop girls, 58, 61, 63-66, 67, 72, 75, 88, 119, 121, 208
sidesaddle riding, 186-87
sidesaddle velocipede, 186
skirt dancers, 16, 19, 142
Smiles, Samuel, 29
Smith, Alys Pearsall, 9
Smitham-Jones, C., 88
smoking: by women, 2, 3, 13, 85, 87, 124, 127, 135-42, 161, 170, 206; as unwomanly, 8, 122
social Darwinism, 27
social distinctions: and education, 104; and improved health for women, 27; of ladies, 5, 92
social insurgents, 2, 8
Society for the Employment of Women, 60
Somerset, Lady Henry, 191
Sorosis, 119
Sothern, Winifred, 89
Spencer, Herbert, 8, 26, 45, 159, 174, 184
spinsterhood, 3, 62, 81, 98. *See also* redundancy, of women
sports: and athletic women, 14, 27, 45, 173, 175-76, 180, 190; and health, 174, 175-76, 179, 180, 185, 190, 197, 199, 206; and sapping of womanliness, 175-76, 181-82; as unwomanly, 8, 122, 176-78

Stevenson, Dr. Sarah Hackett, 130
Stewart, Edna Seass, 6
Stotesbury, W.A., 181
suffrage, for women, 2, 13, 14, 17, 22, 122, 134, 135
suffragettes, 88, 119
Sullivan, Sir Arthur Seymour, 80, 90, 122, 123, 153, 167
Sullivant, T.S., 20
Swedish exercises, 182, 202
Swinburne, Algernon, 169

tandem bicycles, 185, 200-201
teachers, women as, 28, 33, 60, 67, 120, 182
telegraph operators, women as, 120
Tennyson, Alfred Lord, 15, 55, 60, 110, 113, 128, 130, 143
Terry, Ellen, 10
Thackeray, William Makepeace, 83, 207
theologians, women as, 76-80, 105
Thomas, M. Carey, 91, 99
Thorne, Rose, 143
thought, as masculine, 7. *See also* intellect, of women
Tilt, Dr. Edward John, 149
*Times* (London): on clothing for women, 149; on courtship difficulties, 32; on education for women, 109, 110; on emigration schemes, 29; on married woman's property rights, 48-49; registry of workers suggested in, 29, 59
*Too Many Women* (pamphlet), 26
toothpicks, use by women, 161
tricycle velocipede, 185
*Tricyclist, The*, 185
trousers, 148, 149, 159, 161, 187, 188, 190. *See also* breeches
*Truth* (London), 2; on clothing for women, 163-66; and education for women, 113-15; and manners of New Woman, 2; on New Woman and Fall of Man, 11; opposition to New Woman in, 17-18, 113, 142, 166-71; on salaries for women workers, 58-59; on use of "woman" versus "lady," 92-93
*Truth* (New York): on athletics for women, 181, 186, 195; on clothing for women, 163, 188, 190-91; history of, 19; on the manly woman,

3, 148; opposition to New Woman
  in, 19
tuberculosis, 26, 48
Tulliver, Maggie, 3

undergarments, 148-50. *See also*
  bloomers
unemployment: blamed on working
  women, 8; emigration as solution
  to, 28-29
unionization, of women, 67, 118, 120-
  21
utopian schemes, 22

*Vanity Fair* (Thackeray), 57
Van Rensselaer, Mrs., 99
varmity woman, 2, 178, 205
Vassar College, 91, 104
vice: charity as solution to, 66; emigration as solution to, 29; in male
  clubs, 127; opposition to, 18, 20. *See
  also* drinking; prostitution; smoking
Vicinus, Martha, 71
Victoria (queen of England), 1, 204-5,
  208-9
*Victorian Family* (Hughes), 10, 33
*Victorian Ladies at Work* (Holcombe), 67
Virginia Slims cigarettes, 135
voting. *See* suffrage, for women
Vynne, Harold, 121, 128, 130, 135

waitressing, 75
Walker, William, 87, 161, 162
Warner, Charles Dudley, 159
wars, and male population decline, 26
wedding rings, 47
weddings, expense of, 32
Weeton, Nellie, 68
Wellesley College, 91, 104
Wells, Carolyn, 151-52
Wesleyan College, 91
Westfield College, 100
*Westminster Gazette*, 83, 92
*Westminster Review*, definitions of
  manliness and womanliness in, 6-7
Whitman, Walt, 125
Whittier, John Greenleaf, 77
wife beating, 76
Wilcox, Edna Wheeler, 51

Wilde, Oscar, 168, 169
wild women, 2, 7-9
Wilkinson, Tony, 81-82
Willard, Miss Frances, 191
Wilson, Oscar, 138
Winchester, Boyd, 7
*Woman and the Demon* (Auerbach),
  10
womanliness: definition of, 4, 6-7, 92,
  118, 204; sapped through education,
  12, 90, 98-99, 100, 102, 176; sapped
  through exercise, 175-76, 181-82.
  *See also* female; womanly women
womanly women, 1, 4, 7, 10, 26, 92,
  155. *See also* womanliness
Woman's Alliance, 119
Woman's Christian Temperance
  Union (WCTU), 119. *See also* drinking
women: life span of, 26; as nurturers,
  4; physical stamina of, 2, 12, 41, 103,
  174, 175-76; physical weakness of,
  10, 12, 18, 42, 48-50, 146, 197, 202;
  self-sacrifice of, 6, 8, 9, 143; superiority within domestic sphere, 7,
  38, 129-30. *See also* childbearing;
  education, for women/girls; gender
  roles; health, of women; intellect, of
  women; mythologizing, of women;
  womanliness
Women's Congress, 119
Wood, Jessie M., 84-85
Woolf, Virginia, 22, 204
Wordsworth, William, 38
work, for women: as competition
  with men, 74; and dress styles, 159;
  economic necessity of, 24-26, 54, 55,
  57-58, 88-89; and exploitation, 58,
  60-62, 67-70; lack of, 22; and salaries, 58-59, 88, 89, 121, 130; as unwomanly, 8, 55, 89. *See also* careers,
  for women; factory work; prostitution; unemployment
Working-Girls' Club, 120
Working Girls' Societies, 119
Wormwood, Edyth M., 134

Young Men's Polytechnic Institute,
  120

Zola, Emile, 100, 101